BEYOND PARTY MEMBERS

COMPARATIVE POLITICS

Comparative Politics is a series for students, teachers, and researchers of political science that deals with contemporary government and politics. Global in scope, books in the series are characterized by a stress on comparative analysis and strong methodological rigour. The series is published in association with the European Consortium for Political Research. For more information visit www.ecprnet.eu

The Comparative Politics series is edited by Kenneth Carty, Professor of Political Science, University of British Columbia; Ferdinand Müller-Rommel, Director of the Center for the Study of Democracy, Leuphana University; and Emilie van Haute, Professor of Political Science, Université libre de Bruxelles.

OTHER TITLES IN THIS SERIES

Institutional Design and Party Government in Post-Communist Europe
Csaba Nikolenyi

Representing the People
A Survey Among Members of Statewide and Substate Parliaments
Edited by Kris Deschouwer and Sam Depauw

New Parties in Old Party Systems
Persistence and Decline in Seventeen Democracies
Nicole Bolleyer

The Limits of Electoral Reform
Shaun Bowler and Todd Donovan

The Challenges of Intra-Party Democracy
Edited by William P. Cross and Richard S. Katz

If Money Talks, What Does it Say?
Corruption and Business Financing of Political Parties
Iain McMenamin

The Gendered Effects of Electoral Institutions
Political Engagement and Participation
Miki Caul Kittilson and Leslie A. Schwindt-Bayer

The Strain of Representation
How Parties Represent Diverse Voters in Western and Eastern Europe
Robert Rohrschneider and Stephen Whitefield

Party Patronage and Party Government in European Democracies
Edited by Petr Kopecký, Peter Mair, and Maria Spirova

Organizing Democratic Choice
Party Representation Over Time
Ian Budge, Michael McDonald, Paul Pennings, and Hans Keman

Challenging the State: Devolution and the Battle for Partisan Credibility
A Comparison of Belgium, Italy, Spain, and the United Kingdom
Sonia Alonso

Beyond Party Members

Changing Approaches to Partisan Mobilization

SUSAN E. SCARROW

OXFORD
UNIVERSITY PRESS

Great Clarendon Street, Oxford, OX2 6DP,
United Kingdom

Oxford University Press is a department of the University of Oxford.
It furthers the University's objective of excellence in research, scholarship,
and education by publishing worldwide. Oxford is a registered trade mark of
Oxford University Press in the UK and in certain other countries

© Susan Scarrow 2015

The moral rights of the author have been asserted

First Edition published in 2015

Impression: 1

All rights reserved. No part of this publication may be reproduced, stored in
a retrieval system, or transmitted, in any form or by any means, without the
prior permission in writing of Oxford University Press, or as expressly permitted
by law, by licence or under terms agreed with the appropriate reprographics
rights organization. Enquiries concerning reproduction outside the scope of the
above should be sent to the Rights Department, Oxford University Press, at the
address above

You must not circulate this work in any other form
and you must impose this same condition on any acquirer

Published in the United States of America by Oxford University Press
198 Madison Avenue, New York, NY 10016, United States of America

British Library Cataloguing in Publication Data
Data available

Library of Congress Control Number: 2014943261

ISBN 978–0–19–966186–2

Printed and bound by
CPI Group (UK) Ltd, Croydon, CR0 4YY

Links to third party websites are provided by Oxford in good faith and
for information only. Oxford disclaims any responsibility for the materials
contained in any third party website referenced in this work.

Acknowledgements

Writing a book is never a completely solo activity. While the errors that remain are certainly my own, the work that follows has been immeasurably strengthened by inputs from a supportive and collaborative community of party scholars. The citations and bibliography recognize my specific debts; here I want to mention a few of the less obvious ones.

This book's arguments have been shaped and refined by workshop and panel discussions with colleagues from all over the world. Special thanks are due to the hosts and participants of several of these gatherings, including Bill Cross and Dick Katz for organizing two meetings in Ottawa on intra-party democracy, and to Luciano Bardi for organizing an APSA round-table on trends in party organizational change. Discussions in these sessions convinced me to revisit the topic of party membership with the aim of answering some puzzles about common patterns in cross-national developments. I benefited from further opportunities to develop my ideas in conversation with scholars at a 2009 colloquium convened by the Party Research Institute at the Heinrich Heine University, Düsseldorf, at a 2011 lecture at the Sorbonne Nouvelle University organized by Emmanuelle Avril, at the ECPR Political Parties Summer School in Brussels in 2012, organized by Jean-Benoit Pilet, Kris Deschouwer, and Emilie van Haute, and at a 2013 workshop on party membership at the University of Copenhagen, organized by Karina Pedersen. I am indebted to the organizers and funders of these forums. Even in an era where e-mails leap over time zones, such gatherings are invaluable for fostering intellectual exchange and trans-national collaboration.

Special thanks are due to Liz Mallet, who collected Facebook data, and to Aldo Ponce, who helped prepare some of the survey data used in this book. Many others generously shared data or answered questions about specific countries or parties, including Elin Haugsgjerd Allern, Katharina Barié, Josje den Ridder, Vesa Koskimaa, Katrina Kosiara-Pedersen, and Emilie van Haute. My brother, chemistry professor Rob Scarrow, gave me a much-needed refresher tutorial on the Bohr model of the atom. The first chapters of this book were drafted during a Faculty Development Leave provided by the University of Houston. The index was subsidized by a grant from the University of Houston's College of Liberal Arts and Social Sciences. I am grateful to my college and my university for their support of inquiry and scholarship.

Last but certainly not least, I am deeply appreciative of those who read and commented on drafts of this manuscript in various stages, including Anika Gauja, Anna Mikulska, Aldo Ponce, Margit Tavits, and Emilie van Haute. Among these readers, one who deserves special recognition is Ken Carty, the exemplary series editor for this book. In addition to his work in expeditiously shepherding this project through the publication process, Ken offered substantive comments at multiple stages that managed to be simultaneously encouraging and challenging, sometimes prompting significant rewrites. I had the good fortune to again work with staff at Oxford University Press and editor Dominic Byatt, who were prompt and supportive throughout.

Contents

List of Figures ix
List of Tables xi

1. Introduction: The Puzzles of Party Membership 1

Part I Party Membership: The Uneven Development

2. Motives and Modes of Party Membership 13
3. Myths and Realities of Mass Membership Parties 36
4. Explaining Enrollment Change: Looking Beneath the Numbers 69

Part II Party Membership: The Uncertain Future

5. What Do Party Members Contribute? 101
6. Multi-Speed Membership Parties 128
7. Making Party Membership Rewarding: Social and Material Benefits 156
8. Making Membership Meaningful: Political Benefits 175
9. The Consequences of Organizational Change 206

References 219
Index 233

List of Figures

1.1	Varieties of party membership	6
2.1	Party affiliation: Duverger's bulls-eye model	27
2.2	Party affiliation: the multi-speed model	33
4.1	Membership density: low initial level	71
4.2	Membership density: medium initial level	71
4.3	Membership density: high initial level	71
4.4	Hypothetical changes in membership density	75
4.5	Party membership density: long term decline	87
4.6	Party membership density: change since 1990s	88
4.7	Party membership density: relative stability	89
5.1	Party member activity	104
5.2	Member impact: % of participants who are party members	106
5.3	Event attenders: participation levels	107
5.4	Event attenders: % of participants who are party members	108
5.5	Campaign participation in the Netherlands	109
5.6	Changing importance of member-based financing	113
5.7	Donors and fundraisers: participation levels	119
5.8	Donors and fundraisers: % of participants who are party members	120
5.9	Voters: % eligible voters who participated in last election	121
5.10	Discussing and persuading: participation levels	123
5.11	Discussing and persuading: % of participants who are party members	124
5.12	Media contacters: participation levels	124
5.13	Media contacters: % of participants who are party members	125
6.1	Membership accessibility: ease of joining	133
6.2	Party affiliation: the multi-speed model	136
6.3	Sustainers: party web pages and fundraising	140

6.4	Party membership and party Facebook friends	143
6.5	Followers: parties advertising digital communication options	144
8.1	Use of intra-party leadership ballots, 1990–2012	184
8.2	Member turnout in intra-party leadership elections, 1990–2012	191

List of Tables

2.1	Party members and party narratives of legitimacy	21
3.1	Removing obstacles to political organization	44
3.2	The franchise and parliamentary elections	48
3.3	Founding of first socialist or labor parties	54
3.4	Democratic parties with membership-based organizations	56
4.1	Change in enrollments, 1960–2008	72
4.2	Party membership density and electoral systems: 1960s	93
A4.1	Total party enrollment	97
A4.2	Membership density	97
5.1	Total party revenues: average % from membership dues	112
5.2	Minimum regular dues rates, 1970–2011	116
5.3	Average minimum dues by party family, 2011 (€)	117
5.4	Average minimum dues by country, 2011 (€)	118
6.1	Party Facebook popularity, spring 2011	142
6.2	Multi-speed attributes: country averages	147
6.3	Multi-speed attributes: party-family averages	148
6.4	On-line accessibility index: country averages	149
6.5	On-line accessibility index: party-family averages	149
7.1	Benefits for party members and supporters	157
7.2	Reasons to join	161
7.3	Self-reported membership activity	165
7.4	Activity on popular party Facebook pages, spring 2011	167
8.1	Benefits for party members and supporters	176
8.2	Participation in party policy votes, 1990–2012	183
8.3	Number of parties using leadership ballots, 1990–2012	185
8.4	Access and inclusion in party leadership ballots, 1990–2012	188
8.5	Turnout in party leadership ballots, 1990–2012	190

8.6	High participation leadership ballots	192
8.7	Sustained Member Turnout in intra-party elections	193
A8.1	Leadership and policy ballots, 1990–2012: turnout	197
A8.2	Leadership and policy ballots, 1990–2012: sources	200

1

Introduction

The Puzzles of Party Membership

This book investigates two puzzles of party membership. The first is the puzzle of what happened to the formerly strong model of membership-based party organizing: when and why did party memberships start falling, and what does this reveal about who benefits in party–member relations? The second puzzle stems from a seeming paradox, the fact that individual party members have been gaining new political rights at exactly the same time that numerical membership strength is eroding, making party membership simultaneously less and more important. This book seeks to shed light on both puzzles by looking more closely at the origins of membership-based party organization, and at parties' current efforts to adapt this model to new circumstances. These twin approaches reveal how parties in contemporary parliamentary democracies are attempting to re-engage with members and other supporters, and how these efforts may affect political life within the parties, and within the wider democracies in which the parties compete.

The templates for membership-based party organizing emerged in the nineteenth century as political parties began playing a bigger political role in developing democracies. By the middle of the twentieth century, member-based parties had become a dominant ideal in many parliamentary democracies, though one which was honored in the breach at least as much as it was realized. Democratic membership parties came to be viewed as institutions which strengthen electoral democracies by linking citizens to governors. One of their most visible contributions was to increase electoral participation, especially by mobilizing resource-poor citizens who were otherwise less likely to vote. By the beginning of the twenty-first century this organizational model seemed to be in trouble. Parties across established democracies faced shrinking and aging memberships, and parties in new democracies failed to create strong extra-parliamentary organizations. These developments sparked debates about whether declining party memberships should be seen as either a symptom, or a cause, of democratic discontents.

The chapters that follow aim to enrich these debates on three levels: by providing a better historical baseline, by creating a broad picture of current party efforts to attract and retain enrolled support, and by proposing a framework for understanding these changes that expand the focus beyond traditional party members. One of the main arguments in the book's first section is that accounts of party change should not uncritically accept the persistent myth of mass-party dominance in some unspecified golden age. Chapter 3 marshals historical evidence to demonstrate that this is an unrealistic standard against which to judge subsequent organizational development. This chapter, like those that follow, focuses on partisan mobilizing in nineteen parliamentary democracies which democratized before the collapse of Communism. Experiences in these countries help explain why and where membership-based parties developed in the first place, and show the different ways that parties reacted once this strategy seemed to be losing its effectiveness.

Building an historically informed baseline to study party membership decline is not just a matter of having more exact membership numbers. Equally important is the recognition that parties' reasons for enlisting members have varied across parties, and have changed over time within single parties. Organizational diagnoses that ignore these ontological differences risk overlooking some of the most politically significant changes in contemporary parties, those affecting organizational norms. Thus, one essential step in solving the puzzle of party membership decline is to understand the status of party members before recent enrollment changes. This can help to explain how and why some parties were originally able to recruit large membership bases; it can also help identify what is new in some parties' efforts to adjust to enrollment losses.

The second section of the book more directly examines party responses to the waning appeal of party enrollment. Chapters in this section seek to answer the puzzle of why declining enrollment numbers might have led to an increasing role for individual party members. The investigation starts by looking more directly at the forces that affect parties' organizational decisions and recruiting success. From the party side, it examines the importance, and substitutability, of party members as organizational resources. From the individual side, it considers what benefits seem most likely to attract and retain future members. Both sides of the membership equation point in similar directions. On the one hand, a highly valuable contribution of party members' activities, and one with no easy commercial substitutes, is to strengthen the political legitimacy of party policy and personnel decisions. On the other hand, political benefits provide some of the most powerful incentives for inspiring intra-party participation. These twin factors help to explain why many parties have been strengthening the political rights of individual party members at precisely the same time that party memberships are shrinking. Moves in this direction are producing politically important changes in how parties select candidates and leaders, and in how they make policy decisions. The resulting new models of representation have the potential to alter patterns of participation and influence within parliamentary democracies. These far-reaching changes provide new opportunities for democratic participation. The new linkage mechanisms may mitigate some of the effects of waning membership, offsetting the risk that dwindling traditional enrollments could become an existential crisis for the parties themselves, or for the representative democracies in which they compete.

Finally, this book argues that analysts who study grassroots party organizing need to get beyond categories that rigidly divide party supporters into members and non-members. Instead, we need to see supporters in the way that parties increasingly seem to view them: as individuals who move between different levels of party activism and interest. Traditional formal membership is only one part of a portfolio of organizational options in which parties can invest when attempting to convert individual political interest into a partisan resource. In recent years many established membership-based parties have introduced new categories of affiliation, often with overlapping rights but with different channels of access to party decision-makers. These initiatives take advantage of opportunities offered by new digital communications technologies. Parties' new affiliation categories generally coexist with traditional membership organizations, supplementing but not supplanting traditional membership. This book dubs these new organizational hybrids *multi-speed membership parties.* For some parties, these new forms constitute a radical change, while for others they merely formalize long-standing practices. Whether newly created or merely renamed, parties' expanding affiliation options raise new questions about how to distribute duties and privileges among different types of affiliates, about lines of intra-party accountability, and about the reasons why individuals opt for any type of partisan affiliation. The book examines the consequences for parliamentary democracies of these ongoing transformations, asking how political parties—and the democracies in which they compete—move beyond party members.

THE IMPLICATIONS OF PARTY MEMBERSHIP DECLINE

The decline in party memberships in established parliamentary democracies is well-documented (Scarrow 2000; van Biezen et al. 2012). Most parties in these countries have seen steadily dropping enrollments over the past two decades. As Chapters 2 and 3 will show, the picture is a bit more complex than these figures suggest at first glance. Above all, some of the biggest apparent losses result from changes in record-keeping practices, not from changes in citizens' behavior. However, even accounting for such discrepancies, it is clear that many parties have seen real membership losses since the 1970s and 1980s. These shrinking grassroots organizations are a cause of concern for party organizers and party analysts.

Declining party membership can matter for individual parties in multiple ways. It may deprive them of organizational resources, including campaign volunteers and partisans who can be persuaded to stand for local government offices. Loss of members can bring a loss of financial resources. Enrollment decline also may be a warning sign, an indicator of a more general decline in a party's support. How much these changes matter for any particular party depends on the extent to which it has relied on members to provide political resources, and on how easily the party can find substitutes for their contributions. It also depends on what roles party members have previously played in party decisions, and whether these losses affect all parties equally.

Whatever the implications for individual parties, there are also potentially grave consequences for the wider polity. If party members have enhanced democratic political competition by strengthening participatory and policy-responsive linkage (Lawson 1980, ch. 1), declining party memberships may erode ties between citizens and those who govern, thus exacerbating processes of electoral dealignment. To the extent that party membership formerly helped to offset resource-linked disparities in political participation (Verba et al. 1978, ch. 7), membership decline could also change the composition of the active electorate. In countries such as Germany, in which party laws define parties as membership associations, shrinking memberships may make it difficult for parties to comply with legal obligations concerning party registration or the practice of intra-organizational democracy (Klein et al. 2011, 27; van Biezen and Piccio 2013). Even where laws are silent on this issue, many parties have come to depend on party members or their delegates to provide legitimacy for important party decisions. Although analysts have been denouncing intra-party democracy as a fiction for almost a century (notably, Robert Michels [1915] 1959; Max Weber [1919] 1946), that supposed fiction has assumed an increasingly prominent place in current party practices. The statutes of most parties in parliamentary democracies give members or their delegates important roles in selecting or ratifying party leaders and party candidates. Party membership decline imperils this legitimating link, which is another reason that dwindling enrollments have been seen as a potential crisis for polities, not just for individual parties.

As this list suggests, the decline of party membership may represent much more than just a change in parties' campaign strategies and electoral resources. It also may mark a radical transformation—though not necessarily a decline—in meaningful opportunities for citizens to participate in politics. The actual consequences of these changes depend on how parties respond to the loss of members, and what participation opportunities and resources they develop to supplement or replace traditional party membership. The impact of such changes is likely to vary across parties. Because of differences in their past reliance on party members, these changes will be much more radical for some parties than for others. In order to understand the implications of falling party enrollments, we need a theoretically and empirically informed understanding of why citizens join and stay in parties, and of why parties seek to affiliate them. We also need an historically informed baseline against which to measure change in what members actually do for their parties.

THE VARIETIES OF PARTY MEMBERSHIP

A fundamental problem that confronts any study of party membership is the variety of ways in which this term is used. Citizens who describe themselves as party members may have in mind very different kinds of relationships with their parties. In 1970s Sweden, a trade union member might have self-described as a party member because his trade union was affiliated with the Social Democrats. In 2013, his grand-daughter would have no reason to feel such a link between union membership and party membership. In contemporary France, a self-described Socialist member might be thinking of the one-time fee she paid several years ago to participate in an internal party election. A New Yorker might be thinking of the party preference she registered with a public agency in order to be eligible to vote in the Democrats' primary election. A Texan might be thinking of the fact that he voted in that state's most recent Republican primary, participation that required no pre-registration of party preference. As these examples suggest, the notion of what party membership means can vary widely across countries and decades, and often among parties within a single country. Thus, before embarking on an investigation of evolving party membership, it is useful to distinguish between basic varieties of membership, and to specify which kinds of party members are the focus of the current study.

Three questions can help sort out the different modes of party membership. First, is it administered by individual political parties, or by the state? The latter is primarily found in some US states, in which public authorities administer rules about eligibility to participate in party primaries. Second, is party membership held by individuals or by affiliated associations? Third, is membership status defined in formal terms (for instance, dues payment), or is it considered a psychological attachment, one that may be demonstrated by certain behaviors (for instance, by voting loyalty)? These categories are not exclusive. A single party may have both individual and organizational membership, and state-administered membership for purposes of primary election participation could coexist with party-administered membership.

In practice, answers to these three questions yield five relevant cells (see Figure 1.1). The three party-administered cells (boxes 3–5 of Figure 1.1) are the varieties that have featured most prominently in discussions of party membership in parliamentary democracies. In the middle of this row (box 3) is the mode associated with mass political parties: individuals enlist by completing formal procedures that are defined and administered by political parties. Common enrollment procedures include filling out application forms and paying annual dues. Those who join in this way are often quite literally "card-carrying" party members. Having formal membership definitions means that there are clear distinctions between members and others. Some parties have avoided such legalistic membership definitions, and

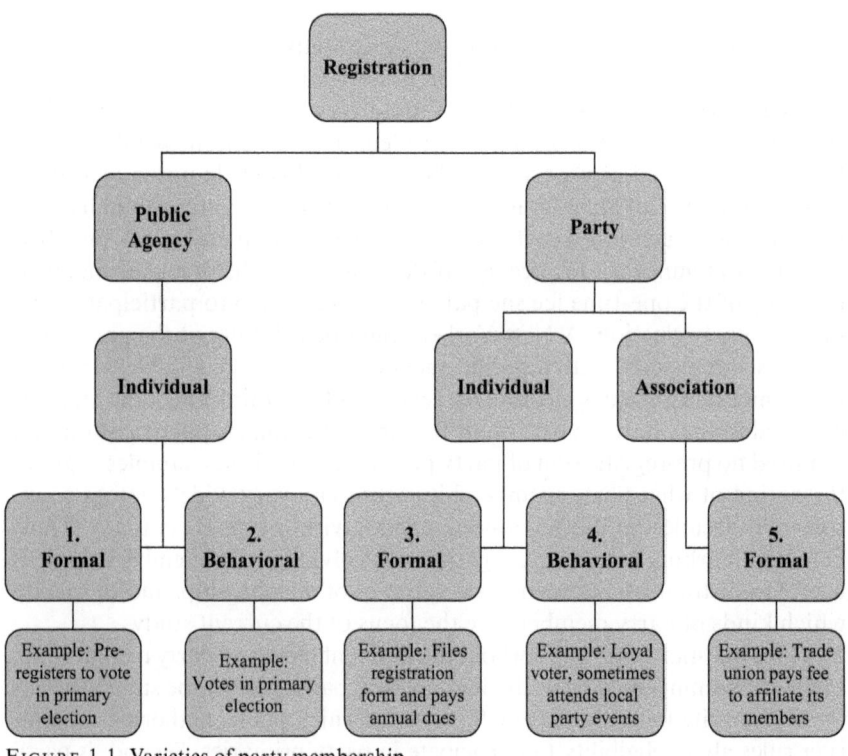

FIGURE 1.1 Varieties of party membership

Introduction

instead have employed behavioral definitions, such as ascribing membership to all who attend the annual party dinner or who contribute to party funds (box 4). Finally, there are parties with organizational members, most usually trade unions, but also other organizations such as farmers' organizations, co-ops, and business associations (box 5). Such affiliated organizations pay fees on behalf of their members. Sometimes these payments give members of the affiliated organizations individual rights within the party; this type of affiliation is described as *indirect* membership. In some parties, indirect members have had the right to participate in local party meetings or to stand as candidates. In other cases, the individual members of the affiliated organization have no personal connection with the party and enjoy no rights within it.

This book focuses primarily on the two varieties of party membership that have been most prevalent in parliamentary democracies: party-administered individual membership, both formally and behaviorally defined (boxes 3 and 4). As will be seen, parties have frequently adjusted their notions of how or whether formally organized individual supporters fit into their overall aims. Some parties have ascribed membership organizations a central role in party development; others have seen party members as, at most, peripheral to party goals. Changes in party membership structures shed light on parties' evolving electoral tactics, and on developing power relations within them.

INVESTIGATING THE EVOLUTION OF PARTY MEMBERSHIP STRATEGIES

The following chapters examine the development of party membership organization in nineteen democracies, most of which are parliamentary systems. These include thirteen European Union (EU) democracies that democratized prior to 1990 (Austria, Belgium, Denmark, Finland, Germany, Greece, Ireland, Italy, the Netherlands, Portugal, Spain, Sweden, and the United Kingdom), two non-EU European democracies (Norway and Switzerland), and three Commonwealth countries whose original political traditions were influenced by British experiences (Australia, Canada, New Zealand). France, currently a semi-presidential system, is included because its party traditions were formed during the country's long period of parliamentary democracy.

There are two main reasons for focusing on the development of popular political organizations within these countries. First, political experiences in established parliamentary democracies have shaped ideas about how strong parties should and do organize. The templates created in these countries continue to influence recommendations about organizational best practices for parties in newer democracies.[1] Second, the parties with the longest experiences of membership-based organizing tend to be the ones which currently are grappling the hardest with the question of how to respond when party membership numbers dwindle, and when new technologies bring new mobilization opportunities. This case selection leaves out most presidential regimes, newer parliamentary democracies, and even some large established parliamentary democracies (most notably, India and Japan). The purpose of limiting the scope in this way is to reduce the contextual variation, while still having variation in key institutional and historical factors which have been linked to party organizational development, including electoral systems and the timing of franchise expansion. The study's conclusions are necessarily limited to the universe of the investigation. However, the larger aim is to develop approaches and frameworks that are more broadly useful for understanding how parties organize relations with their supporters.

Even when employing a most-similar-system design, it is a challenge to trace party organizational development in such a large group of countries. The chapters that follow use historical, qualitative, and quantitative sources to map the evolution of party membership organizations. This task has been greatly facilitated by historians' growing interest in political party emergence as one aspect of the nineteenth century's burgeoning associational life. In political science, studies of more recent party organizational development were stimulated by the massive multi-country collection of party organizational data known colloquially as the "Katz/Mair Data Handbook" (Katz and Mair 1995a). The contributors to this and a companion volume (Katz and Mair 1994), and other scholars who have subsequently used this data or built upon it, have helped to fill in many details about party organizational life in specific countries. In addition, in the past two decades a growing number of surveys of party members have greatly expanded our understanding about the motivations and behaviors of individual party members. These endeavors were spurred by the ground-breaking surveys of British party members conducted by Patrick Seyd and Paul Whiteley (including Seyd and Whiteley 1992 and Whiteley et al. 1994). Other important data sources for this comparative overview are the cumulating waves of multi-country surveys which ask questions about party membership, including the European Social Survey, and the World Values Survey. Last but not least, part of this study is based on a systematic comparison of party web pages. Party web pages are a type of visual manifesto that represent and summarize parties' public images and outreach priorities. Moreover, in contrast to most traditional election manifestos, these web pages are on the front lines of parties' interactions with members and non-member supporters. As such, they are a new and valuable resource for the comparative study of party organizational strategies. The quantitative and qualitative information from these varied sources sheds historical light on parties' current struggles to retain, and to expand, formal links with their supporters.

A LOOK AHEAD

Before investigating contemporary trends in party membership, this study begins by tracing the advent and evolution of membership-based party organizing. Chapters 3 and 4 present historical data that qualify prevailing assumptions about the past strength of democratic membership parties. These chapters suggest that parties' current organizational difficulties are neither unprecedented, nor are they necessarily signs of parties' diminishing capacity to connect with those whom they seek to represent. The chapters in the second section of the book examine contemporary decisions about party membership from the perspective of the parties that recruit them, and of the supporters who might be persuaded to join. Using perspectives introduced in Chapter 2, these chapters show how and why parties have been experimenting with new ways to connect with party supporters. These experiments are leading to the emergence of multi-speed membership organizations, ones which offer multiple ways for supporters to affiliate, and which cater to supporters' shifting levels of partisan engagement. The ongoing changes hold the potential to increase the extent and consequences of individual partisan participation by moving parties beyond traditional forms of party membership.

NOTES

1. See, for instance, the *Guidelines on Political Party Regulation* agreed to by the Venice Commission in 2010 (OSCE 2011).

Part I

Party Membership: The Uneven Development

2

Motives and Modes of Party Membership

Creating membership-based local organizations was a radical idea when it was first introduced by a few parties in the nineteenth century. In many cases, it was also a highly effective approach. That is a main reason why other parties began to emulate this new organizational strategy. By the second half of the twentieth century, most parties in parliamentary democracies had established formal membership organizations to support their electoral efforts. Although parties varied widely in how they defined membership, and in the extent of their recruiting success, membership-based organizing gradually became the norm in these countries. Eventually, some countries even incorporated membership into their legal definitions of political parties.

The growth of party membership organizations generated familiar pictures—even stereotypes—of what it meant to be a party member. In Britain there were the redoubtable Conservative Party ladies who raised funds for the local party through jumble sales and the annual fête. In many countries in continental Europe, there were Socialist and Social Democratic party members who turned out on May 1 to march in demonstrations alongside their trade union comrades. There also were the doorstep dues collectors, gathering monthly or weekly dues from members of the Dutch Worker's Party or the German Social Democrats. And everywhere there were the proverbial smoke-filled rooms in which local parties held monthly membership meetings to discuss party policies or to prepare for the next local or national election. Prior to elections, voters were likely to see at least a few party loyalists (probably party members) standing at campaign stalls in local markets, going door-to-door to distribute leaflets, displaying party colors in their windows, or putting up endorsement signs. In the 1950s and 1960s, such party members were a familiar sight in most parliamentary democracies; because of this, even apolitical citizens were likely to have some image of what it meant to be a party member.

By the beginning of the twenty-first century, the future of this organizing model seemed to be in doubt. In countries where party membership once flourished, parties were finding it increasingly difficult to maintain existing membership organizations. In both new and established democracies, parties were experimenting with new organizational styles and new ways to strengthen links with supporters. These changes potentially affect parties' capacities to represent voters and to mobilize supporters. The task for this chapter is to outline several frameworks that will be used throughout the book to assess the magnitude and likely impact of these ongoing organizational shifts.

The first challenge is to understand the forces that shape parties' organizational initiatives and successes. The following account adopts both an economic and an ideological perspective to illuminate the considerations that are involved in these relationships. These perspectives help to answer the "why" questions: why might parties seek to enroll members, and why might supporters join? The second challenge is to understand the different ways that parties have used membership to relate to their supporters: what have parties meant by membership, and how has this varied? To answer these questions, later sections of this chapter describe important relational nodes that can connect political parties and their supporters. This new schema rejects rigid distinctions between party activists, other party members, and looser supporters. Instead, it presents these categories as being both dynamic and overlapping. It depicts party membership as merely one way in which supporters may affiliate (i.e. create formal links with) their preferred party. From this perspective, supporters are conceived to be constantly choosing between multiple modes and intensities of partisan action. Conversely, political parties face ongoing decisions about which activity modes to cultivate. Answers to the "why" and the "what" questions are intertwined. Taken together, these approaches provide a useful context for understanding recent changes in party organizational styles. Most importantly, they help to explain why many contemporary parties have been investing in creating alternatives to traditional party membership, and why this trend coexists with other reforms that are elevating members' political rights.

WHY PARTY MEMBERS?

Why did some parties enroll members in the first place? And why did this organizational form endure better in some countries than in others? Previous studies have approached these questions from many angles. Here, the emphasis is on two types of explanation. The first, an electoral economy approach, highlights the costs and benefits that parties and individuals derive from a membership relationship. The second approach, one that has received less attention, views party organizational choices from an ideological perspective. While this approach is completely compatible with a cost/benefit interpretation, its emphasis is different because its calculus of benefits transcends electoral considerations. Instead, it focuses on how membership organization fits into a party's proclaimed political worldview, and what role (if any) members are seen to play in bolstering the party's political credibility.

Organizational Choices as Cost/Benefit Calculations

Party organizations are commonly seen as the product of cost/benefit calculations, albeit ones that may be constrained by historical legacies. From this perspective, two types of consideration explain the strength of party membership organizations: party elites' calculations about the net utility of this organizational form (demand-side explanations), and party supporters' calculations about whether it makes sense to join (supply-side explanations) (cf. van Haute 2011a, 12–13). Both supply-side and demand-side explanations of party membership levels portray party organization as a solution to collective-action problems, and as a resource that benefits those who invest in it. Despite these similarities, it is important to distinguish between the two perspectives when diagnosing reasons for change, because the different origins have different long-term implications about what (if anything) might reverse waning organizational strength.

Demand-side explanations have long dominated academic analyses of party organizational development. These accounts view top–down decisions as the primary influence on parties' organizations and organizational evolution. According to them, party leaders and party organizers respond to changing competitive circumstances by pushing for organizational change. This tradition finds some of its earliest expression in the works of analysts who described how informal parties of notables were being displaced by more bureaucratically organized and professionalized parties. Max Weber labeled the new types of parties as "the children of democracy, of mass franchise, of the necessity to woo and organize the masses" ([1919] 1946, 102). In Weber's view, political leaders developed such organizations in response to new electoral conditions. Weber's analysis quoted Moisei Ostrogorski's monumental account of party organizing in Britain and the United States, a demand-side analysis which portrayed British Liberal and Conservative Caucus parties as nefariously top–down creations. These apparently democratic organizations enlisted newly enfranchised voters but remained in the control of those whom Ostrogorski called the wire-pullers: "The popular form of the party Organization merely enables the latter to penetrate deeper into the masses for the purpose of capturing them more easily, and not for giving them independence" ([1902] 1982, 302).

A half-century later, the famous exchange between Maurice Duverger and Leon Epstein on the nature of organizational contagion shared a similar assumption about the organizational primacy of demand-side forces. Duverger argued that middle-class parties adopted the Socialists' branch-style organization, trying to attract "the masses... by the very methods that were making the working-class parties so successful" (1954, 25). Epstein countered with a prediction of organizational contagion from the right due to the growing importance of mass media communications and large financial contributions, both of which offered party organizers substitutes for the resources potentially provided by party members. According to him, party campaigners have little need for members if they have these other resources (1968, ch. 9). Neither Duverger nor Epstein saw this as an exclusively demand-side process. Both agreed that supply-side forces played a role, not least because different types of organization appealed differently to working-class or to middle-class adherents. Yet for both analysts, decisions about the utility of such organizations were primarily top–down ones dictated by electoral goals, and based on the availability of other means for attaining these goals. Otto Kirchheimer similarly described the switch towards catch-all parties as a demand-side process resulting from political leaders' acquiescence to "the law of the political market." Whereas prior to the Second World War some parties enjoyed access to state resources independent of their electoral success, by the 1960s such a link had become inescapable. As a result, party leaders introduced organizational changes to make their parties more competitive (1966, 184).

More recent attempts to understand when and how parties change have given greater attention to the circumstances and constraints that affect party organizational choices. They also have taken a more nuanced view of the main aims that drive party adaptation. Yet many still give primacy to demand-side considerations. For instance, Angelo Panebianco's genetic theory takes a path dependency approach to organizational development, arguing that initial organizational choices constitute long-term constraints. He rejects the notion of parties as unitary actors motivated solely by electoral goals. Like Michels and Weber, Panebianco (1988) depicts established party organizations as self-defensive bureaucracies whose main aim is organizational continuity: electoral victories are but one means to that end. Although Panebianco portrays party elites as having multiple and even competing goals, his theories still emphasize the organizational primacy of top–down decisions. Similarly, Robert Harmel's and Kenneth Janda's theory of party change depicts alterations in organization and policies as a deliberate and top–down process. It may be spurred by environmental changes such as the availability of new resources, or electoral losses, or threats to other party goals. However, "party change does not 'just happen';" rather, it is the result of internal decision-making (1994, 263). Joseph Schlesinger (1991) and

John Aldrich (1995, 2011) also depict party organizational development as a result of goal-driven elite behavior, although for them the most relevant goals are those of individual politicians pursuing their own self-interest. In their accounts, considerations about party electoral success may also matter, but perceived utility to individual political careers is the primary engine of organizational development.

Importantly for the subject at hand, none of these demand-side views of party organization depict party membership as an end-in-itself. This is one key way in which parties differ from many voluntary associations for whom membership is synonymous with their mission: a Rotary Club or Girl Scout troop or trade union cannot exist without members. Even elite clubs need to have a few members. For clubs, membership recruitment must be a constant concern. In contrast, members are an optional means to an end for political parties: indeed, some parties exist and flourish without them (von Beyme 2002, 104). This difference may affect parties' responses to membership losses. Thus, James Q. Wilson's observation about members' centrality to organizational survival does not necessarily apply to political parties: "Those responsible for maintaining the organization will be powerfully constrained in their actions by the need to conserve and enhance the supply of incentives by which the membership is held in place" (1973, 27). In the case of parties, if members do not contribute to a party's electoral success—or if they come to be seen as vote losers because of their extreme behavior—the party's leaders may feel little or no need to invest in membership recruitment or retention. For election-oriented political parties it is voters, not members, who are the organizational bottom line.

Demand-side explanations generally link declining membership to the declining value of benefits that members provide to their parties. Many scholars have argued that new communications techniques and resources, and new electoral strategies, are helping to make membership-based organizing obsolete. As early as 1956, Epstein described the persistence of membership-based campaigns in Britain as a legacy of that country's nineteenth-century limits on constituency campaign spending, not as a feature of a "modern" organizational template (1956, 122). For Kirchheimer, the downgraded importance of membership was not just a result of parties having better *means* for spreading this message; it was also because members were no longer the most important *targets* for the party message. Parties which sought to overcome an image as the protector of a specific social class or confessional group could find membership to be an obstacle to their attempts to appeal to new constituencies (1966, 190). In Panebianco's account, electoral professional parties emerge in part due to changing communications techniques, particularly television. It takes professional experts, not amateur volunteers, to run campaigns using these new media. This change has consequences for party voluntary organizations: professionalized parties have less need to cultivate membership (1988, 266). Similarly, cartel parties are said to emerge in part because established parties are able to rely on resources other than their own voluntary organizations to protect their privileged positions. Established parties enjoy high access to mass media, including free coverage. They also benefit from institutional rules that work against the emergence of new parties, and from growing public subsidies that undercut the value of party members' donations of time and money (Katz and Mair 1995b, 15–17). Such parties lose incentives to formally enroll their supporters; in fact, parties may come to view members as a liability if members oppose leaders' electoral strategies.

Demand-side accounts do not inevitably predict the demise of membership-based party organizing. Indeed, and as will be shown in more detail in later chapters, there is growing evidence that members can help win votes even for professionalized parties. If so, there may be important demand-side incentives for contemporary parties to invest in developing their grassroots organizations. For present purposes, however, the salient point is that arguments from this perspective see the fate of membership organization as linked to perceptions by those at the top of a party as to whether members are an electoral asset for either the party or for its individual candidates.

Supply-side explanations for party membership decline to look at the same equation from the point of view of potential party members. They link dwindling enrollments to citizens' changing preferences, and to the advent of competing outlets for civic engagement. For instance, some see current trends as a reflection of citizens' growing distrust of governing parties (Dalton and Weldon 2005). Other supply-side explanations focus on lifestyle causes, depicting organizational change as the result of new and more attractive political and free-time alternatives. As societies became more affluent in the second half of the twentieth century, citizens gained access to more educational and leisure opportunities, and better housing encouraged increased individualism. Whereas parties could once attract members by the social opportunities they afforded, and by excursions and vacation clubs they organized, by the 1960s party meetings were competing with television and package holidays and non-political sports clubs. At the same time, by the 1970s some active citizens were becoming interested in new styles of political participation, ones that focused on single issues, and which gave participants more direct influence. Rising social movements now competed with parties for the attention of politically engaged citizens. Some of the new organizations also had the appeal of being less hierarchical associations. Thus, in several senses traditional party organization came to be perceived as old-fashioned or even irrelevant (Barnes et al. 1979; Dalton 1996; Katz and Mair 1995b, 15; van Deth 2000; von Beyme 2002, 32–7). In a variant of this lifestyle argument, Panebianco stresses the impact of social changes on party electoral and organizing strategies, arguing that parties find it harder to organize an "electorate of belonging" due to shifts in the labor market, rising education, and secularization. Parties need to adjust their strategies because voters (and potential members) have become more individualistic (1988, 266–7).

Whatever the underlying reasons for this supply-side shift, the supposed results are that today's citizens are less inclined to make long-term organizational commitments to political parties. Supply-side explanations for membership decline thus portray party organizational changes as the result of social and political changes to which parties could attempt to respond. However, trying to recruit and retain party members in this new environment means swimming upstream in cultures that are now less attuned to partisan identities.

Although demand-side and supply-side explanations for party organizational change are compatible, they have rather different implications about what (if anything) might halt or reverse the diagnosed decline in party membership enrollment. Demand-side explanations suggest that this trend is unlikely to change unless parties lose access to other resources (for instance, public subsidies are cut), or unless party strategists re-evaluate how members enhance electoral success. In contrast, supply-side explanations suggest that parties will be unable to revitalize membership organizations unless they drastically change the experience of party membership in order to compete with more attractive associational and free-time options.

Both approaches view organization through an economic lens, depicting party membership in terms of its costs and benefits for the organization, or for the individuals who enroll. They illuminate some of the causes of change, and also make it easier to see what external shocks or internal efforts could possibly alter current trajectories. Later chapters will explore these explanations in more detail, investigating the relative importance of specific supply-side and demand-side factors in reshaping membership recruitment and retention. Yet there are limits to an electoral economy approach to party membership. Importantly, this perspective excludes the normative context that shapes decisions about organizational priorities. Norms matter, not least because parties' perceptions about the benefits provided by members may reflect more widely held views about the appropriate sources of party mandates. In fact, political legitimacy and confidence in a party's chosen policy alternatives may be the most important benefits that party members can provide. Such long-term legitimacy is overlooked in models that focus on short-term electoral calculations. Whether members actually confer such legitimacy on a party depends to a great extent on how that party defines its own purposes, and on the values of the wider society.

Organizational Choices as Ideological Products

Political parties are distinguished from other political organizations by the fact that they contest elections, but their organizational choices usually reflect aspirations and values that go beyond immediate electoral success. These values may be expressed in a well-defined ideological worldview, or they may be only implied in the rhetoric that party leaders invoke to explain why they and their parties deserve to govern (for instance, Gauja 2013, ch. 3). These explicit or implicit accounts can be dubbed *narratives of legitimacy*. Such narratives identify the sources of party credentials, which may come from a combination of sound ideology, superior policy prescriptions, excellent leadership, and the strength of links to social groups or individual citizens.

There is a direct connection between the sources of a party's self-identified credentials and its organizational choices, including how it defines party members. These different narratives of legitimacy imply different statutory relations between party leaders and party members, and different procedures for gaining party membership. Table 2.1 lays out some of these relations between organizational choices and narratives of legitimacy. The table gives examples of how party claims about the main sources of party credentials have implications for their understandings of the roles for party members (if any). These assignments are not necessarily permanent, nor do they necessarily rigidly reflect party origins as internally or externally created (Duverger 1954; Daalder 2001). Indeed, the evolution of party members' roles is worth studying precisely because it reveals a great deal about party efforts to adapt to societal understandings of parties' linkage roles in representative democracies.

The rows in Table 2.1 are arranged according to their implications for the size of the group that has ultimate authority in the party, ranging from narrow (a single party leader) to broad (the entire party electorate). The parties with the most tightly circumscribed leadership groups are *Personalistic Parties* (Diamond and Gunther 2001, 28; Gunther and Diamond 2003; Hartleb 2013, 7–8). These parties derive their legitimacy from the quality of a single charismatic leader. At the beginning of the twenty-first century, Silvio Berlusconi's People of Italy Party offered an example of a personalistic party in a parliamentary setting, as did some nationalist and far right parties (most notably, the Dutch Party for Freedom, whose leader was the sole member of his party). If these parties have members, the role assigned to them is that of the *fan*. Fans are a type of member who are valued for their loyalty, but who are not expected to exercise voice. Fans join to show support for the leader and his or her party, and they may be willing to pay a fee to demonstrate this support (just as listeners demonstrate support for US public television stations by becoming donor "members"). A leader's popular standing and position within his party may be bolstered if he

TABLE 2.1 *Party members and party narratives of legitimacy*

Party Type	Source of Political Legitimacy	Role of Party Members	Nature of Affiliation
Personalistic	Legitimacy comes from the leader's political vision and popularity.	**Fans**	Loose membership rules.
Ideological	Party aims are defined by ideology.	**Adherents**	Exclusive membership. Members must pass ideological tests; dissenters are ejected.
Elite	Party leadership group embodies a social order.	**Fans**	Loose membership rules.
Cleavage Representation	Parties represent the interests of a defined group.	**Community Members**	Membership (if any) primarily for cleavage group members. Members are vetted prior to joining, and can be expelled for mis-interpreting party aims.
Subscriber Democracy	Parties are clubs representing the interests of their members.	**Stakeholders**	Well-defined membership rules. All full members are equal.
Political Process	Legitimacy is guaranteed by internal processes.	**Stakeholders**	Membership rules vary in strictness, balancing tradeoffs between boosting participation and protecting party identity.
Political Market	Parties represent political consumers (i.e. voters); sometimes stakeholders.	**Fans**	Loose membership rules designed to increase participation.

helps to attract a large number of fan-members, but the leader is not formally accountable to them. To the extent that personalistic parties offer their members few rights, and impose few responsibilities, they can afford to have loose membership rules. Such parties may have a more exclusive level of membership, governed by tighter entry rules, out of which the party draws its candidates and functionaries.

Ideological parties are ones which justify their current politics by referring to a long-term historical mission. This group includes Gunther's and Diamond's Leninist, Ultra-nationalist, and Fundamentalist Parties (2001, 10–11). Like personalistic parties, they may be dominated by a leader or small group, yet the appeal of these leaders rests on their authoritative interpretation of party doctrine, not solely on personal popularity. Unlike personalistic parties, ideological parties seek *adherents* who believe in party doctrine and are willing to help advance its cause. *Adherents* share a political vision, and they agree on the basic implications of its diagnosis. Such parties may limit full membership to acolytes who have demonstrated their commitment to the ideology, and who are expected to work towards achieving ideologically defined aims. Leaders' primary accountability is to the mission, not to the membership. In order to limit potential conflict between these sources of authority, party statutes may include procedures for ejecting members, including elected representatives, who are deemed to stray too far from prevailing interpretations of party ideology. This model describes a traditional Leninist cadre party. Although genuinely ideological parties are rare nowadays in established democracies, the model may apply in milder form to some contemporary parties on the far-left and far-right of democratic electoral competition. In these parties, it is the overall mission that provides the main source of party legitimacy.

Elite is the term that Gunther and Diamond use to describe local notable parties and clientelistic parties (2001, 12–13). The former are electoral alliances whose appeal rests primarily on the general economic and social sway of local and regional leaders, while the latter are based on specific transactional relations between local patrons and clients. In elite parties, as in personalistic parties, members are optional. If the party has them, they are generally regarded as *fans*. *Fans* may be electorally useful, and some may be mobilized to help with campaign tasks, but they are not central to a party's claims about why it should govern. As a result, there is no reason to give the members ultimate authority over party decisions. Because elite parties tend to be more decentralized than parties dominated by a single leader, their fan-members may enjoy some opportunities to exert informal influence in dyadic relations with local party leaders. However, their party statutes may look like those of personalistic parties in terms of specifying loose membership procedures and limited formal membership rights.

Cleavage Representation Parties present themselves as defenders of pre-existing interests, be these economic, ethnic, or religious. (These include Gunther's and Diamond's Class-Mass, Denominational, and Ethnic Parties; 2001, 10–11). They define politics more as a matter of group conflict than of contending individual claims. They cultivate visible ties to the group(s) they claim to represent. Having strong party membership organizations is one way to embody and cement such links, although there are other ways to achieve the same end. For instance, some have few members of their own, and instead rely on milieu organizations and leaders to nurture partisan identity and to mobilize popular support. But many cleavage parties have been classic mass parties, and have placed strong emphasis on their membership organizations. For parties of this type, one of the chief reasons to create their own membership organizations is to reinforce the political implications of group identity. Members of such parties are viewed as *Community Members*. They are co-religionists, trade union comrades, or ethnic group members.

Cleavage parties with their own membership organizations are ones that the German political scientist Sigmund Neumann described as "parties of democratic integration" ([1932] 1965, 105). Maurice Duverger also had this type of organization in mind when he remarked that a mass party without members "would be like a teacher without pupils" (1954, 63). Such parties often give members an indirect role in party decisions, letting them select delegates to party conventions. Indeed, Katz and Mair claim that such parties have valued extensive membership organizations precisely because they have viewed mass participation in party policy formulation as crucial to their legitimacy (1995b, 7). Cleavage party statutes tend to make leaders ultimately accountable to party members, who are seen as representatives of the larger interest group. At the same time, however, Cleavage parties generally have well-defined notions of the group interest to which members are expected to defer. To ensure such loyalty, parties may restrict membership to those with demonstrated ties to the cleavage group, such as religious affiliation or trade union membership. They also may impose a probationary period on new members, requiring them to demonstrate their commitment to the predefined group interest before they are granted full membership rights. Finally, cleavage parties may have mechanisms for expelling members who are perceived to be disloyal to the party's major aims. These elaborate rules on membership are designed to protect the party from takeover by those who misunderstand, or who seek to undermine, community interests. In short, such parties may employ the mechanisms of representative democracy, and their narratives of legitimacy may emphasize the virtues of these procedures. However, deference to members is restricted when that is seen to conflict with the party's proclaimed goal of representing the fundamental and predefined interests of a specific group.

In contrast, *Subscriber Democracy* (Bermeo and Nord 2000; Morris 1990) *Parties* define themselves through their members. These organizations are heirs to the civic associations that proliferated in the mid-nineteenth century. Such associations enrolled a dues-paying (subscribing) membership, and gave members an equal vote in internal affairs. Organizational leaders were accountable to the membership, and often were required to report to them at the organization's annual meeting (Morris 2000). Among the first parties to adopt this organizational style were the nineteenth-century British, German, and Swedish Liberals. Neumann described these as *Parties of Individual Representation*. Parties in this mold depict themselves as formed by, or on behalf of, individual citizens with shared values. Unlike cleavage parties, which put a premium on shared social group identity, they are in principle open to all who broadly share their values. At the same time, it is party members, not pre-existing commitments to ideology or to social groups, who ultimately determine party aims. As in the nineteenth-century civic associations on which they were originally modeled, leaders of subscriber democracy parties are formally accountable to members. Members of such parties are viewed as *Stakeholders*, with clearly defined rights to help determine party goals and to help select party leaders. These rights are most often exercised indirectly, through layers of delegates and representative assemblies. In practice such organizations may function as oligarchies dominated by office-holding leaders, but statutorily they are mini-republics. As the subscriber democracy label suggests, such parties tend to have clear rules to distinguish members from non-members; these rules usually require regular payment of a party subscription (dues).

Political Process Parties resemble subscriber democracy parties in that they look to enrolled supporters to validate the superiority of their proposals. The difference is that these parties emphasize supporters' direct involvement in party decisions. As a result, they are likely to place more direct responsibility in the hands of individual members than to leave decisions to delegate assemblies. (Gunther's and Diamond's Left-Libertarian Parties fit into this category; 2001, 10–11.) This ideal of participatory democracy within parties was popularized by Green and Alternative parties in the 1980s. More recently, it has been embraced by populist parties such as the German Pirates Party and the Italian Five Star Movement, both of which based their political credentials on their extensive use of internet-based policy formulation (Hartleb 2013; Passarelli and Tuorto 2013). Green and Alternative parties have had varied approaches to membership rules, differing on whether to make them maximally open to encourage participation, or to limit membership to those who share fundamental party values. Some of the newer populist parties have made broad popular participation in party decisions a paramount principle, one that is at least as important as other (often loosely defined) party priorities.

Finally, *Political Market Parties* are ones whose leaders rest their mandate on party responsiveness to voters' wishes. Kirchheimer's catch-all parties fall into this category (1966), as do Panebianco's electoral professional parties (1988), Koole's modern cadre party (1994), and Gunther's and Diamond's "electoralist" catch-all party (2001, 10–11). Parties of this sort place electoral success at the center of their narratives of legitimacy: good election results signal that a party is on the correct course. In keeping with their name, political market parties may use market research tools to determine what ideas have popular support. Such parties suffer doubly from big electoral losses, because they lack an alternate political justification. This sets them apart from ideological parties and cleavage-based parties, which may soldier on for years winning relatively few votes, but nevertheless retaining a firm identity and purpose. Just as personalistic parties can find it difficult to continue when their founding leader leaves the scene, political market parties lose their *raison d'être* if political consumers reject their brand: a catch-all party faces an existential crisis when it catches little.

As long as they are winning elections, political market parties may treat their members as fans and volunteers, but not as stakeholders. When a party is governing, leaders may think that members' primary job is to help rally voters at election times, not to help make decisions. However, once that party finds itself outside of government, its leader may make greater efforts to develop member support as an alternative source of legitimacy, for instance by highlighting members' roles in party decision-making. Thus, whereas Kirchheimer (1966) predicted that catch-all parties were likely to downgrade the role of members, when such parties suffer major losses they may re-examine these decisions, and may instead expand intra-party democracy in order to buttress their claims to represent the popular will. In political market parties, membership empowerment can be a tactical response designed to increase the party's electoral popularity; it is not an ontological need, as with political process parties. Because political market parties stress their accountability to voters rather than to their formal members, they may be willing to consider opening these processes to non-member supporters, if such openness seems likely to win votes. In other words, political market parties may treat traditional members as stakeholders, but not necessarily as the only stakeholders.

The party types shown in Table 2.1 illustrate common ways that ideology interacts with party goals to affect the status of, and need for, party members. The rows show how party organizational decisions can be shaped not only by electoral considerations, but also by the ways that parties frame their political appeals. They also show that party members are not created equal. Differences in the roles that parties assign to their members are likely to affect how much the parties can or will invest in reforming their existing membership organizations. Parties which view members primarily as fans should find it relatively easy to substitute other resources for the financial and volunteer benefits that members once provided. Fan-based membership parties also tend to have looser affiliation rules, making it easier for parties to expand alternative forms of affiliation. In contrast, parties that have viewed members as stakeholders may find it more difficult to cope with waning enrollments. For these parties, dwindling membership undercuts one basis of their claim to political legitimacy. As a result, such parties may make greater efforts to offset these losses, for instance by elevating the status of members in hope of attracting or retaining more members. On the other hand, such parties may find it more challenging to introduce new forms of affiliation, especially ones that potentially compete with dues-paying membership.

The preceding discussion shows how ideological considerations may interact with the more familiar political economy logic that is often applied to party organizational development. Electoral competition and electoral rules play a big role in shaping organizational decisions, but ideological filters can affect the organizational calculus. Moreover, because organization is tightly linked to ideology, some organizational shifts may signal, or may precipitate, shifts in ideological commitments. Thus, even if short-term tactical reasons explain why a party experiments with holding an open leadership vote, its use of the procedure may have the longer-term impact of altering intra-party (and wider) assumptions about the proper source of the party leader's mandate. Subsequent chapters will examine these relations more closely, looking at how parties' organizational adaptation is affected by their claims about whom they represent, and at how ongoing organizational changes can signal altered claims about the sources of party legitimacy. First, however, it is worth looking more closely at the new forms of affiliation that some parties have been exploring, to see what they entail for parties and for individuals, and how they relate to traditional types of party membership.

THE EMERGENCE OF MULTI-SPEED MEMBERSHIP PARTIES

Most definitions of party membership center on the question of what distinguishes party members from other party supporters. In parties with very formal membership rules, there may be behavioral distinctions between members and other supporters, and even between different groups of members (e.g. activists vs. other members). One classic and influential attempt to capture these distinctions is found in Maurice Duverger's description of party participation as consisting of four concentric circles. Member-militants occupy the center of his bulls-eye diagram. They are distinguished from other members by their activities, and by the strength of their partisan sympathies. Electors occupy the outermost ring. (See Figure 2.1.) Supporters occupy an intermediate position. They have stronger partisan sympathies than mere voters, and they may occasionally help their party by making a donation or joining an ancillary organization, but they do not take up full party membership. In Duverger's colorful language, "the relation of supporter to member resembles the relation of concubinage to marriage" (1954, 102). Ordinary members are much more involved in party life than supporters, but are less active than militants (1954, 90–1). Although Duverger applied this model specifically to mass parties, this notion of

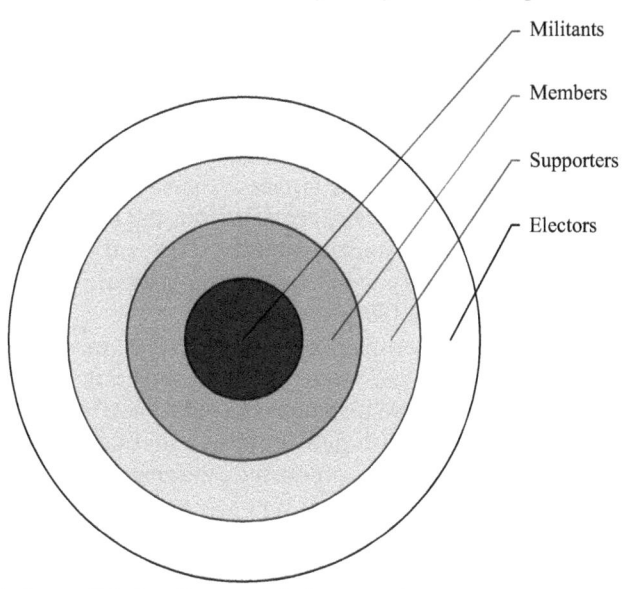

FIGURE 2.1 Party affiliation: Duverger's bulls-eye model

concentric levels of activism is commonly used to distinguish between different levels of partisan commitment and partisan participation in all types of membership-based parties.

Duverger's neatly ordered model resembled the Neils Bohr model of the atom, still current when he was writing, in which electrons are conceived as circling a central nucleus in concentric orbits that are decreasingly attached to the nucleus. According to this classic chemical model, electrons occupy orbits with different average distances from the nucleus. Electrons stay in their fixed orbits unless there is a chemical reaction in which energy is released or absorbed. In the party equivalent of this model, elected officials and party leaders are the nucleus. Active members occupy the innermost orbit, followed by other members, then party voters. All activists are presumed to be members. All supporters always vote for the party. Like their atomic equivalent, the central activists in this model are seen as more tightly bonded to the party. These strong bonds make them act differently than other party supporters, giving greater time and energy to the cause.

This traditional concentric circle model of activists, members, supporters, and voters continues to be a useful starting point for thinking about the role of individuals within parties. (For instance, see Hazan and Rahat 2010, and Kenig et al. 2013 for a model that revises these circles). More generally, many studies of partisan activity still accept the assumptions of this model, and make a simple distinction between formal party members and other supporters. Yet this model has always been incomplete, in part because it ignores supporters who have been attached to the party in other ways, for instance as family members or as members of trade unions. Moreover, viewing different ways of relating to the party as fixed and discrete orbits obscures some of the most interesting aspects of party life: the movement between, and overlap among, these circles. Whereas diagnoses that focus on party membership numbers may see exit from the party as a symptom of partisan disaffection (for instance, Whiteley 2011), a dynamic model sees movement in and out of party membership as a normal part of organizational life (Selle and Svåsand 1991).

In fact, parties themselves may seek to erase the boundaries between these support categories. As Chapter 6 will describe in more detail, in recent years many parties' have responded to voter disaffection, and to the advent of new technologies, with new initiatives that deliberately blur the lines between members and other supporters, making it easier for supporters to link to the party, even if only in very loose ways. Some of these new affiliates may be designated as "sympathizers" or "friends" instead of members. Other opportunities to connect with a party may be as informal as subscribing to a party blog or linking to a party's Facebook page. Some of these new modes of affiliation are alternatives to traditional membership; others complement it and can be enjoyed either separately from, or in addition to, old-style affiliation.

It is not a new idea for parties to create alternative affiliations for those who do not want to join the party proper. Indeed, Duverger described the creation of such options as "the latest stage in party technique" in the early 1950s (1954, 106). Yet today's new affiliation modes differ from the ancillary organizations that Duverger described. The latter were often only loosely linked to the national party, and many pursued seemingly non-partisan ends (sports clubs, tenant associations, small gardener associations). In contrast, today's affiliates are generally linked directly to the central party and their activities center on partisan politics or issue advocacy. National parties can use relatively inexpensive new technologies to stay in touch with these new affiliates, including e-mail, electronic newsletters, blogs, text messages, and Facebook postings. Affiliates sign up to receive these electronic messages. Parties then try to mobilize them to act as "digital ambassadors," urging them to pass along partisan messages to their friends and to declare their political affiliations on Facebook pages (Margetts 2006; Marschall 2001). In addition, a few parties have created categories of affiliation that are designed as half-way steps to traditional party membership, including trial memberships with reduced dues and reduced membership privileges.

When we broaden the membership lens in this way, it becomes clear that parties have always had multiple categories of permanent affiliates. These include self-identified supporters who may or may not be dues-paying party members in the traditional sense. As with the members of older-style party-linked sports clubs and choirs, self-identified and registered partisanship is one of the characteristics that distinguishes these affiliates from more casual supporters who may receive mass mailings or a doorstep political visit. Different types of affiliation may generate different types of contact from the party, and may lead to different types of engagement. For instance, traditional party members are most likely to interact with local parties, and are most likely to have face-to-face contacts with other party supporters. On the other hand, those who affiliate solely as Facebook friends or blog followers will be in touch with the central party or national party leader. They have fewer opportunities for personal interaction than traditional dues-paying members, but they are more likely to receive central party messages on a weekly or even daily basis—far more partisan contact than most traditional members received in the past. In other words, patterns of contact with the party differ across types of affiliation. Similarly, one type of affiliate is not necessarily more engaged than another; instead, levels and types of activity vary across individuals. Furthermore, these types of connections are not mutually exclusive, meaning that individual partisan experiences will vary according to a person's portfolio of affiliations.

The imperfect overlap between partisan activists and party members is a second factor that muddies the clean lines of the concentric circle model of activism, membership, and supportership. Multiple affiliation modes create potentially overlapping circles of support and contact. The idea that all activists were party members was probably never accurate, particularly for cleavage-based parties that traditionally drew campaign volunteers from other organizations aligned with the group interest (such as trade unions, churches, or farmers' organizations). But, as will be shown in more detail in Chapter 5, it seems to be increasingly the case that party activists are not necessarily just a subset of party members. Many who are active *for* a party also choose to be a member *in* the party, but this link is neither automatic nor necessary. Moreover, many contemporary parties are encouraging supporters to get involved, regardless of their membership status. For instance, non-member supporters may be asked to donate to the party, and they may be urged to distribute party materials to their digital friends; they may even be invited to help select party candidates or leaders.

Finally, a third factor that complicates the concentric circle picture is that the size of the circles does not correspond to the required level of commitment. Thus, for most parties the newer affiliation categories still attract relatively small numbers, although these numbers are growing along with the spread of new technologies. Low-intensity participation opportunities do not necessarily attract higher numbers of participants.

One way to summarize this discussion is to differentiate affiliation modes in terms of the economic calculus of membership: what are the costs to the individual of joining, and what rights do individuals gain when they affiliate in different ways? As a group, political parties in parliamentary democracies are now offering at least six main ways of joining, listed here from most to least costly. These represent a repertoire of affiliation modes from which parties choose; few parties promote all of them to an equal extent.

1. **Traditional individual membership** This type of affiliation is traditional in the sense that the mass party model has been an organizational inspiration for many parties in parliamentary democracies. When there are multiple ways to affiliate, traditional membership is the mode that confers the most political rights within the party, and also carries the heaviest obligations. Such members are generally required to pay dues, and may also need to sign an explicit declaration of support for party principles. Traditional members may have to serve a probationary period before they are granted full political benefits. Most parties specify that traditional membership is an exclusive status: members are prohibited from joining more than one party at a time.

2. **Light membership** This category, sometimes designated "party friend" or "party sympathizer," is a kind of second-class membership. It charges lower dues than traditional membership, but also carries fewer benefits, especially political benefits. Light members are generally ineligible to stand as candidates, but sometimes are allowed to vote in intra-party decisions. Parties may view light membership as a potential gateway to full membership. They may give individuals the option of remaining in this category indefinitely, or they may set it up as *trial membership*. This is a time-limited status for those who are curious about the party but not yet ready to fully commit.

3. **Cyber-members** These "virtual members" are formally registered party supporters who are recruited through a party's web page or other on-line portal. In some parties, they also must fulfill criteria other than simple self-registration, such as proclaiming support for the party goals, requirements that set them apart from those who are merely on-line followers. This category may include traditional members, who have all the rights and obligations of other traditional members, but who sign up through on-line cyber branches rather than having the more customary link with a geographically-based local party. Cyber-members of all types are encouraged to use on-line tools to campaign on the party's behalf, and to help spread the party message to others. They also may receive special benefits, such as password-protected access to websites that provide resources for building websites and Facebook pages to promote party goals.

The preceding categories share certain similarities, in that they create communities reserved for loyal supporters. They also usually involve an exchange of rights and obligations. These features distinguish them from the affiliation modes described next, ones which impose no duties, and which generally do not require exclusive membership. Those who affiliate to a party in the latter ways may sometimes gain opportunities to exercise voice within the party, but because the affiliation is so loose, they have little to gain by threatening to exit. These looser affiliation categories contain some who would have been labeled "supporters" in Duverger's distinctions. While this label still applies, the definitions identify relationships with parties that go beyond psychological attachment, in that they involve some kind of formal registration with the party. Because of this registration, party organizations can communicate with these affiliates much more effectively and frequently than with more casual supporters.

4. **Sustainers** These are supporters with financial links to their parties. Their gifts may be small, one-time, donations, they may be ongoing contributions via automatic bank withdrawals, or they may be large gifts. Even when the amounts are small, digitally solicited contributions can reinforce partisan ties that exist apart from traditional membership categories and traditional member activities. In making on-line donations or contributing via text message, contributors provide contact information, which parties can use for future communication and mobilization. Parties are likely to return to one-time donors in hopes that they will give further financial support.

5. **Social media followers and friends** These join party-led digital communications networks; they do not pay fees to affiliate in this way. Followers receive messages from the party headquarters or party leader via Twitter or other blogs, or the party Facebook page. These media are designed as two-way communications technologies. Parties may emphasize this participatory angle by encouraging followers to speak back, for instance urging them to comment on Facebook postings or to answer web-polls on topical questions. Followers do not have any obligations towards a party, nor is this status exclusive: no rules prohibit individuals from "liking" more than one party, or from receiving Twitter messages from competing politicians.

6. **News audience** This is the audience for one-way communications from a party. Audience members may sign up to receive updates from one or more of the party's official outlets, such as newsletters and news feeds. Those who access the party web page directly are also part of the wider audience. However, they are not a registered part of this audience, and therefore the party cannot initiate communication with them. Parties' news communications are generally distributed for free. Like social media followers, registered audience members incur no obligations towards the parties from which they receive the information. Even if followers and news audience members never communicate back to the party, they are not necessarily

politically passive. Indeed, one reason for parties to enlist such affiliates is the hope that targeted party communications will mobilize broader public opinion. Such mobilization may be accomplished when news recipients forward story links to friends; it also could occur through conversations between friends and colleagues. Thus, even though these loose affiliates do not have obligations to the parties, having such affiliates may enhance parties' ability to shape public perceptions, and may provide them with valuable data about their supporters.

We could conceive of these different modes of affiliation merely as new rings in Duverger's concentric circle model. In such a model, activists would still be seen as a subset of traditional members, and partisan engagement would progressively diminish when moving towards the outer rings. However, this modified concentric circle model would not be a good representation of how people actually affiliate, because those in the inner circles do not necessarily belong to all of the outer categories. Most importantly, supporters can volunteer for a party without actually joining it. Moreover, the size of the groups does not necessarily expand when moving from the inner to the outer circles.

In a way, this lack of fit should come as no surprise, because the atomic model once used to describe levels of party activism has itself been obsolete for decades. It has been replaced by a model which conceives of atoms as nuclei surrounded by clouds of particles whose locations are described probabilistically rather than depicting them as confined to fixed orbits. Similarly, the model of party activism proposed here sees supporters' activities and commitments as much more fluid than the activism-orbits in Duverger's model. This quantum model of activism assumes that individuals will alter their degree of participation in party activities at different points in their lives, or even within spans of months rather than years. When there are important elections or internal primary contests, the affiliated supporter may temporarily take her activism to a different level, for instance by joining the party in order to vote in party-internal elections, or by volunteering to work in local campaign efforts. Indeed, parties may encourage supporters to move temporarily from one circle into another, for instance by inviting "instant members" to participate in party decisions (an incentive to formally join), but then offering them few reasons to keep paying membership dues once the vote has passed. Today's Party Friend may never become a full-fledged party member, but she may serve as a digital ambassador, for instance by forwarding Twitter messages to her friends, sharing a link to a partisan YouTube video, or letting her Facebook friends know that she "likes" her party and its leader. She might even be inspired to make a one-time donation by text message, making her a Sustainer, even if she never pays regular membership dues. Whether or not she is a registered party member, she is closely linked to the party project, receiving messages

Motives and Modes of Party Membership

from the central party, and possibly participating in two-way communications in the form of party-organized discussion groups and surveys. Her level of partisan engagement between national elections may not predict what she will do in the months leading up to an important political contest. This dynamic model implies that we need videos, not snapshots, if we want to study individual experiences of partisan activity and affiliation across different points in electoral cycles, and across different life stages.

Another important difference from Duverger's model of partisan engagement concerns the size of the various groups. In his classic model, there is a direct and inverse relation between the level of partisan activity and the group size: those in the large outer ring are least active, those in the small inner ring are most active. In this new model, high activity is not confined to those in the central rings: most importantly, some non-member supporters may be very active on behalf of their party. Conversely, some traditional members who self-recruit and pay dues on-line may be only very loosely linked to the party, especially to local party branches. Parties can benefit by mobilizing various types of affiliates at election times, particularly if they can move loose affiliates into higher levels of activism.

Figure 2.2 illustrates this new organizational structure with the overlapping circles of a Venn diagram rather than as a bulls-eye. The sizes of the various circles are only suggestive. In practice, the relative sizes of the different groups would need to be established empirically. We would expect this to vary across parties, and across time in a single party. What will not change is the fact that these circles overlap: some individuals are in several circles at once; some in only one or two. The entire diagram encompasses

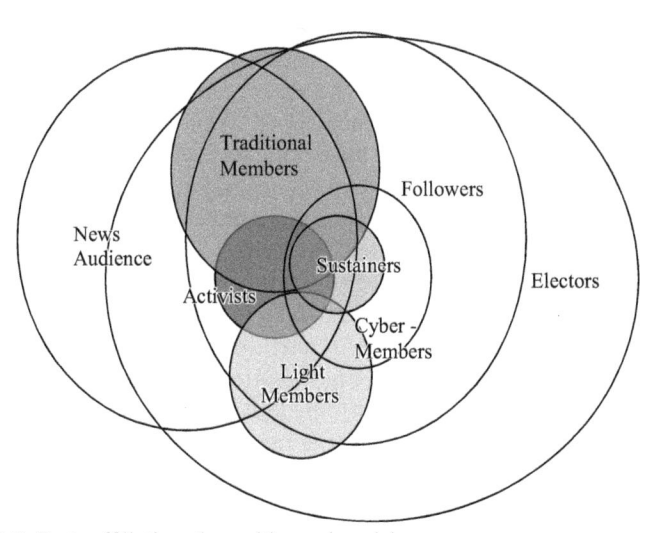

FIGURE 2.2 Party affiliation: the multi-speed model

a larger universe than Duverger's circles, which were bounded by party voters, because the news audience of the newer model potentially includes non-citizens and others who never will vote for the party. In addition, the lines between these new circles are fluid: individuals are likely to shift between them, sometimes within very short periods. Many supporters may join for a few years and then leave. Unless they are very disillusioned by their experiences they may remain more loosely bound to the party through political and personal ties; they potentially could be reactivated under the right political circumstances.

The fluid affiliation categories depicted in Figure 2.2 characterize today's *multi-speed membership parties*. These are parties which differ from traditional membership parties by deliberately linking to their supporters in a variety of ways, and by promoting varying types of activity for affiliates. Multi-speed membership parties offer supporters multiple ways to engage with their preferred party, and to be active on its behalf.

CHANGING PARTY STRUCTURES AND DEMOCRATIC CHANGE

How do these organizational changes affect the interests that get represented in parliamentary democracies, or the strength of popular support for contending parties? Do shrinking party memberships and the changing nature of party affiliations alter the choices that parties offer, or the way these choices are perceived? Before answering questions about the impact of these party organizational changes, it is important to clearly understand parties' prior experiences with membership-based organizing. As the discussion of party representation narratives indicated, some parties have never enrolled members, and even those that did have done so for varied reasons. We need to take account of this, and to start with an historically informed baseline before assessing the extent and likely impact of recent changes.

Constructing such a baseline is the task for the next two chapters. They begin by mapping the development of membership-based parties in parliamentary democracies. These historical accounts make clear that it has been relatively rare for parties in parliamentary democracies to have numerically strong membership organizations. Although many parties have paid lip-service to the subscriber-democracy ideal, and although a few well-known parties did enlist large memberships, there was no point in the twentieth century when it was common for democratic parties to enroll as many as 10 percent of their voters as individual dues-paying members. Moreover, even though the use of membership-based organizing grew throughout the twentieth century, parties have invested these members with roles that vary widely in terms of their organizational and political importance. For most of the twentieth century, the largest membership parties were ones which included indirect membership in their totals. Those that enrolled large numbers of direct members tended to have areas of geographic strength and weakness, making membership-based party politics more of a regional than a national phenomenon. These points are important correctives to accounts that portray contemporary parties' small and declining membership numbers as novel developments. Exaggerated visions of once-thriving membership parties provide a poor starting point for judging what has changed, or how the change might matter. The accounts of the next two chapters thus examine historical data to offer an amended view of the oft-described phenomenon of party membership decline, showing that losses are not as dramatic as is sometimes suggested, and that current enrollment levels are not greatly different from past experiences. This picture provides a more optimistic background to subsequent chapters' examination of current reforms, because it sets the bar a little lower for parties that want to rebuild past organizational strength.

3

Myths and Realities of Mass Membership Parties

The decline of mass membership parties is simultaneously true and exaggerated. As is well known by now, party memberships in established parliamentary democracies shrank during the last third of the twentieth century, and this decline has continued into the twenty-first century. Chapter 4 will look more closely at these numbers to clarify the extent and timing of the changes. The earlier part of this story is less well known, but it, too, deserves to be critically examined in order to understand what preceded the apparent drops at the end of the twentieth century. As will be seen, in most countries and in most eras party members had never been a large part of the electorate. Adding more complexity, some of the parties that have lost members now have tighter links with those who do enroll. Thus, one of the first steps for understanding organizational changes in contemporary political parties is to look more closely at the apparent divergence between the idealized vision of once-dominant mass membership parties, and the historical realities of party development. Disentangling the ideal from its realization is the goal for this chapter. The historical accounts presented here survey the uneven emergence and growth of membership-based party organization. Investigating where and why this organizational template took root helps to explain its enduring appeal, even in circumstances in which it has proven difficult to implement.

When summarizing the evolution of membership-based parties in parliamentary democracies, one of the most striking facts is that democratic parties with large individual memberships have been the historical exception. In Europe, overall party enrollments rose sharply in the first third of the twentieth century, but much of this increase related to the success of anti-democratic parties. Prior to the 1950s only a few parliamentary democracies had strong membership parties on both the democratic left and right. This began to change immediately after the end of World War II. However, as early as the 1960s scholars were already diagnosing the demise of membership-based political organizing, and were portraying this organizing technique as an old-fashioned vestige. Since then, this diagnosis has become widely accepted. However, it is one which rests on shaky historical foundations, because it seems to imply that large party memberships were once the norm. In fact, the mass membership party may be better understood as an ideal to which many parties aspired, particularly parties on the left, but which was only sporadically achieved. Nevertheless, it was and is important, because the ideal proved to be persistently attractive, and because it continues to guide many parties' internal organizational decisions.

THE EMERGENCE OF PARTY MEMBERSHIP: MULTIPLE PERSPECTIVES

The idea of membership-based parties is about 150 years old. Prior to the 1860s few European political parties had any sort of parliamentary caucus; even fewer had extra-parliamentary support structures. Almost none of them enrolled supporters in members' associations. In contrast, by the 1960s almost all parties in parliamentary democracies were membership-based organizations (at least nominally). This transformation, which began in the last third of the nineteenth century, can be understood as the result of cultural, functional, and ideological pressures and incentives.

The Cultural Context: Political Parties and Other Voluntary Associations

From a cultural perspective, the emergence of membership-based political parties is merely one aspect of the nineteenth century's associational efflorescence, part of a much broader trend in changing social structures. As recent historical scholarship has underscored, the nineteenth century was the age of the voluntary association, especially the second half of the century. This context shaped the development of political parties on both the left and the right (Bermeo and Nord 2000; Hoffmann 2003). Some of the first parties of the right had their roots in religious guilds; many liberal parties had their roots in middle-class associations. Parties of the left often employed structures that resembled those used by middle-class associations, even though they appealed to different social groups.

Associational life expanded across Europe in the first half of the nineteenth century, growing despite strict state supervision of private societies. After the defeat of Napoleon, most of the restored regimes in continental Europe imposed repressive limits on civic and political life. Under these rules, associations of all sorts were tightly regulated, and were not allowed to espouse political aims. Even so, their increasing popularity had political implications, because they altered the fabric of civic life by strengthening networks in the private sphere. Among the most common of the early voluntary associations were exclusive literary societies and private clubs, including Free Masons. Associational life gradually opened up to broader constituencies, though the pace of such change depended on the extent of each regime's toleration for private associations. Thus, Britain developed an active and open associational life by the 1830s. In contrast, this developed more slowly in much of continental Europe, when it was hampered by legal restrictions, and by government censorship. Nevertheless, even here civil society became more active by the 1840s, briefly bursting forth in full force during the revolutionary years of 1848/9 (see chapters in Bermeo and Nord 2000; Laven and Riall 2000; Morris 1990; Morton et al. 2006).

After 1848 the restored regimes banned all associations that were perceived to have revolutionary sympathies, but many showed increased tolerance for groups that were considered regime-supportive or non-political. As a result, by the third quarter of the nineteenth century voluntary associations were spreading through all fields of European life, spurred by what has been dubbed "association mania" (*Vereinswut* in German). In some countries the growth of civic groups can be traced to specific legal changes, such as the 1867 relaxation of association laws in the Habsburg lands. Yet growth also occurred in countries like the Netherlands, where associational life had been under few legal restrictions in the previous decades. It also happened in France, which did not recognize the legal right of free association until 1901. Non-legal explanations for this organizational flowering include increased urbanization, rising literacy rates, growing prosperity that expanded access to leisure time, and the heightening of social conflicts that fragmented prior associations (Hoffman 2003; Nord 2000).

Whatever the causes, by the second half of the nineteenth century, civic realms in Europe and the British colonies were characterized by increasingly dense associational networks. Groups promoted all aspects of life, from entertainment, to self-improvement, to public improvement. Typical examples included literary societies, gentlemen's clubs, musical associations and choirs, museum associations, women's organizations, temperance societies, sports clubs, and self-insurance organizations. Associations first flourished in urban settings, but by the end of the nineteenth century they were a feature of small towns and rural areas as well. They were also spreading to different social layers: by mid-century they were no longer primarily a middle-class phenomenon, with new associations forming to cater to the growing urban working class. Although their aims and constituencies varied widely, many of these associations adopted similar organizational forms, ones that recognized written rules as the basis of associational legitimacy. Carl Strikwerda describes this as the spreading embrace of bureaucratic methods, a trend that accelerated by the end of the nineteenth century, by which point "[f]ormal membership, written rules, organized meetings, and designated officers were utilized by everyone from big business corporations to farmers' leagues and coalminers' unions" (1997, 11).

This bureaucratic embrace was manifest in the fact that most voluntary organizations published statutes and issued annual reports on their activities. Indeed, some countries enacted laws that required private associations to have statutes designating who was in charge, thus ensuring that there were individuals who could be held legally accountable for associational activities. Civic associations generally articulated membership rules in their charters or by-laws. Such rules might require members to support the organization's aims and to pay an annual subscription; sometimes they included requirements that reserved membership for targeted populations. Associations might select or elect executive committees; these usually had the obligation to report to annual membership meetings. Robert Morris dubs such member-based associations "subscriber democracies" (1990, 184). In practice, most subscriber democracies may have operated in ways that were neither democratic nor open, but on paper at least they affirmed the importance of rule-based procedures and the equality of members-in-good-standing. In this way the associations pioneered the practice of liberal democracy on a small scale, practices that took hold even under autocratic regimes. The widespread adoption of similar structures across multiple countries and in organizations serving multiple purposes attests to a rapidly developing consensus about which organizational practices gave leaders authority to act on behalf of the group.

Thus, when membership-based political parties began to emerge in the last third of the nineteenth century, their leaders were not just inventing organizational models from thin air: there were plenty of examples for them to follow. Some parties emerged out of existing membership-based organizations, be these economic organizations (local workers' associations and trade unions) or religiously affiliated ones. In other cases, the new membership-based parties emulated the efforts of other groups to enroll citizens in communities of interest. On the left, this organizational formalism led to what Geoff Eley describes as "the crucial democratic breakthrough of the nineteenth century's last four decades": the elevation of the socialist mass party model (2002, 27). A mass party was characterized by campaigning publicly for parliamentary representation, and by "organizing its own affairs by the internal democracy of meetings, resolutions, agreed procedures, and elected committees" (Eley 2002, 27).

To be clear, most civic-oriented associations did not become political parties, and indeed, prejudices against political parties remained strong through the end of the nineteenth century. Liberal political thought portrayed voluntary associations as communities which aimed to improve individual virtue and civic welfare. In contrast, political parties still tended to be viewed as factions, in other words, as organizations more focused on the achievement of narrow self-interest than of the common good. Nineteenth-century conservative political thought remained hostile to partisan organizing, sometimes pointing to the excesses of the French Revolution as proof of the dangers of organized politics (Hoffmann 2003; Huard 2000; Rosenblum 2008; Scarrow 2002). Nevertheless, as elections became an increasingly important part of political life, even supposedly non-political local associations could assume functions linked to parties, such as candidate selection and voter mobilization (see e.g. Hiebl (2006)'s description of associational life in a small city in Austria). As a result, local leaders who constituted de facto "parties of notables" may not have held formal membership in local party organizations, but they may have been personally linked by their memberships in other associations.

The cultural perspective suggests that organized membership parties should be understood as products of a specific time, and as ones whose original forms and practices were influenced by those of other voluntary societies. This rapid growth of partisan and non-partisan groups in the late nineteenth century was fostered by changing economic conditions, and by the growth of national transportation and communications networks. The organizational styles favored by these groups reflected an emerging belief in the importance of rules rather than customs as the basis of civic life.

Cultural pressures have continued to shape parties' more recent development. In the middle of the twentieth century, the *Zeitgest* may have helped to convince some non-socialist parties to adopt membership-based organizational models. In this period, popular organizations seemed more modern than organizations premised on deference to local notables. Similarly, the spreading use of direct democracy for public decisions in the late twentieth and early twenty-first centuries may have nudged political parties to begin using more direct democracy within party structures. Just as the ideal of membership-based party organization grew out of, and was strengthened by, broader ideas about civic life, so too has this ideal been undermined by ongoing value shifts which put a higher premium on individual autonomy and the private sphere. Because political parties are organizations which are seeking broad popular support, their organizational decisions inevitably reflect cultural perceptions about how individuals should connect with their wider societies.

Political Organization as a Functional Response

Functional and institutional explanations for the emergence and development of extra-parliamentary organizations portray organizational outcomes as solutions to problems facing political elites: how to win elections, how to coordinate activity in legislatures, how to advance political careers, how to handle political recruitment (for instance Aldrich 1995; Cox 1987; Harmel and Janda 1994; Panebianco 1988; Schlesinger 1991). The demand-side views of party membership change discussed in the previous chapter are a subset of broader functional perspectives on party organization.

Institutional accounts tend to emphasize how electoral systems and political opportunity structures affect incentives for legislators and aspiring politicians to invest in creating and maintaining local party organizations. For instance, in the first decades of the twentieth century the widespread switch to proportional representation spurred the strengthening of national party organizations. The new ballot structures meant that local committees could no longer manage candidate selection and campaigning on their own; instead, they needed to coordinate with national or regional co-partisans. Proportional representation also created new incentives for parties to campaign even in areas where their support was comparatively weak. Similarly, in the many countries with very limited franchises in the nineteenth century, one of the original purposes of local partisan organization was to identify supporters and make sure they were on the electoral register (Ertman 2000; Gash 1977; Huard 2000). Organizational needs changed when the franchise broadened.

Institutional explanations for the emergence of strong extra-parliamentary party organizations also highlight legal obstacles to organizing. For instance, in many countries party organizational growth was hindered by laws restricting free assembly and curbing free speech. Such laws more heavily affected parties which were perceived to be anti-regime, particularly those associated with socialism.

Perspectives which focus on rules and incentives help explain cross-national differences in the timing of party development, and in some organizational choices. There was less need for well-organized local campaigns prior to the advent of contested elections and a relatively large franchise. Even after the franchise expanded, restrictions on organization and on free speech could delay the emergence of strong partisan structures (as in France). These types of explanations for organizational development continue to be invoked to explain decisions by today's parties, such as arguments that link the introduction of party subsidies to changes in party organizational practices. On the other hand, institutional and functional arguments are generally less useful for explaining why parties within a single country respond differently to similar environments. To understand this, it is also helpful to understand how political organizers' different worldviews shape their organizational preferences.

Ideology and Organization

As Chapter 2 argued, parties' organizational choices are not purely matters of electoral strategy and internal power struggles. They are also the product of implicit or explicit beliefs about the nature of politics, and about how parties ought to function as channels of democratic representation. Some parties draw a clear link between their organizational choices and their narratives of legitimacy, asserting that parties must have the right type of organization in order for them to contribute towards building a better society. Thus, Green parties in the early 1980s touted their novel organizational practices as being essential for achieving their programmatic goals, because these included opposition to governance by entrenched political elites. Similarly, some of the emerging cleavage-based parties in the late nineteenth and early twentieth century explicitly portrayed their popular organizations as communities for reshaping the social order, not just as campaign resources. For parties of the left, networks of leisure societies, women's and youth organizations, and co-operatives were workshops for *creating* socialists. These associations, which were embedded in a larger framework of trade unions and mutual aid societies, were supposed to educate urban workers about the inequitable distribution of economic and political power, and to provide solidary ties to reinforce class loyalty (Eley 2002, ch. 2).

In the nineteenth century, politicians on the left were not the only ones who hoped to use grassroots associational membership to create and reinforce political identities. In Belgium and the Netherlands they were not even the first to do so. Some of these first efforts at exerting popular political pressure drew inspiration from the success of earlier popular movements, including the British Anti-Corn-Law League of the 1830s and 1840s, or the Irish Catholic Association of the 1820s. In the final decades of the century Catholics began forming Church-sanctioned associational networks to protect Catholic culture and institutions against the perceived threats of liberal (secular) modernizing states, and of growing socialist mobilization. Political organizing was not the initial aim of many of these lay associations, even though some of them eventually provided essential support for Catholic candidates, and for nascent Catholic political parties. The lay Catholic associations helped to turn Catholicism into an identity that acquired political overtones when the Church felt under attack (Kalyvas 1996). Where Catholic parties formed, they usually could rely on support mobilized by non-party associations; because of this, they had little need to construct party-specific popular organizations. Indeed, in their early years some Catholic parties did not recognize individual party membership, and relied solely on corporate membership of functionally defined subgroups (small business associations, etc.)

In the last decades of the nineteenth century, orthodox Calvinists in the Netherlands formed their own political and social sub-organizations for reasons similar to those of their Catholic counterparts. They were first spurred to political action by a secularizing state, and later by the perceived threat of socialist organizing. In 1879 this movement gave birth to one of the first membership-based political parties, the Dutch Anti-Revolutionary Party (ARP) (Ertman 2000: 168–9). Whether Catholic or Protestant, the parties which emerged out of religious subcultures, like their socialist counterparts, viewed organization as a tool to cultivate group identity, not just (or even primarily) as a means to mobilize for elections.

Cultural, institutional, and ideological pressures all shaped the introduction and spread of membership-based political parties. Such parties formed as part of a wider cultural shift in the nineteenth century, one that spurred the growth of all sorts of membership-based associations. Parties' organizational choices responded to country-specific electoral incentives and legal obstacles. Finally, ideology played an important role: the parties that created the strongest mass organizations were those that viewed politics as a struggle to preserve or transform dominant social orders. All three forces have continued to influence party organizational development from the nineteenth century through the present day.

WHEN WERE DEMOCRATIC MEMBERSHIP PARTIES AT THEIR PEAK?

Although the idea of membership-based political parties had begun to spread by the end of the nineteenth century, actual political practices were a different matter. This discrepancy deserves closer scrutiny, because it is at the heart of the puzzling gap between the myth and the historical reality of mass member parties. Diagnoses of contemporary party change need to carefully distinguish between these two aspects of political development. Above all, accounts of party change should avoid comparing today's empirical realities with yesterday's ideal types.

In keeping with this, the next sections seek to establish when and where membership-based party organizing became established in practice as well as in aspiration. To this end, these investigations will examine the evolution of popular partisan organizing in the regions and countries that became the nineteen democracies which are at the center of this study. As will be shown, membership-based party organizing was relatively rare outside of left parties until the second half of the twentieth century. Even on the left, the development was uneven, both within and across individual countries.

Pre-1848: Obstacles to Popular Organization

Public political organizing was slow to emerge in continental Europe in the nineteenth century, hampered first by reactionary laws adopted in the shadow of the French Revolution, and then further restricted by anti-revolutionary measures that spread across post-Napoleonic Europe. In the 1820s and 1830s autocratic regimes actively repressed anything resembling political opposition. Under principles propounded by the Austrian minister Prince Metternich, formalized in the Carlsbad Decrees of 1819 and in subsequent expansions of these laws, the Habsburg Empire and its allies prohibited all forms of political and labor organizing, and tightly restricted other types of association (Tenfelde 2000). As Table 3.1 shows, most of the future parliamentary democracies maintained legal restrictions on assembly and association well into the nineteenth century. These rules prevented all gatherings which authorities viewed as having a subversive political purpose. For example, the 1808 French Law on Association required associations with twenty members or more to register with authorities, and

TABLE 3.1 *Removing obstacles to political organization*

	Press Freedom			Organizational Freedom	
	End of prior censorship	End of severe post-publication censorship	End of special press taxes	Free association guaranteed	Legalization of trade unions
Austria	1867	Post-1914	1899	1867	1867
Belgium	1830	1830	1848	1830	1866
Denmark	1849	1846		1849	1849
Finland		1917		1906	1906
France	1814	1881	1881	1901	1864
Germany*	1848	Post-1914	1874	Post-1918	1869
Great Britain	1695	c. 1830	1861	1689	1824
Greece				1911	never banned
Italy**	1848	c. 1900		1848	1859
Netherlands	1815	1848	1869	1848	1872
Norway	1814	1814			never banned
Portugal	1834	1852		1911	1910
Spain	1837	1883		1867	1868
Sweden	1809	1838			1846
Switzerland	1848	c. 1830		1830	never banned

* Prussia before 1871.
**Piedmont before 1860.
Source: Goldstein 1989, 33.
Notes: Australia, Canada, and New Zealand: British rights extended to free settlers in 19th cent. Ireland: British controlled but more limited political freedoms. Empty cells = information missing.

organizations regarded as potentially subversive would have their registrations denied (Huard 1996, ch. 1). This law was in place throughout the nineteenth century. As the same table shows, most countries also banned labor organizing until at least the latter third of the century.

Most of these regimes also censored all political speech, using both pre- and post-publication sanctions. The impact of such laws went well beyond their actual use, because the threat of fines and imprisonment encouraged self-censorship. All the future parliamentary democracies except Norway retained legal restrictions on press freedom at least into the 1830s (see Table 3.1). High taxes on newspapers posed an additional deterrent to the development of a popular press even in countries like Belgium and Great Britain that abolished censorship relatively early. Liberties of speech and association developed unevenly, and progress towards achieving them was seldom linear. Many countries strengthened restrictions on political activity after the revolutionary uprisings of 1830 and 1848 (Goldstein 1989). Wherever restrictions on speech and assembly applied, they hampered the development of political parties as well as other civil society organizations.

There were a few exceptions to these restrictive practices in the first half of the nineteenth century. Not surprisingly, these exceptions coincided with the first efforts at popular organizing on behalf of political parties and other movements. This was most evident in Britain, a country with a long-established constitutional monarchy, and one that was not under the sway of the reactionary politics of Metternich's Europe. Yet even here political liberties developed slowly and unevenly. For instance, although England relaxed censorship restrictions by the 1830s, it did not develop a nationwide popular political press until the 1860s, after the reduction of previously high newspaper taxes and the relaxation of libel laws (Goldstein 1983, 33–68). However, in comparison with most of its European neighbors, the obstacles to political organizing were low in nineteenth-century Britain. Because of this, partisan organizations and other political associations were able to develop rapidly when political controversies and institutional changes created new incentives for political coordination inside and outside the Westminster Parliament. The utility of popular organization for electoral mobilization was dramatically demonstrated in Ireland in the 1820s, when Daniel O'Connell and the Catholic Association used a network of local branches to fundraise and to support candidates who favored their cause of winning full political rights for Catholics. Soon thereafter, the redistricting and slightly increased franchise of the Reform Bill of 1832 created new incentives for political organizing in Great Britain, because these reforms made parliamentary elections more competitive (Bulmer-Thomas 1967, ch. 8; Salmon 2002),[1] and because the struggles surrounding the passage of the First Reform Bill sharpened partisan divisions in British politics. These changes spurred the formation of Britain's first national party committees, which took the form of informal election organizations run out of private clubs. They focused primarily on the legal task of ensuring that known supporters got on (and stayed on) the electoral register.[2] These proto-party organizations did not enlist members or have formal statutes, so in that sense they did not lay the groundwork for later membership-based parties, but they did again demonstrate the potential electoral benefit of coordinating election efforts. Such efforts went largely dormant by the mid-1840s, undermined by the increasingly blurred lines of partisan division within the legislature (Gash 1977; Hanham 1978). However, in the late 1830s and early 1840s the Anti-Corn Law League had taken up the model of non-violent political mobilization pioneered by the Catholic Association; the success of both movements demonstrated the potential clout of large membership-based political organizations.[3]

Organized partisan politics slowly spread to Britain's settler colonies in the first half of the nineteenth century. By the 1850s European immigrants in the territories that became Australia, Canada, and New Zealand lived within the framework of English law, and their territorial legislatures had gained some measure of self-government.[4] However, it was only in the second half of the century that their legislatures began to organize along clear partisan lines (Engelmann and Schwartz 1975; Milne 1966; Overacker 1952; Robson 1967).

Outside of the Anglo democracies, partisan divisions also crystallized as legislatures became more central to political life, and once restrictions on political association were eased. Belgium was the other parliamentary democracy that experienced big strides in this direction prior to 1848. From the founding of this new constitutional monarchy, in 1830, legislative elections were consequential for determining the complexion of the government. The importance of these elections fostered party development. Divisions between Liberals and religious conservative forces soon emerged as a central dividing line in Belgian politics, although the electorate remained small until the end of the nineteenth century. In 1846 the Belgian Liberal Party became the first in that country to formally establish a nationwide network of local electoral associations (Delwit 2009, 26–7; Irving 1979, 170).

Elsewhere, even where restrictions on political organization were loosely applied, the absence of competitive legislative elections meant that there was little reason for parliamentary allies to organize outside of parliament. Most legislative assemblies that existed prior to 1848 had little or no influence (for instance, France, Spain). Some were still based on "estate" models of representation (including Austria, Finland, and Sweden; Carstairs 1980). In all of these legislatures, members were elected or selected by extremely small constituencies, meaning there were few votes to be gained from extra-parliamentary partisan organization.

In short, prior to 1848 Britain and Belgium developed early examples of both parliamentary and extra-parliamentary party organization, but this was an exceptional story among the future parliamentary democracies. The nascent party organizations that emerged in these two countries engaged with relatively small electorates. In all countries in this era, "party" remained a term that was more associated with intellectual currents (liberal, conservative, monarchist, ultramontane, etc.) than with formal organizations.

1848–1914: The Spread of Civic Association and Cleavage Representation Parties

The organizational face of politics changed quickly in the second half of the nineteenth century as parliaments gained new political powers, as electorates expanded, and as restrictions on political organizing were lifted. Some countries got a first taste of the new politics in 1848, when middle-class liberals temporarily joined cause with urban workers to demand greater economic and political rights. Revolutions spread across Europe, toppling monarchs and replacing them with republics or constitutionally limited monarchies with broad suffrages and new political freedoms. In Denmark and the Netherlands, monarchs defused the revolutionary pressures by granting new, constitutionally protected, political freedoms. Elsewhere, most of the changes were short-lived, as the revolutionary regimes proved unable to construct new political institutions that could cope with the challenges of post-revolutionary governing. By 1850 all but one of these new regimes had collapsed.[5] The restored monarchies quickly imposed renewed restrictions on political liberties. Yet many of them maintained some of the institutional changes precipitated by the revolutions, including greater sovereignty for legislatures and, in some cases, an expanded franchise (Goldstein 1983; Sperber 2005). As a result, by the end of the 1860s a majority of the countries in this set were constitutional monarchies, and most had direct elections for their lower chambers of parliament (see Table 3.2).

Even so, few countries had truly competitive elections until at least the 1880s, and through that decade most retained relatively small electorates. Table 3.2 shows the expansion of the national electorates, calculating these figures both as percentages of the entire population, and as percentages of the adult population. To interpret these figures, it is worth remembering that the countries studied here excluded women from the franchise throughout the nineteenth century,[6] and that most of them combined high voting ages with youthful demographics.[7] Under these conditions, a country with full manhood suffrage would have enfranchised about 40 percent of the adult population, or about 25–30 percent of the entire population.

TABLE 3.2 *The franchise and parliamentary elections*

	A Enfranchised as % of Population		B Enfranchised as % of Adult Population		C Nationwide Manhood Suffrage	D First Direct Legislative Election	E First Competitive Legislative Election
	1865	1895	1860s	1890s***			
Australia					1902	1901	1901
Austria	6	7	0	13	1907	1873	1907
Belgium	2	22	7	37	1893	1831	1847
Canada	15	15			1920	1867	1867
Denmark	15	16	25	29	1915	1849	1884
Finland	6	5			1906	1907	1907
France	25	29	41	42	1848	1876	1902
Germany*		21	35	38	1871	1848	1848
Great Britain	4	16	8	29	1918	1832	1885
Greece	23	23			1864	1844	1926
Ireland+					1919	1921	1923
Italy**	2	7	4	17	1912	1848	1895
Netherlands	3	6	5	21	1917	1848	1888
New Zealand	17				1879	1856	1890
Norway	8	11	9	17	1898	1906	1882
Portugal	9	10			1918	1852	1915
Spain	3	24			1890	1832	1876
Sweden	6	6		12	1907	1866	1887
Switzerland	22	22		38	1848	1848	1896

* Prussia before 1871.
** Piedmont before 1860.
*** Highest figure of the decade.
+ Founded as the Irish Republic in 1919.
Sources: Column A: Goldstein 1983; Australia, New Zealand, Canada: Mackie and Rose 1991; column B: Bartolini 2000, 583; column C: Mackie and Rose 1991; column D: Rokkan and Meyriat 1969; column E: Mackie and Rose 1974. Empty cells = information missing.

As columns A and B show, by the 1860s only a few countries in this group were close to these levels, including France, Greece, and Switzerland. Of these, only Switzerland also had a sovereign parliament. France had manhood suffrage but actively repressed political opposition throughout the Second Empire period. The country's legislative elections and plebiscites had predetermined outcomes (Huard 1996). Greece also had manhood suffrage, but its political system had only limited political competition (Korisis 1966). Prussia and Denmark offered voting rights to half or more of their adult male residents by the 1860s, but Prussia's property-based suffrage was not equal. Canada and New Zealand enfranchised more than one-third of European-origin adult males for their colonial legislatures. Elsewhere, electorates remained quite small in the 1860s, generally under 10 percent of the population.

After 1880 many countries rapidly expanded voting eligibility, with most instituting full manhood suffrage in the first two decades of the twentieth century (see Table 3.2, column C). Even before full manhood suffrage was achieved, most electorates had become so numerous that elections could no longer be determined solely by signals from local notables. In addition, the spreading use of secret ballots further hampered traditional local control mechanisms. By 1900 more than 10 percent of the total population was enfranchised in all but three of the countries in this set. These expanded franchises created new incentives and new opportunities for parties to systematically organize their popular support.

Other changes in this half-century also affected the speed and degree of party organizational development. By the 1870s most of the future parliamentary democracies in this study had removed both pre-publication and post-publication political censorship, though exceptions remained. The Austro-Hungarian lands and Germany retained post-publication censorship until 1914, and Austria continued to levy special press taxes until 1899, restricting the development of a popular press (see Table 3.1). By the 1870s most of the countries also had introduced guarantees of free association, and had legalized trade unions and strikes (in law, if not always in practice). The loosening of such restraints provided more room for political debate and for the development of organized popular politics. There were important exceptions to this trend. For instance France, one of the first countries to have manhood suffrage, did not guarantee freedom of association for political purposes until 1901. Portugal did not legalize trade unions until 1910. In addition, explicitly anti-socialist laws and police actions hampered organization on the left in some countries. These restrictions were lifted in Germany in 1890, in Italy in 1900, and in Austria in 1911 (Bartolini 2000, 321).

One result of the broadening suffrage and the increasing status of parliaments was that legislative elections became more competitive and more likely to be organized along party lines. Coordination became more obviously useful when more was at stake in the elections. Mackie and Rose date the advent of competitive partisan parliamentary elections as the first one "in which the great majority of seats for the national parliament were contested, and most candidates fought under party labels common across constituencies" (1991, p. x). Under this definition, only three of the future parliamentary democracies had experienced their first competitive partisan elections by 1870.[8] By 1900 only five countries were holdouts from this trend: Austria, Finland, France, Greece, and Portugal. All of them held their first competitive legislative elections prior to 1918. In Austria and Finland, parliaments were still organized by estates in 1900, a pattern that changed shortly thereafter (Austria in 1907, Finland in 1906; Carstairs 1980). In Portugal, a small electorate had directly elected the parliament since the middle of the nineteenth century, but elections were dominated by two very similar parties which generally negotiated a division of the electoral spoils (Costa Pinto and Tavares de Almeida 2000). Thus, Mackie and Rose designate 1915 as Portugal's first competitive election. Well into the twentieth century Greek elections were contested on the basis of personalities more than of parties (Hering 1992; Koliopoulis and Veremis 2002; Korisis 1966). Extra-parliamentary party organizations emerged more slowly in countries where competitive elections arrived relatively late.

Variations in organizational obstacles and electoral incentives help explain why extra-parliamentary parties emerged at different times in different countries. Partisan popular organizations could not develop until associations had the right to assemble, and until restrictions on political speech were relaxed. There was little point in organizing extra-parliamentary support organizations until parliamentary elections mattered, and until large number of citizens were eligible to participate in them. But even favorable institutional and political conditions did not guarantee that organized parties would emerge. In Switzerland, for instance, national party organizations only began forming in the late 1880s and early 1890s, decades after the Alpine republic granted manhood suffrage and guaranteed freedom of assembly and freedom of speech. Yet even if broad enfranchisement was not always sufficient to spur popular political organizing, the transition to mass electoral politics made it increasingly worthwhile for political leaders to invest in grassroots political organizations.

This general background provides the context for answering the more specific question about the state of membership-based party organizing in the late nineteenth and early twentieth centuries. One good place to start when tracing membership party emergence is to rule out the countries which lacked nationally coordinated partisan membership organizations prior to 1910. This includes Greece and Portugal, which had not yet held competitive elections. It also includes three countries which had some or much experience with competitive elections, but in which parties had yet to introduce or cultivate permanent membership-based organizations: Canada, New Zealand, and Spain (though by 1910 the Spanish Socialist Workers Party did enroll a small corps of militants: Gillespie 1989, 19–20; see also Edwards 2003, ch. 6; Engelmann and Schwartz 1975; Milne 1966).

To understand developments elsewhere, it is useful to look at party organizational patterns by party families. This is because parties' organizational strategies were shaped by the nature of their political bases and by their ideologies. Liberal parties and parties on the non-religious right were among the first to develop membership-based organizations. Nineteenth-century Liberal parties developed in response to country-specific conflicts, but in general they shared an appeal to the growing urban middle classes. Given that this milieu took the lead in embracing subscriber-democracy civil society associations, it is not surprising that many liberal parties consciously adopted similar organizational structures, with formally enrolled members and statutes that specified members' rights and obligations.

Once again, British parties led the way, with both the Liberals and the Conservatives being among the first to develop strong networks of locally organized party members. Their efforts were spurred by the relatively early expansion of the British electorate, a change which rewarded parties which were able to mobilize their supporters. In the 1860s Liberal clubs in Manchester and Birmingham touched off this development when local campaigners began coordinating supporters to win extra seats in multi-member districts. Their successes prompted Liberal associations around the country to adopt the so-called "Birmingham Model" of political organization. Under this system, any male local resident who supported the party's principles could join a ward party by paying an annual subscription. Ward members elected a ward committee at a public meeting, and the ward committees sent representatives to a citywide association. In 1877 the Liberal Party established itself as a national federation, governed by an annual meeting of delegates sent from the municipal parties. Despite this highly developed procedural democracy, in Birmingham and elsewhere municipal parties were often dominated by a few powerful leaders. In addition, an internal power struggle in the early 1890s made clear that the parliamentary party would not be bound by the national federation's policy decisions (Bulmer-Thomas 1967, 120–1; McKenzie 1955; Ostrogorski 1982 [1902]; Vincent 1976). Yet even though the party base did not gain *de facto* control over party office-holders, these structural experiments made the British Liberal Party a pioneer in adapting the subscriber-democracy template originally developed by civic associations. By employing this model, the party demonstrated that enrolled supporters could be both an electioneering resource and a source of party legitimacy.

In 1883, after a further expansion of the electorate, the British Parliament became pioneers in adopting political finance legislation, strictly limiting the amount that candidates could spend on their campaigns. These restrictions, coupled with the expanding electorate, radically altered prevailing campaign practices. They eliminated the use of paid canvasser corps and voter "treating" (providing food and drink on election day), and rewarded candidates who could recruit volunteers to mobilize supporters (McKenzie 1955, 165; Pinto-Duschinsky 1981). Spurred by this legislation, and by the obvious success of the Liberal's labor-intensive organizing, Conservatives slowly began developing their own network of local parties. They began this task in 1867 by creating the National Union of Conservative and Constitutional Associations. The National Union was a federation of local parties that functioned under the subscriber-democracy template, enrolling members who elected local leaders. Local parties sent delegates to a national meeting. However, in the Conservative Party the reach of organizational democracy was always explicitly limited by the formal separation between the National Union and the party's parliamentary wing, and by the National Union's loose membership rules (Bulmer-Thomas 1967, 112). Moreover, in the early 1890s many of the party's individual supporters enrolled not in the party itself, but in the Primrose League, a pro-Empire association that was only loosely affiliated with the Conservative Party. This organization counted over one million members by 1891 (Bulmer-Thomas 1967, 129).

In the British cases, as elsewhere, the organizations of Liberal and non-religious Conservative parties developed in response to new electoral challenges. Where such parties could rely on local notables to organize support, they often did so, but they formed their own organizations when they needed more coordinated efforts. In Belgium, the Liberal Party began forming local membership-based associations in the mid nineteenth century, but these remained small until well after the 1893 introduction of manhood suffrage (Delwit 2009). In Imperial Germany, the Left Liberals and National Liberals were the first non-socialist parties to adopt membership-based organizing models. They shifted in this direction in the 1890s, spurred in part by the resurgence of socialist organizing after the lifting of the anti-socialist laws. By 1914 Germany's National Liberals claimed over 2,000 local branches and 200,000 members (Nipperdey 1961, 89–105; Sperber 1997, 135). In Denmark, it was the Right (later, Conservative Party), that was the first to experiment with membership-based local organization (Miller 1968, 59). In Sweden, both the Liberal Party and the Farmers' Party were formed at the beginning of the twentieth century. From the start both employed membership-based organizing based on local branches. The Swedish Liberal Party counted over 40,000 members by 1910. This country's Farmers' Party developed more slowly, but its Center Party successor enrolled tens of thousands of members by the 1930s (Aberg 2011, 222; Christensen 1997).

Yet it was certainly not the case that all liberal and secular conservative parties relied on membership-based organizing in the pre-1914 period. For instance, in this period the Norwegian Farmers' Party was one of the rare parties of the secular center-right that relied on corporate membership by milieu organizations rather than recruiting individual members of its own (Christensen 1997). In Finland, non-socialist parties established extra-parliamentary organizations around 1906, when manhood suffrage was introduced along with a new electoral system. However, through the 1930s these parties remained weak electoral associations, lacking strict membership definitions and with branches that were largely inactive outside of election periods (Allardt and Pesonen 1960; Sundberg 1995). Likewise, in pre-1914 Switzerland, the Radical Democrats lacked their own individual party members, and were instead a loose federation of many affiliated groups. In France, Republicans and Radicals remained parties of notables, with little organized grassroots support. Their structures reflected both the parties' identities as loose electoral coalitions, and the restrictions on political organizing that were in place prior to the French Associations Law of 1901 (Huard 1996, 2000).

In countries like Belgium, the Netherlands, and Germany, religious communities generated electoral organizations as a result of struggles over secularization that brought them into conflict with liberal parties. One chief organizational difference between various religiously-based parties was whether they established party associations to identify and mobilize supporters, or whether they relied solely on milieu organizations to reinforce supporters' political and social identities. Catholic parties in Austria, Belgium, Germany, and the Netherlands fell into the latter camp through the first years of the twentieth century. Rather than cultivating their own memberships, these parties derived support from networks of confessional organizations, including trade unions and newspapers (Ertmann 2000; Evans 1981; Kalyvas 1996; Sperber 1997). In the Netherlands, orthodox Calvinists in the 1880s were the first to organize a political party that used membership enrollment and ancillary organizations to boost its political influence (see Ertman 2000; Evans 1999). The situation was quite different in Italy, where the conflict between the new state and the Catholic Church was so extreme that the Church initially discouraged good Catholics from participating in the country's national politics. Overtly Catholic party organization only emerged in Italy in the early twentieth century, once the Church began loosening this restriction in the face of rising socialist power (Banti 2000, 54; Kertzer 2000, 198; Duggan 2000, 156).

Liberal and religious parties were thus some of the first to establish membership-based party organizations, and to try to translate popular organizing into electoral strength. Liberal parties tended to develop these organizations in keeping with subscriber-democracy templates. In contrast, the religious parties adopted a more holistic approach to partisan associations: for them, political life was only one aspect of an encompassing ethos that encouraged individuals to live their lives in ways that were inspired by divine authority.

For very different reasons, some of the emerging socialist parties built party structures which not only recognized and formally empowered grassroots members, but which also included a full range of ancillary organizations to structure all aspects of supporters' working lives and private hours. Early socialist parties developed before most of their supporters were eligible to vote, which is one reason that they did not begin as purely electoral organizations (see Table 3.3). Indeed, socialists built some of their strongest organizational networks in two countries where they faced particularly tough obstacles to electoral participation: in Germany, and in regions of Austria-Hungary. In these two countries, repression of socialist political

TABLE 3.3 *Founding of first socialist or labor parties*

			Years until (after) Manhood Suffrage
Australia	1891	Australian Labor Party	11
Austria	1889	Austrian Social Democratic Party	18
Belgium	1885	Belgian Workers' Party	8
Denmark	1876	Danish Social Democratic Association	39
Finland	1899	Finnish Labor Party	7
France	1880	Federation of the French Socialist Workers' Party	(32)
Germany*	1875	German Social Democratic Party	(4)
Great Britain	1883	British Social Democratic Federation	35
	1900	British Labour Party	18
Greece	1920	Socialist Party of Greece	72
Ireland	1912	Irish Labour Party	7
Italy**	1892	Italian Socialist Party	20
Netherlands	1881	Dutch Social Democratic League	36
New Zealand	1901	New Zealand Socialist Party	(22)
Norway	1887	Norwegian Labor Party	11
Portugal	1871	Portuguese Socialist Party	37
Spain	1879	Spanish Socialist Workers' Party	11
Sweden	1889	Swedish Social Democratic Workers' Party	18
Switzerland	1888	Swiss Social Democratic Party	(40)

Sources: Bartolini 2000, 246; Eley 2002, 63.

organizations forced parties to focus their (legal) efforts on creating ostensibly non-partisan associational networks such as groups for women and youth, sport clubs, singing clubs, and mutual aid societies. When the parties were permitted to emerge as extra-parliamentary associations, these ostensibly non-party organizations helped to foster rapid growth in party membership (Bartolini 2000; Eley 2002).

Outside of Austria-Hungary few parties of the 1890s came close to imitating this organizational success. Some left parties did not even try, adopting very different organizational models. One of them, the British Labour Party, was a latecomer to its country's political scene. Established in 1901 as the Labour Representation Committee, and renamed the Labour Party in 1906, this new party grew out of the trade union and co-operative movements and remained organizationally tied to them. Initially the British Labour Party was not an organization for individual members; instead, individuals were affiliated to the party indirectly, as a result of their membership in one of several other associations (primarily affiliated unions and co-operative societies). In adopting indirect membership, the British Labour Party became one of several social democratic and labor parties that initially focused on corporate membership of union members rather than on individual and direct affiliation. Other adaptors of this approach included the Belgian Socialist Party and the Swedish Social Democrats (Strikwerda 1997, 20). It also included Australia, where a national political wing of the labor movement emerged in the 1890s, even before the creation of federal Australia. This was established as a federal party in 1901 (and in 1908 took its modern name, the Australian Labor Party). Unlike the British Labour Party, from its start the ALP combined direct individual membership with indirect membership through affiliated trade unions (Jupp 1964; Overacker 1952).

In contrast, the Dutch Socialist Party adopted only a direct membership model. However, this party grew very slowly, with growth blocked in part by late industrialization, and by competition from confessional parties which were making their own appeals to the working classes (Andeweg and Irwin 1993). Socialist party membership also grew slowly in France and Italy, countries where socialist parties did not use affiliated membership (Huard 1996, ch. 10; Banti 2000, 55). The more Marxist socialist parties did not even want large memberships. For instance, through the 1920s the Spanish Socialist Party remained a deliberately small party of militants, admitting only the most fervent adherents as party members (Gillespie 1989, 20–6).

The first column of Table 3.4 summarizes this discussion, showing the spread of membership-based party organization prior to World War I. As it makes clear, by 1910, most—but not all—of the emerging parliamentary democracies had membership-based socialist or social democratic parties, even if in France, Italy, and Switzerland these organizations were relatively weak, and in several countries this membership was mostly or entirely indirect. In contrast, only one-third of the countries had non-left parties with established broad-based membership-based structures. Only Denmark, Germany, and the Netherlands had large parties of the left and right that had successfully recruited large numbers of *individual* members. Even this overstates the case, because by 1910 one of Germany's largest parties, the Center Party, still did not recruit its own members. In short, at the beginning of the twentieth century the idea of member-based political organizing had yet to be widely embraced. Among parties that did enroll individual members, success in recruiting large memberships was even rarer. We thus need to look further to find a true hey-day of membership-based party organizing.

1918–1939: Popular Mobilization in the Inter-War Years

During the inter-war period, parties in parliamentary democracies initiated major organizational reforms in response to institutional and ideological

TABLE 3.4 Democratic parties with membership-based organizations

	A	B	C	D
	c.1910	c.1930	c.1960	c.1990
Membership Parties: Left and Right	Australia* Denmark Germany Netherlands Sweden* UK**	Australia* Belgium***+ Denmark Germany Netherlands Sweden* UK*	Australia* Austria+ Belgium Canada Denmark Finland Germany	Ireland* Italy Netherlands N. Zealand* Norway* Sweden* UK*	Australia* Austria Belgium Canada Denmark Finland France Germany Greece Ireland*
Limited Membership Parties: Primarily in one party, usually on the Left	Austria Belgium** Finland France Italy Norway* Switzerland	Austria Finland France Ireland N. Zealand** Norway* Spain Switzerland	France Switzerland		Italy Netherlands N. Zealand* Norway*¹ Portugal Spain Sweden*¹ Switzerland UK*
No Membership Parties	Canada N. Zealand Spain	Canada Greece	Greece	
No Competitive Elections^	Greece Portugal	Italy Portugal	Portugal Spain	

Parties with statutory recognition of membership and some real development of membership structures.
* Left: Indirect and Direct Individual Membership.
** Left: Primarily or exclusively indirect membership.
\+ Right: Primarily or exclusively indirect membership.
¹ Indirect membership abolished: Norwegian Labor Party 1997; Swedish Social Democrats 1990.
^ Mackie and Rose 1974.

changes in their electoral environments. This was a period of rapid political and economic changes, particularly in the new republics in Central Europe, and in Southern Europe. By the mid-1920s many European countries were governed by some form of dictatorship, including Italy, Portugal, Spain, and Greece. Elsewhere, these democratic collapses loomed large, as did the revolutionary example of Communist-led Russia. Democratic politics of the era were dogged by the apparent promises of various revolutionary alternatives, visions which were actively promoted by populist parties on the left or right.

In most parliamentary democracies, parties of all types faced newly competitive and highly mobilized electoral environments after World War I. Whereas half the countries in this study lacked full adult manhood suffrage in 1900, by 1920 all of them had implemented this. The expanded electorates meant that all parties had much more to gain by cultivating grassroots organization. In addition, many countries adopted more proportional electoral systems in this period, which also increased incentives for party organizing and coordination. These institutional conditions formed the background for new waves of popular organization by both democratic and anti-democratic parties.

To see how these changes affected the creation of democratic membership-based party organizations, we can once again start by ruling out countries in which such structures played little or no role during the inter-war period. This was most clearly the case in Italy and Portugal, which were dictatorships for most of the 1920s and 1930s. It was also true in Greece and Spain. Both countries held some contested elections in these two decades, but political parties had little chance to develop their organizations during the short democratic episodes.

On the democratic left, parties often worked in tandem with increasingly powerful trade union movements. The socialist parties in the countries studied here were equally split between those in which most or all of the nominal members were indirectly affiliated through trade unions, and those which had only individual members. In seven of the countries in this set (Australia, Belgium, Ireland, New Zealand, Norway, Sweden, and the UK),[9] trade unions affiliated to the main party of the left, financially supporting party work in some way, and in return receiving representation in party decision-making bodies. These parties also admitted individuals directly, but in the 1920s their affiliated members far outnumbered individual members. About the same number of socialist parties admitted only individual members (in Austria, Denmark, Finland, France, Germany, Netherlands, Spain, and Switzerland). With or without indirect membership, most of the democratic left parties cultivated milieu organizations, including sports clubs, women's organizations and youth organizations. These organizations aimed to construct and reinforce political identities based on shared interests.[10] In the 1920s, parties such as the Austrian Socialists and the German Social Democrats epitomized the vision of the democratic mass party that was described by Sigmund Neumann as "parties of democratic integration," and that would later be described by Maurice Duverger as the *parti de masse*—party-of-the-masses, or "mass party" (Neumann [1932] 1965; Duverger 1954). Yet in Germany, and even more so in Austria, these strongly organized parties were dominant only in large urban centers (Dachs 1995, 158).

Most center-right and right parties only slowly revised their organizational strategies in the face of post-war changes in the electoral environment. This meant that in the 1920s most Conservative and Catholic parties still based their local mobilization efforts on informal networks and non-party groups, except for those like the Dutch ARP that had strong pre-war membership traditions. A few of them began moving towards membership-based organizing, but with mostly modest success. For instance, the German Center Party was a rare Catholic party that tried building a membership organization in the 1920s. However, this party's organization dwindled quickly as its electoral support faded. The Dutch Catholic Party introduced direct individual membership in 1926 (Evans 1999, 147). In contrast, the Belgian Catholic Party formally introduced *indirect* membership in 1921, organized around corporate sub-organizations (van Haute 2011b, 36). When the New Zealand center-right parties merged after an electoral defeat in 1936, one of the changes introduced by the new party was to begin recruiting individual members organized on a branch party basis (Edwards 2003, ch. 6). In Canada, the Conservative Party first established a national organization in 1924, but for a while this was largely inactive; it did not formally establish a dues-paying membership until 1943 (Williams 1956). In 1929 the Danish Liberal Party took initial steps to strengthen what had been a very weak and decentralized membership organization, but these changes did not bear fruit immediately. In Norway and Finland, non-left parties often benefited from the support of well-organized popular social movements (for instance, farmers' or temperance associations), but if they had their own memberships these were, at best, loosely organized (Allern 2010: 106–13; Christensen 1997; Nousiainen 1971). In the new Irish state, Fine Gael and Fianna Fáil were initially only loosely organized at the constituency level, but by the election of 1932 Fine Fáil had made great strides in establishing a nationwide network of local party clubs. These locally focused networks would become important to the party's ongoing electoral success (Carty 1981: 104–8; Chubb 1970; Moss 1933).[11] In this era the French center-left Radicals offered a rare exception to the generally weak membership basis of non-religious and non-socialist parties. By the mid-1930s, this party claimed up to 120,000 members. These figures were inflated by memberships purchased in bulk by competitors trying to gain advantages in intra-party votes, but the high numbers are nonetheless indicative of aspirations to create a membership-based organization (Larmour 1964, 22).

In sum, the 1920s and 1930s brought changes in the ways that some center-right and Catholic parties approached the subject of party membership. Yet for most of the non-socialist parties, the new steps in the direction of membership-based organizing models did not yet translate into big actual enrollments. Moreover, it is worth noting that parties which lacked formal memberships in this period were not necessarily electorally weak. Indeed, quite the opposite could be the case: several center-right or religious parties began experimenting with formal membership enrollment only after experiencing electoral losses. In countries like Canada and Finland, parties which lacked extensive formal party membership organizations were nevertheless able to mobilize high levels of partisan participation at the local level.

Column 1 in Table 3.4 summarizes these developments, showing the extent to which the electorally large parties of the left and right were attempting to cultivate links to supporters through membership-based organization. A comparison of columns A and B shows only modest change from the beginning of the twentieth century to the middle of the inter-war period in terms of the spread of membership-based party organizing. The list of countries with competitive elections was slightly altered, bolstered by the entrance of newly independent Ireland, and by the absence of several countries that had moved from partial democracy to dictatorship (Italy, Portugal, Spain). Even leaving aside these new and removed cases, the story of Table 3.4 is quite clear with regards to the growth of party membership organizations. In the 1920s and 1930s more parties of the center-right and religious right began to endorse the idea of parties as membership associations, but among the democratic parties of the period it was primarily (some) of the left parties that actually achieved this ideal.

The anti-democratic parties were another story. In this period some anti-system parties on both the left and right aspired to build strong membership organizations, and some had notable success. This was less true on the left, because many revolutionary left parties favored Leninist cell-based structures, which were inherently select and secretive. However, a few built broader popular organizations, though their memberships remained relatively small even where they enjoyed electoral success (including in Finland, France, Germany, and the Netherlands; Bartolini 2000, ch 2). For instance, in 1931 the German Communist Party—at that time probably the electorally strongest Communist Party outside of the Soviet Union—had an estimated 200,000 members (Nipperdey 1961, 397). This was a large number of members, but it represented only a very small portion of the more than five million votes the party received in the elections of 1932. Equally striking were the Greek Communists, who never enlisted a large membership, even though in electoral terms they were the main party of the left in this period (Hering 1992, ii, ch. 7).

Fascist and other anti-regime parties on the right actively enrolled large memberships as part of their strategies of populist mobilization. These parties tended to be more open to mass recruiting than the Communists, in part due to differing concepts about the role of the party base. Whereas the democratic centralism of Communist parties ascribed members a role in party decisions, Fascist parties made no pretense of intra-party democracy. They viewed members as fans, whose role was to support the leadership and to learn its worldview; leaders were not accountable to them. Like the socialist and Catholic milieu parties, the Fascist parties of the 1920s also tried to augment party organizing with a variety of ancillary organizations (including party militias), giving supporters multiple options for joining. The most successful of the far-right and right populist parties and movements enrolled hundreds of thousands of supporters, sometimes exceeding the enrollments of the left socialist parties. These included the nationalist Croix de Feu organization in France in the mid-1930s—renamed the French Socialist Party in 1936—and the National Socialists in Germany at the beginning of the 1930s (Soucy 1991). Thus, although some European democracies did experience surges in party enrollment in the late 1920s and 1930s, part of this growth occurred in anti-democratic parties; some of the rest was stimulated by this, as pro-democratic forces reacted to the marches and violence of anti-democratic parties. Such party membership growth was not the mark of healthy civic participation.

Faced with deep economic crises in the early 1930s, weak democratic governments in Germany and Austria succumbed to fascist nationalist movements. In Spain, the republic that was founded in 1931 struggled to survive. It was soon toppled and was replaced by General Franco's fascist dictatorship. Greek democracy dissolved in 1936 after the king appointed a prime minister who aimed to create a fascist state. At points in the 1930s, fascist and corporatist regimes in Austria, Germany, Greece, Italy, Spain and Portugal all used regime-controlled political parties as tools to boost visible support for the regime. Unlike the autocratic monarchies of post-Napoleonic Europe, the new dictatorships used parties to link themselves directly to the people, and these parties organized large rallies and other large-scale demonstrations to provide evidence of their popular mandate.

Thus, the 1930s witnessed the spreading use of party membership organizations by non-democratic parties, but with wide variations in the tasks that parties assigned to their members. The most ideological of the parties (the German National Socialists and the Communists) viewed members as adherents who needed to subsume individual interest to the (centrally defined) common good. The less ideological, more personalistic dictatorships of the 1930s generally created much looser party membership organizations, with members serving more as fans than as well-schooled followers. Both visions concerning the proper roles for party members contrasted with the stakeholder-members of the subscriber-democracy parties, and with the community-building members of cleavage representation parties.

The 1950s and Beyond: The Brief Apogee of Democratic Membership Parties

As the preceding accounts make clear, the first half of the twentieth century was not the golden age of party membership—at least not of *democratic* party membership. Such an age, if there was one, must be sought in the immediate aftermath of World War II. Yet if it existed then, it was at best a short-lived phenomenon, fuelled at least as much by electoral strategy as by a normative commitment to membership-based structures.

The late 1940s and early 1950s brought a surge in party organizing in many European countries after the wartime election hiatus. Even in countries with war-ravaged infrastructures and economies, new and re-established political parties scrambled for electoral advantage. In many countries party enrollments reached all-time peaks in this period, reflecting a pent-up demand for political participation.

Social democratic and labor parties profited from popular support for social welfare reforms that promised to prevent a return to the economic hardships of the 1920s and 1930s. Trade union membership surged immediately after the end of the war, helping to boost left party enrollments, an effect most evident in—but not limited to—parties with affiliated memberships for trade unionists (Judt 2007). For the most part the division between left parties with and without affiliated memberships remained the same as during the inter-war period, reflecting party origins. In some parties with affiliated memberships, enrollment growth largely reflected trade union expansion, while individual membership numbers remained relatively weak. For example, in the mid-1960s a report by the Australian Labor Party described the size of its individual membership as "appalling" (quoted in Overacker 1968, 184). One exception to this static division between parties with and without indirect membership was the post-war Belgian Socialist Party, which dropped affiliated membership and moved exclusively towards direct individual membership. It was the first left party to make this shift, but it would not be the last.

Big factors in the post-war surge in party membership numbers were the efforts of many center and right parties to build new or stronger membership networks. Whereas prior to World War II most Catholic parties had relied primarily or exclusively on Catholic lay organizations to mobilize popular political support, after the war many of them began building their own membership-based structures. This included the newly founded Christian Democratic parties in Italy and Germany as well as Belgium's Catholic Party. The latter party, newly renamed the Social Christian Party, switched to an exclusively direct membership, though it did retain some of its earlier links with farmers' and trade union groups (Irving 1979, 173). The new Christian Democratic party in France also attempted to build a membership organization, but its efforts were not very successful (Kalyvas 1996; Leonardi and Wertman 1989; Warner 2000). The Austrian People's Party was a holdout from this trend, opting to retain the corporatist structure of its predecessor, the Christian Socialist party. Rather than joining the party directly, its supporters joined sub-organizations representing sectoral interests (e.g. farmers, middle class); these sub-organizations formed the basis of the party federation.

Some secular center and right parties also showed new interest in membership-based organizing. By the end of the 1940s the Australian Country Party abandoned attempts to create affiliated membership structures and focused solely on individual membership. The new Australian Liberal Party also based its organization on dues-paying individual members. The Norwegian Farmer's Party began organizing its own membership in 1938, and its membership grew rapidly in the late 1940s (Allern 2010: 111; Christensen 1997). The Danish Liberal Party saw a big spike in its membership in the first post-war years, reaping the benefits of organizational reforms that it had initiated in the late 1930s. In contrast, in both Canada and Ireland the largest parties retained very weak membership structures at least through the early 1960s. Their statutes formally recognized party membership, but their membership procedures remained loose and localized.

Table 3.4, column C, summarizes these developments. It shows that by 1960 most of the democracies in this group had parties on both the left and right that recognized direct membership. In aspiration, and to a lesser extent in practice, these parties had the support of enrolled individual members who participated in local party associations. In most such parties, members were the nominal basis of authority within the party. At the beginning of the 1960s Greece was the only country in the group without at least one major party that had embraced membership-based organizing.[12]

This shift towards individual membership continued from the 1970s through 1990s, as several parties moved away from affiliated memberships, while others took their first steps towards formalizing membership requirements. The Austrian People's Party began to move away from an exclusively indirect membership in 1972, when it introduced the option of direct individual membership. After 1980 the party changed its rules so that all members of party sub-organizations would also hold direct party membership. Even after these changes, most members of the Austrian People's Party retained primary contact with a party sub-organization rather than with the local or national party (Müller and Steininger 1994). In the 1990s socialist parties in Sweden and Norway made more radical structural changes, abolishing affiliated membership altogether. The parties made these decisions after both party and trade union leaders came to view their long-standing institutional links as obstacles to growth for both organizations. The British Labour Party retained affiliated membership into the twenty-first century, but from the 1980s onwards it enacted a series of party reforms that steadily reduced the voting power of the affiliated trade unions in favor of individual members. In the small Irish Labour Party, unlike in the British Labour Party or Swedish Social Democrats, affiliated members had never held a block vote and had never been a major source of party finance, although most party members were themselves union members. Yet here, too, things shifted from the 1970s onward. The Irish Labour Party inaugurated a central membership registry in 1971 so that it could keep track of its individual members. This move coincided with the party's growing independence from trade unions (Mair 1987, 103). By the beginning of the twenty-first century, the left parties in which affiliated members (trade unions) remained most dominant were the Australian Labor and New Zealand Labor parties. Trade unions also retained great influence in the UK Labour Party, but this influence had waned in the preceding two decades. In other left parties, to the extent that party membership was important, it was individual membership.

The last decades of the twentieth century saw a new interest in membership-based organizing even in some parties which had previously made few moves in this direction. In the 1970s Swiss parties of both the center and right amended their constitutions to create clearer membership rules and enhanced membership rights, reforms which were justified as ways to alter the parties' local notable images (Grüner 1977, 269–303). Yet these efforts were not very successful in transforming either of the parties into membership organizations. Two decades later the Social Democrats were still the only Swiss party with centralized membership records and uniform national membership requirements (Ladner 2001, 138). More important were the changes within Canadian parties. They began strengthening their identities as membership organizations in the mid-1960s, although at that point party membership still remained a local or provincial party matter. In the 1980s and 1990s, Canadian parties across the political spectrum began instituting uniform national membership requirements and record keeping (Carty et al. 2000). These changes were largely spurred by national parties' newfound interest in intra-party democracy. In order for parties to give members votes in internal decisions, they had to know who their members were, and to have stricter rules on who was and was not eligible to participate. A similar change took place in France on the Gaullist right, and for similar reasons. Whereas from the mid-1950s to the mid-1970s Gaullist support had been organized around notables, not activists, by the 1980s the Gaullists were attempting to build up membership-based party structures. By the 1990s the Gaullist RPR had statutes with formalized membership requirements, and which gave members a direct vote in leadership selection. This was a marked change in a party that was originally built around the personality of a strong leader who did not like strong parties (Haegel 1998). In Ireland, Fine Gael took steps in the 1970s to formalize membership and to elevate the status of individual members, and introduced a central membership registry (Mair 1987, 103). The most electorally successful Irish party, Fianna Fáil, was slow to follow suit, and continued to rely on support from loosely coordinated local clubs. However, after the party's devastating electoral defeat in 2011, it instituted sweeping organizational reforms, including giving individual members more rights to participate in leadership and candidate selection. In order to implement these new procedures, the party also introduced a national schedule for annual dues, and mandated that all membership applications and dues payments would be collected and processed at the national level. As a result, for the first time in its long history, Fianna Fáil leadership was in a position to identify, and to communicate with, its own party members (Little and Farrell 2013).

Given that party structures based on individual membership were becoming so widely embraced across the established parliamentary democracies, it is not surprising that parties in newer parliamentary democracies have enshrined similar organizational models in their statutes. In the 1970s and 1980s parties in the new Southern European democracies formally embraced membership-based organizational models, but their memberships grew slowly. In Spain and Portugal, local and regional parties relied on patronage to spur recruiting efforts. In Greece, too, patronage-based parties dominated during periods of Greek democracy in the 1920s and 1950s, and after the restoration of Greek democracy in 1974. However, even here, party leaders began to put a new emphasis on creating membership ties, reacting to past political turbulence by attempting to nurture partisan identities that could outlast individual leaders. In 1970s Greece, the center-right New Democracy instituted a top-down democratization that expanded the role for the extra-parliamentary party, at least on paper. PASOK, the newly established Greek Social Democratic Party, also built an organization based on individual membership (Pappas 1999). Whatever the actual strength of the membership organizations in these three Southern European democracies, it was a notable shift to have many of their parties establishing party structures based on subscriber-democracy models.

Many of the newer parties that have emerged in established democracies since the 1970s have also followed a subscriber-democracy template, or else have embraced more participatory formats. Parties in the latter category included the Green and Alternative parties that came to the fore in the late 1970s and 1980s, and the populist internet-based parties of the early twenty-first century, such as the German Pirates Party and the Italian Five Star Movement. The early Green parties aimed to eliminate hierarchy in favor of more bottom–up procedures, in some cases envisioning that decisions could be made in plenary sessions open to all supporters (Kitschelt 1988; Koelble 1989; Pogunkte 1987). Over time, however, even the most open Green parties tended to become more restrictive in order to exclude those who were not committed to party causes; as a result, their structures began to resemble subscriber democracies, though ones in which leaders' accountability to subscribers is taken more seriously than in some other parties.

More radical were the internet-based parties that made waves in Germany and Italy at the beginning of the second decade of the twenty-first century. For these populist parties, their unique organizational structures were a big part of their political message. The German Pirates Party touted the "liquid democracy" (internet discussion panels) that it used to frame its platform, and made the novelty of its organization a central part of its political appeal. Its members joined on-line, and the internet was the primary locus of membership activity. Yet in keeping with German Party Law, the Pirates had formal membership rules which distinguished members from others, and it staged in-person (not just on-line) party conferences. The Italian Five Star Movement organized an internet-only membership. Both parties made attention-getting use of on-line membership, and of very flat structures that directly connected membership with top party leadership. Both also featured their use of on-line policy discussions in their electoral messages. The parties clearly considered these structures to be one of their selling points, even if in practice it was difficult or impossible for members to control how party leaders interpreted the results of internal deliberations (Hartleb 2013; Niedermeyer 2012; Passarelli and Tuorto 2013). In a final similarity, both parties found it difficult to translate their initial popularity and publicity into durable organizational strength. Whatever their longer term political impact, the initial popularity of these internet-based parties presents a possible lesson to other parties about the appeal, and the potential pitfalls, of on-line political participation.

A few of the newer parties on the center-right and populist far-right have remained holdouts from the subscriber-democracy or political process models. If these parties recruit members, it is as fans who are asked to demonstrate support for what the party is doing without being given a say in party affairs. One of the most successful of the recent leader-dominated parties was Silvio Berlusconi's People of Italy, the loose electoral organization that helped propel him to his second term as Prime Minister of Italy. Its predecessor, Forza Italia, even took its name from the slogan chanted by fans of Berlusconi's soccer club. The statutes of these parties give members little role (direct or otherwise) in the party decisions. Their claims to govern are based on ideology, or on the leader's popularity and charisma, not on the democratic credentials provided by intra-party procedures. In the early twenty-first century the Dutch Party for Freedom of Geert Wilders stood out as an extreme example of this type of leader-dominated party, being a party that had only a single member (Wilders himself). This was a rare example of a party in a contemporary parliamentary democracy that completely eschewed traditional membership enrollment for supporters.

In short, by the end of the twentieth century almost all the major parties in this book's universe of parliamentary democracies—and most of the smaller ones—had adopted membership-based organizational forms. They had formal rules about how to join, and most national parties kept digital records of individual members. Most also had detailed internal constitutions which made party leaders accountable to party members in some way, whether through direct ballots or representative structures within the party. Party members had become a widely respected fount of political legitimacy, one to which most parties paid homage, whatever the actual extensiveness or authority of their membership organizations. In some countries, this bias towards party membership was reinforced by party registration laws and party finance laws that required parties to have memberships, or which rewarded successful recruiting efforts (van Biezen and Piccio 2013).

There seem to be many reasons why the shift towards member-based party organizing gathered steam after the Second World War. As functional explanations would suggest, electoral considerations were probably an important impetus for individual parties to implement these changes. Initial efforts may have reflected the kind of organizational contagion that Duverger described, with parties of the center-right adopting branch party structures based on individual membership in order to compete with the post-war surge in left-party enrollments (1954, 25). Yet this surge was short-lived. By the early 1960s most of the European parties of the left were abandoning a purely class-mass electoral strategy in favor of more inclusive appeals based on issues, not on social class identity. The organizational corollary of this shift in electoral strategies was that party leaders became more interested in trying to attract voters by delivering policy benefits rather than by encapsulating supporters in partisan networks. These changes removed some of the old arguments in favor of organizing supporters between elections (e.g. for building community identity). Eventually, however, the declining importance of ideological identities also created new pressures for parties to invest in their membership organizations. In today's less-ideological political environment, parties are seeking electoral advantages by highlighting the formal links between party leaders and grassroots supporters. Such accountability may be embodied in subscriber-democracy and political process structures that treat members as stakeholders, or in the more open structures of political market parties. Either way, however, it seems to be the case that many parties no longer judge the worth of membership organization solely in terms of its contribution to campaigning or party finances. Parties—especially opposition parties—also seem to judge it by how well it contributes to the credibility of party decisions.

Thus in the contemporary era, as in the past, the emergence of extra-parliamentary organizations, political institutions, political culture, and ideological norms remain entwined forces that are shaping party organizational choices. It is the combination of these forces that has kept the ideal of membership-based organization alive, whatever the strength of its realization.

ADJUSTING THE BASELINE: BEYOND THE MYTH OF THE GOLDEN AGE OF MASS PARTIES

The account in this chapter is meant as a corrective to more pessimistic discussions of the decline of membership-based political organizing. These histories clearly show that democratic parties with large individual memberships have been relatively rare. In the decades immediately after World War II parties on both the left and the right adjusted their statutes to fit this norm, formalizing individual membership and using membership bases as symbols of their connections to grassroots support. Even at this point, however, the reality seldom matched the stated aspirations of organizational reforms. Moreover, parties with similar enrollment numbers and even similar enrollment procedures might still differ widely in the rights that they ascribed to these members (e.g. fans vs. stakeholders), and in the cohesiveness of their organizational networks.

This kind of organizational variation across countries, and within party families, is hard to reconcile with artificial and undifferentiated invocations of the former age of mass party dominance. A more complex story emerges from emphasizing the gap between parties' organizational rhetoric and their organizational practices. These varied historical experiences raise the question of whether today's apparent organizational trends also mask important differences, ones that are not easily explained by macro-level forces such as cultural or technological changes. The next chapter thus continues this investigation into the timing and causes of change in partisan enrollments. It closely examines party membership figures and public opinion data, using both types of evidence to construct a more precise picture of when membership losses occurred, and of the magnitude of these shifts. These accounts are then used to consider the plausibility of common explanations for party membership decline.

NOTES

1. This trend towards competitive elections should not be overstated: as late as the mid-1880s more than half the Members of Parliament won their seats in uncontested elections (Bulmer-Thomas 1967, 83).
2. The Carleton Club for Tories (Conservatives) and the Reform Club for Whigs (Liberals).
3. My thanks to Ken Carty for pointing out the demonstration effect of the Irish Catholic Association's organizational style.
4. Self-government was recognized for Canada by the late 1840s, for most Australian states in 1856, and for New Zealand in 1853.
5. All except the Kingdom of Piedmont/Sardinia, formerly under the control of the Habsburg monarch, but now an independent constitutional monarchy.
6. With the exception of New Zealand, which introduced female suffrage in 1893.
7. e.g. at the beginning of the 20th cent. the voting age for men was 25 in Belgium, Prussia, the Netherlands, Norway, and Sweden, 24 in Austria, and 30 in Denmark (López Pintor et al. 2004, 15).
8. Counting only those countries in this study that were independent in 1870.
9. In the 1920s Canada's Cooperative Commonwealth Federation (CCF), a regional party centered in Canada's prairie provinces, attempted to build a European-style membership-based organization, the only Canadian party to set this goal. However, it never recruited many members (Carty et al. 2000, 20). In the 1960s, Canada's new New Democratic Party (NDP) formed out of remnants of the CCF. This party had trade union affiliated members as well as individual members.
10. The Spanish Socialist Party (PSOE) was a partial exception to this, due to ideology as well as political circumstances. In the first decades of the 20th cent. it saw itself as a party of militants rather than as a mass party, and did not invest in creating a strong network of party-linked associations. The party had around 58,000 members as of 1921. Its membership declined rapidly in the face of economic and political crises in the 1920s, but temporarily revived during the short-lived Spanish Republic of the 1930s (Gillespie 1989, 20–6).
11. This complicates the placement of Ireland in Table 3.4, given that in 1930 Fianna Fáil was in the process of building up its local (membership-based) clubs.
12. Georgios Papandreou's newly founded Centre Union made tentative steps in this direction in the early 1960s, but in practice this remained a leader-dominated populist organization (Spourdalakis 1988, 22–5).

4

Explaining Enrollment Change

Looking Beneath the Numbers

By the beginning of the twenty-first century, there seemed to be little doubt that party enrollments were shrinking in most established parliamentary democracies. Although a few parties appeared to escape this trend, the overall pattern seemed clear. This declining enrollment was no surprise to scholars, because it had been amply foretold by theories of party change. At least since the 1960s political scientists had been diagnosing the demise of socialist-style membership parties and volunteer-rich patronage parties, both of which were to be replaced by professionalized organizations conducting mass media campaigns (Epstein 1968; Kirchheimer 1966; Sorauf 1960; Sundberg 1987). These predictions were not universally embraced (for instance, Reiter 1989; Sainsbury 1983; Selle and Svåsand 1991). More recent authors have provided new arguments explaining why such changes occurred and were to be expected. They point to changing individual preferences as well as to further changes in parties' resource needs (Katz 1990; Katz and Mair 1995b; Mair and van Biezen 2001; Sundberg 1987; Whiteley 2011). The title of one of these articles neatly summarizes the verdict: party membership is "going, going, gone" (Van Biezen et al. 2012). Whether or not past trends presage further enrollment declines, the change is notable, with most established parliamentary democracies now having overall rates of party membership which are lower than any time in the past six decades.

Yet although the enrollment data seem to tell a clear story of decline, the aggregate trends conceal a great deal of variation. The drops have been much greater in some countries than others, and some individual parties have even experienced membership growth in recent years. Moreover, upon closer inspection, some of the apparent reductions may have more to do with measurement issues than with behavioral changes. Unfortunately, these data problems are too often ignored, possibly because the available figures so nicely match the overdetermined predictions of party membership decline. In the absence of reliable data, it is difficult to sort out the depth of the decline, or when the drops occurred.

Getting better data is the first step towards clarifying the relative importance of the institutional and environmental changes that have been identified as causes of party membership decline. As will be shown, there are many inconsistencies in aggregate enrollment figures, and most are systematically biased in ways that inflate the apparent longitudinal decline. The first sections of this chapter identify and correct for some of these inconsistencies in order to generate a more accurate picture of country- and party-specific trajectories of enrollment decline. The analysis then uses these cleaned-up data to assess the importance of causal factors commonly associated with such changes. The messages of the adjusted figures are clear and somewhat surprising. First, they show that overall party membership decline has been much less dramatic, and much less uniform, than is sometimes portrayed. Second, they raise questions about the causal importance of several factors commonly linked to membership decline, particularly public subsidies for political parties. The chapter concludes by looking more closely at enrollment differences across countries, considering why some countries have had consistently high or low enrollments, and why some parties have been able to temporarily reverse downward momentum. These investigations provide valuable clues about the sources of party membership strength, and about the plausibility of future opportunities for growth.

PARTY MEMBERSHIP TRENDS: AN OVERVIEW OF PARTY DATA

How much has really changed in terms of citizens' participation within political parties? Figures 4.1–4.3 present a first overview of trends in membership enrollment in all nineteen of the countries covered by this study. These figures, based on party-reports and reports by party experts, compare total party membership with each country's eligible electorate. This ratio, commonly used to standardize enrollment levels for cross-national or longitudinal comparisons, is known as the member/electorate or M/E ratio (Katz et al. 1992).[1] For clarity of presentation, these figures divide countries into three groups based on the approximate rate of membership enrollment in the initial period for which membership figures are available (which varies by country). In the "low enrollment" group are countries in which total party enrollments started at under 8 percent of the electorate. The "medium" group includes those with initial enrollments from 8–15 percent. Those with high enrollments started with an M/E ratio of over .15, or 15 percent of the electorate. These figures suggest that many countries have experienced a membership decline that stretches back decades, beginning as early as the 1960s. The losses are particularly pronounced in the countries that began with medium and high membership ratios.

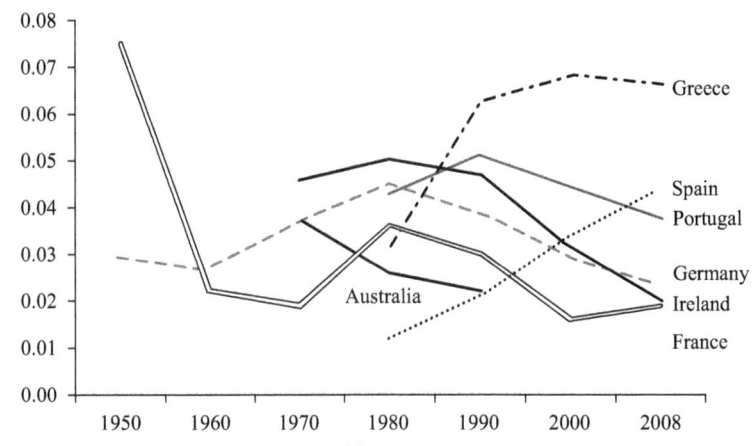

FIGURE 4.1 Membership density: low initial level

Sources: Figures 4.1–4.3: See Tables A4.1 and A4.2

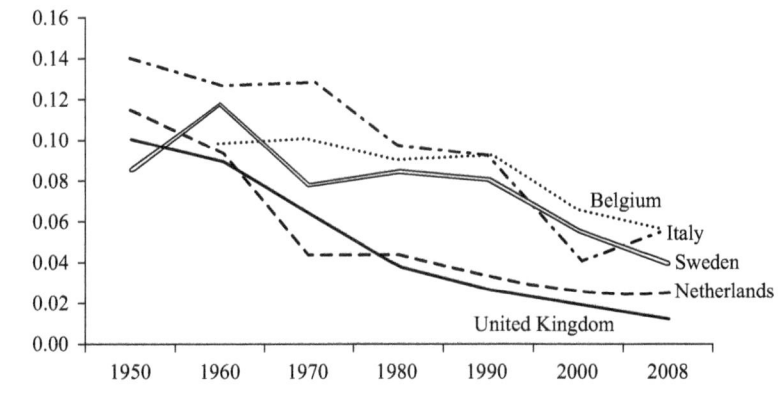

FIGURE 4.2 Membership density: medium initial level

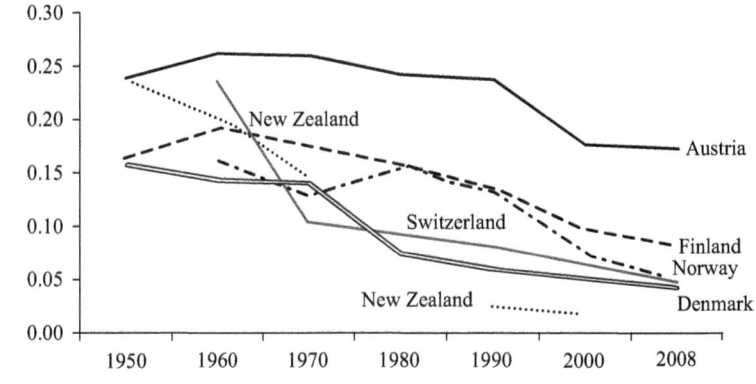

FIGURE 4.3 Membership density: high initial level

TABLE 4.1 *Change in enrollments, 1960–2008*

United Kingdom	−82.5%
Denmark	−72.3%
Netherlands	−58.4%
Sweden	−54.0%
Norway	−46.9%
Italy	−38.7%
Switzerland	−36.3%
Finland	−28.5%
Austria	−16.4%
Belgium	−10.9%
Portugal*	−5.9%
Ireland	6.8%
France	38.0%
Germany	39.8%
Greece*	148.9%
Spain*	374.0%

* Change 1980–2008.
Source: Table A4.1.

Yet while these graphs present clear pictures of decline in *relative* membership, the decline in *absolute* numbers is less uniform. Table 4.1 compares percentage changes in overall party enrollments between 1960 and 2008 (or from 1980 to 2008, for the newer Southern European democracies). Of the countries for which such figures are available, half lost 25 percent or more of their original numbers. On the other hand, five of them had *more* citizens enrolled in parties in 2008 than at the start of the period, and another three had suffered enrollment losses of less than 25 percent. The questions, then, are not only why party enrollment ratios have declined at different rates, but also why absolute membership numbers have been more stable in some countries. To answer these questions, it is useful to start by reviewing the factors that often are linked with global trends in membership development. These macro-level factors should affect all parties within a single country at about the same time, although there may be cross-national differences as to when each factor becomes relevant.

MEMBERSHIP DECLINE: OVERDETERMINED AND UNDEREXPLAINED?

Scholars have identified so many factors as being responsible for the decline in party membership that it can seem surprising that parties have any remaining members. Party enrollments are said to be the victim of global social and technological forces, all of which exert pressures pointing to similar outcomes. Demand-side pressures reduce parties' incentives to recruit and retain members. Supply-side pressures reduce individuals' interest in joining parties or in making long-term participation commitments (see Strom and Svåsand 1997, 10–11, for a summary of some of these arguments). One problem with this over-explanation of downward trends is that it becomes difficult to discern which forces are most important in particular cases, or to recognize other relevant explanations that may have been overlooked. The focus on macro-trends also makes it impossible to explain some of the outliers to these patterns. Thus, it is useful to look more closely at specific cases to see how well various explanations apply. One good way to do this is to ask whether actual membership losses have occurred before or after the factors that are said to cause them, and whether the pace of those losses is consistent with their predicted effects.

This chapter's investigation will consider five such factors, each of which should produce distinctive patterns of change in enrollment figures.

Demand Side I: Public Subsidies The introduction of generous public financing for political parties is commonly blamed for the demise in membership enrollments. Such subsidies are said to make parties less financially dependent on members, and to reduce their incentives to recruit (for instance, Bartolini 2000, ch. 3; Katz and Mair 1995b, 16; Panebianco 1988, ch. 14; Pelizzo 2004; Whiteley 2011). If this effect is at work, we would expect to see enrollments start to fall in all parties within two or three electoral periods after the introduction of substantial public subsidies. If there are limits on the extent to which money can substitute for volunteer hours, this effect should be finite: its impact should be manifest as a steady decline followed by a new equilibrium at lower enrollment levels.

Demand Side II: Media-Intensive Campaigning The spreading importance of television campaigning since the 1960s, and the concurrent rise in parties' reliance on media professionals, are both said to have reduced the importance of volunteer campaigning (Bartolini 2000, ch. 3; Panebianco 1988; von Beyme 2002; Wiesendahl et al. 2009). Once parties acquired easy access to national communication platforms, locally organized efforts began to seem less useful, or even as unwanted distractions from the carefully crafted messages of the national party. In this new environment, parties became much less interested in cultivating the type of volunteer resources that members once provided. As with the impact of party subsidies, we would expect demand-side changes produced by new campaign styles to slowly erode membership. This change should be evident within a decade of the rise of televised campaigning, at least by end of the 1970s. Similar to the predicted effect of party subsidies, we would expect new styles of campaigning to produce a punctuated equilibrium rather than an ongoing slide. If so, the slopes of changes produced by the introduction of public subsidies for parties, and by shifting campaign styles, would look very similar. However, it might be possible to disentangle the impact of the two factors in countries where direct public subsidies were introduced long after the rise of televised campaigns.

Supply Side I: New Leisure Competitors Growing affluence in the second half of the twentieth century gave citizens many new opportunities for leisure pursuits. This affected parties' voluntary organizations, because they were less able to attract members with enticements used in the past, such as providing social or educational activities, or organizing cheap holiday excursions. Not only were parties now competing with many other groups vying for citizens' leisure time and discretionary spending; new amenities such as television and then the internet made it much more attractive for individuals to just stay home. Such broad lifestyle changes have been linked with reduced interest in politics and in party membership, and indeed, in group membership of all sorts (Bartolini 2000, ch. 3; Putnam 2001; van Deth 2000). As with the demand-side effects described above, the impact is likely to be felt gradually. It should affect all ages. Even those who once enjoyed socializing at party events now may decide that they prefer to stay home and watch a movie. This supply-side change may lead to slower enrollment changes than demand-side effects (producing a flatter slope). However, like them, it is also likely to lead to a new equilibrium. Thus, even if party membership generally pales in comparison with other free-time activities, it may remain attractive to some, including those who aspire to hold public office.

Supply Side II: Changed Participation Preferences Value changes may also diminish interest in party membership, or indeed, in any type of group membership. It has been argued that, in an age of individualism, citizens are becoming less interested in making long-term organizational commitments, and that those who participate for political reasons are more interested in project-oriented participation related to specific causes (Katz and Mair 1995b, 15; Whiteley 2011). Those who are politically interested are "doers," not "joiners". These changes are said to be partly caused by a generational shift in values, meaning that the impact of behavioral changes should be gradual and long-term, and should be first evident among younger citizens (Inglehart 1990; Jennings et al. 1990). Unless something happens that once again produces a new set of generational value shifts, the membership decline produced by the new values should be steady, and should take decades to be fully digested. The result should be ongoing decline, with no new equilibrium in sight.

Supply Side + Demand Side: Political Causes A fifth explanation for party membership decline identifies political factors as a major cause for the enrollment drop. A demand-side example of a politically induced

Explaining Enrollment Change

enrollment drop is when total party membership plummets after a once-strong party disappears. That could occur in the wake of a major electoral defeat, due to a political scandal, or because factional in-fighting leads to a party split. These effects would be magnified if many parties collapsed at the same time, for instance because of an economic or political crisis, or due to the adoption of a new electoral system. These demand-side scenarios have closely related supply-side counterparts: citizens may flee a particular party due to a scandal, or as a result of political in-fighting. They may stray from all parties if they become disaffected with the political system as a whole as a result of scandals, or because existing parties prove incapable of dealing with economic crises (Norris 1999; Poguntke and Scarrow 1996). Membership losses due to specific political crises should occur rapidly. If they affect only one party, the slope of a country's overall decline in party membership would not be steep. In contrast, if the crises affect a broad spectrum of parties, the national M/E decline may be both rapid and large. Unlike the other supply-side and demand-side explanations, enrollment changes as a result of political causes are not necessarily unidirectional. After the decline caused by the political shock, enrollments could stabilize or even increase as new political parties gain support with promises to reform the tainted political system

Figure 4.4 presents an idealized depiction of the impact of these various scenarios. The top line shows steady linear change (generational change). The middle line shows medium-term change leading to a punctuated equilibrium. The third, dashed, line shows rapid decline (political upheaval) followed by limited recovery. While we would not expect to see pure cases that exactly correspond to any of these patterns, these hypothetical scenarios

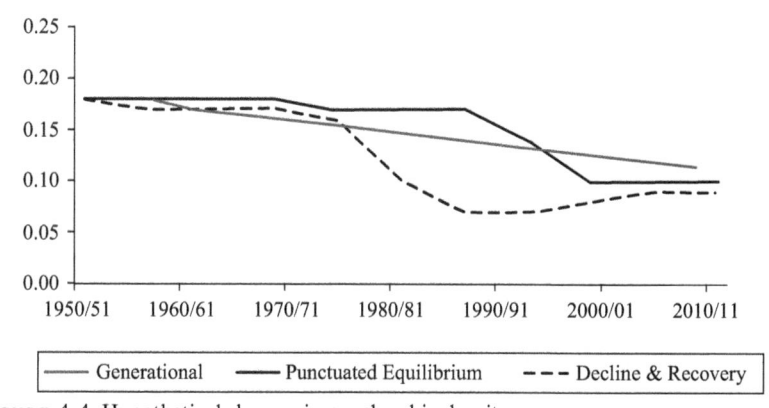

FIGURE 4.4 Hypothetical changes in membership density

illustrate how differences in the timing and speed of change may reflect the relative power of the different factors that are at work.

Do actual patterns of membership change resemble any of these idealized pictures? Before we can answer this question, we need to look more carefully at the enrollment data, with the aim of reducing the impact of measurement error on these long-term patterns. As will be shown, both self-reported membership data (survey responses) and party-reported membership data are affected by measurement problems that must be taken into account before using them for this (or for any) purpose.

PARTY MEMBERSHIP FIGURES: IDENTIFYING THE INCONSISTENCIES

When examining party membership figures, it quickly becomes clear that party-reported numbers are unreliable guides to the exact timing and magnitude of enrollment changes. That is because this seemingly straightforward measure is derived from figures that have been compiled in inconsistent ways. These problems are more serious because the errors are not random, but instead are distributed in ways that exaggerate apparent losses. The most important measurement errors and inconsistencies can be divided into five main categories.

Type 1. Truncated Data Series

Most parties' membership figures are truncated due to lack of data from earlier periods. In many cases, figures are not available until after 1945 even for parties that were founded much earlier than this. This data gap is not just accidental, or the result of poor record keeping. As Chapter 3 made clear, one reason for the lack of membership data for the first half of the century is that many political parties did not formally enroll individual members in those decades. In many countries, it was only parties of the left that had large (or any) individual memberships prior to the 1950s; in some countries, even parties of the left did not have individual members. In other words, most parties' enrollment numbers had a parabolic shape across the twentieth century. Data series that start mid-century miss the upward half of the slope. If we could accurately plot individual membership enrollment across the entire twentieth century, we might give as much weight to the question of why party memberships suddenly grew in the 1950s and 1960s as to the question of why they have declined in more recent decades.

Type 2. Deliberate Overstating

One reason to distrust parties' reported membership figures is that parties have incentives to inflate these numbers. National parties want to publicize the highest possible figures because these numbers (especially *increasing* numbers) are symbols of popular support. This problem can be compounded when national party figures are based on reports from local or regional parties, because these units often have additional reasons to artificially boost their own membership counts.

Type 3. Poor Data

Parties' published data may be unreliable because parties themselves lack good information. This is always true in parties with loose or undefined national membership rules, and in those without regularly updated rosters of individual members. In these parties, all membership numbers are necessarily estimates. Even where rules for joining are better defined, national party data may be less accurate if they are compiled from regional or local party reports, because these sub-units may have idiosyncratic counting practices. Parties' own figures have tended to become more accurate over time. The most important reason for this is that many parties have introduced national membership databases and centralized dues payment procedures. Additionally, many parties have introduced stricter rules about minimum dues levels, and for deciding how soon membership lapses as a result of non-payment. These changes produce more consistent decisions about who counts as a member.

Type 4. Inconsistent Membership Definitions

Parties sometimes register big enrollment shifts when they change their membership definitions. The biggest changes of this type result from decisions about how to count—and whether to have—indirect members. Reported enrollment figures change drastically if parties eliminate this class of members, or even if they just start reporting separate figures for direct and indirect members. This type of record-keeping adjustment could produce big apparent enrollment fluctuations without any change in individual behavior. In other parties, membership figures could be affected by different types of definitional changes, such as the elimination of family membership categories. Inconsistent membership definitions also affect cross-party comparisons. Unless the differences are taken into account, they can lead to misleading conclusions about the relative strength of parties' grassroots organizations.

Type 5. Changing Eligibility

Both absolute enrollments and member/elector (M/E) ratios may change if the pool of eligible members grows or shrinks. The absolute number of members (the numerator in M/E ratios) may grow if parties redefine who is eligible to join. For instance, they may reduce the minimum age for full membership, or may admit new categories of supporters (e.g. women, or non-citizen residents). As these examples suggest, the potential number of party members could exceed the size of the electorate if residents who do not have the right to vote are eligible to join the party. The denominator in member/electorate calculations has changed even more frequently, affected by population growth as well as by changing voting ages (von Beyme 1985, 183). Distinguishing whether movements in the M/E ratio are caused by the numerator or the denominator is important, because these changes usually have different causes and different implications.

The experiences of the two largest British parties provide pertinent illustrations of the impact of various types of measurement changes on the apparent timing of membership drops. Until 1979 the British Labour Party's constituency parties were required to affiliate (pay membership fees for) at least 1,000 members, leading to Type 2 measurement errors (deliberate overstating). When the party lowered the constituency party affiliation requirement to 256 members, in the early 1980s, reported individual membership fell by almost 50 percent within a year (from 666,000 to 348,000 individual members) (Scarrow 1996, 75). Although the party was suffering from deep unpopularity in this period, much of this sharp loss was undoubtedly due to the new rules rather than to a wave of resignations from the party. Local parties were now able to affiliate at levels which more closely reflected their actual membership—and in some or even many Constituency Labour Parties these levels may long have been below the 1,000 member minimum. This rule-related drop continued in the 1980s, as the party further reduced, then abolished, minimum affiliation levels. At the same time it also introduced centralized registration of individual members, which led to more uniform (and stricter) accounting of when an individual's membership lapsed because of non-payment (addressing Type 3 errors). Given the Labour Party's poor electoral fortunes from the late 1970s through the 1980s, it would be easy to assume that plunging official numbers were solely a by-product of political unpopularity, and were signs of the party's growing organizational weakness. In fact, the actual losses were undoubtedly smaller than the official figures suggest. Moreover, to the extent that losses occurred because of the new centralized enrollment procedures, they partly reflected the central party's *increased* organizational capacity.

Until the mid-1990s, British Conservative Party membership figures were distorted by a different type of bias: poor record keeping as a result of loose membership rules and decentralized membership administration (Type 3 errors). For most of the twentieth century the national Conservative Party was formally separate from its extra-parliamentary units. These were organized by the National Union of Conservative and Unionist Associations, a federation which did not collect central membership records or require constituency parties to pay per-member fees to the central organization. There were no national rules on minimum dues levels or other membership requirements; local parties made their own decisions about which supporters counted as members. As a result, the central party's membership estimates were based on unverifiable claims of constituency parties. In the early 1990s the Conservative Party created a new, centralized, system of party registration and renewal. This new system included standard and formalized application procedures, and specified minimum dues levels. The party finally had clear and uniform rules for distinguishing between members, non-member supporters, and lapsed members. Because these new rules were implemented at a time when the party's electoral popularity was falling, it is hard to disentangle the effects of each. However, both factors played a role when the party's estimated membership figures plunged from one million in 1987 to 500,000 in 1992 (Webb 2000, 193). Again, this eye-catching drop was certainly fueled by political pressures, but it should not be interpreted solely as a reflection of changing public support.

To be clear, both the Conservative and Labour Parties experienced real membership losses between the mid-1970s and the end of the 1990s. However, this discussion shows that available figures for these two parties overstate the severity of the plunges, and probably misidentify their timing. These examples show how various types of discrepancies and errors can compound the difficulty of interpreting time series records of party membership. Interpretive problems multiply when aggregating reports from several parties, each with their own types of errors. The question, then, is whether these inaccuracies justify ignoring the numbers that we do have: are inaccurate data better than no data? As one pair of observers described the dilemma, "The choice for the analyst is therefore either to accept at more or less face value those figures that are made available by the party organizations, while accepting that these are probably exaggerated or, in some cases merely crude estimates; or simply do without, and to accept that little meaningful work can be done on party memberships on a comprehensive cross-national basis" (Mair and van Biezen 2001, 8). Those scholars opted for the former choice, though they acknowledged that party reports should sometimes "be treated with a pinch of salt." Yet there is a third alternative to the take-it-or-leave-it approach: estimating how much "salt" to use for specific figures, and then correcting for known measurement inconsistencies.

Two critical questions for those who use these data should be whether such inconsistencies have a directional bias, and whether measurement errors are uniformly distributed over the entire period. Even a cursory examination suggests that the latter is not the case: in most parties, data on individual enrollment have become much more accurate since the 1960s. In regards to the former, most measurement errors in party data are in a single direction, with earlier reports tending to overstate enrollments. This combination of unidirectional errors, and of improving data quality, means that parties' membership figures generally overstate the extent of the recent decline.

ACCOUNTING FOR MEASUREMENT DISCREPANCIES

The implication of the preceding discussion is that at least some of the decline shown in Figures 4.1–4.3 reflects changes in measurement practices, not changes in individual behavior. Identifying these counting changes would make it easier to identify the timing of real enrollment drops—and therefore, perhaps, to better understand why such drops occurred. This section thus presents a brief inventory of known data-reporting discrepancies that affect the country-level patterns shown in the figures that open this chapter.

Type 2. Deliberate Overstating

It is difficult to determine which parties have at some point systematically encouraged local parties to overstate membership, whether by making them pay for a minimum number of members, or by rewarding local parties which reported (and paid for) nominally larger memberships. However, the British Labour Party example already described was certainly not unique. For instance, the Austrian People's Party used to award votes at the national party conference based on the paid-up membership of regional parties and of the party's constituent Leagues (Farmers', Business, Worker subgroups). Until the national party began collecting information about individual members, there were no limits on the number of annual memberships which party subgroups could purchase. The net result was a regular spike in reported membership in years with party conferences, one that probably was unrelated to individual enrollment patterns (Müller 1994, 60–4; Müller and Steininger 1994). Similarly, in the 1970s and 1980s the Italian Christian Democrats' membership figures were boosted by a combination of factional competition and the awarding of party conference votes based on local membership. These conditions encouraged clientelistic practices in which factional leaders directly or indirectly subsidized dues payments for real or fictional supporters (Leonardi and Wertman 1989, 130).[2]

Type 3. Poor Data

Between the mid-1960s and mid-1990s the spreading use of central membership registries and centralized dues payments reduced the likelihood of deliberate overstatement at either the national or local levels. These registries also largely eliminated Type 3 problems. They forced parties to set clear rules for what it meant to join a party, and at what point membership lapsed through non-payment. They also made it more likely that membership numbers were linked to individual names and addresses. Even parties with national membership databases can be more or less conscientious about removing lapsed members from the files. For instance, Portugal's largest parties reported big losses in official membership figures when they cleaned up their membership files. Membership in the Portuguese Social Democrats fell from 183,000 in 1996 to 77,000 in 1999; membership in the Portuguese Socialists dropped from 120,000 in 2001 to 66,000 in 2002. In both cases, these sudden losses reflected changes in party organizational practices rather than a sharp shift in citizens' behavior (Jalali et al. 2012, 315). As these examples suggest, having a central membership database does not guarantee that a party has accurate records, but it at least gives the party the capacity to be accurate if it so chooses.

If we know when a national party began using a national registration system, we can assume that membership numbers became more accurate and consistent after this point—and accuracy has generally meant lower figures. Without delving into party archives it can be hard to establish precise dates for such changes. However, we know that most of them happened between the late 1960s and the end of the 1990s, spurred by cheaper technology that made it much easier to maintain central databases. Whereas in 1985 one commentator could write that "[r]elatively careful records on membership...are still the exception in European democracies" (von Beyme 1985, 169), by 2005 this was no longer the case. Only a handful of parties in this set did not have central individual membership records as of 2012. Remaining exceptions included the Austrian People's Party, as well as most parties in France, Italy, and Switzerland. Of the Swiss parties, by the start of the twenty-first century only the Socialists were keeping national membership records and had relatively accurate figures (Ladner 2001, 138). In France, researchers' estimates of party membership have been notoriously unreliable and inconsistent as a result of parties' own lack of information, particularly for the non-socialist parties (Billordo 2003). By now, however, these are exceptions rather than the rule.

Type 4. Inconsistent Membership Definitions

The timing of Type 4 discrepancies due to changing membership definitions is generally much easier to pinpoint, because such changes tend to be written into party statutes. For instance, both the Swedish Social Democrats and the Norwegian Labor Party traditionally had two classes of membership, individual and corporate (indirect affiliation through trade unions). In the 1990s both parties eliminated their provisions for corporate membership. These changes led to huge drops in these parties' official membership reports. After the Swedish Social Democrats abolished corporate membership in 1990, the party's reported membership numbers dropped sharply (Widfeldt 1997). The Norwegian Labor Party elimination of indirect membership accounted for about half of the party's membership decline in the mid-1990s, which fell from 128,000 in 1990 to 64,000 in 1997 (Mair and van Biezen 2001, 19). These changes raise the question of whether longitudinal data for these countries should be based on direct membership only, or whether they should also include indirect membership. The different approaches yield very different answers. For instance, a publication which included corporate members lists Sweden's 1979 M/E ratio as .24 (Katz et al. 1992, 344), while a publication which excludes corporate members calculates the 1980 ratio as .15 (Mair and van Biezen 2001, 16). For the sake of consistency it would seem sensible to exclude the affiliated membership in a data series that spans this procedural change. However, this would be impossible to do for the Norwegian Labor Party, which did not keep separate counts of direct and affiliated members prior to 1979. In such cases, mixing the different figures may be inevitable; however, it is important to recognize that at some point there will be a big drop in the party's membership figures due to removing indirect members from the individual membership data.

A similar problem arises with data on Swiss parties, which sometimes have included party estimates of "sympathizers" as well as more strictly defined members. For instance, the figures presented in Mair and van Biezen 2001 include "sympathizers" as part of total party membership, while the tally in a subsequent article (van Biezen et al. 2012) specifically excludes such followers (see Grüner 1977, 238 and Ladner 2001, 138, for explanations of the figures). Because a different and narrower measure was used for the later period, a comparison between them makes it look as if there was a sharp drop in total membership between 1977 and 1997. In fact, Ladner reports that Swiss parties' *total* membership (i.e. members plus sympathizers) went from about 390,000 in the mid-1970s to about 400,000 in the mid-1990s (Ladner 2001, 138). This still represented a (smaller) relative drop in membership, but it was not an absolute decline. Again, it is not that one measure is inherently more accurate than the other; however, comparisons between figures gathered in different ways are potentially misleading.

Type 5. Changing Eligibility

Type 5 discrepancies may generate apparent changes in relative membership regardless of any changes in individual behavior. For instance, one source of secular decline in M/E ratios in the 1970s was a widespread reduction in the voting age (to 18 years old), coupled with a bump in the voting-age population as the baby boom generation entered the electorate (denominator). This increase in the denominator of M/E calculations may have triggered a one-time drop in relative enrollment in most parties.[3] Even more dramatically, Switzerland had a huge increase in its electoral denominator in 1971, when it finally allowed women to vote in national elections. This change is the main reason for the plunge in Swiss M/E ratios between the 1960s and 1970s. German party membership figures include another Type 5 discrepancy as a result of German Unification in 1990. This vastly expanded the denominator for relative membership calculations.

Most of these errors and discrepancies bias the figures in a single direction: they inflate earlier numbers compared to recent, more accurate, reports. Because of this, in most countries the drop in party memberships from the 1960s to the present is smaller than shown in party-reported membership figures; in some cases it may be much smaller. Thus, part of the answer to the puzzle of party membership decline is a story about changing measures and changing measurement instruments. Some of the changes shown in Figures 4.1–4.3 undoubtedly reflect changes in individual-level behavior, but imprecise or deliberately inflated measures make it difficult to know when party data are good guides to the timing of these changes.

Self-Reported Party Membership: Comparing Sources

One way to counter-balance the inconsistencies in party-reported data is to examine self-reported (survey) data on party membership (van Haute 2011a, 11). Such data can be particularly helpful for studying changing patterns of individual participation in party life. Questions about party membership have been included in some national election studies since the 1960s, and they began to be used in several cross-national surveys in the 1970s. Unfortunately, some countries' election surveys rarely or never included party membership questions. Even where they were once used, some surveys are discontinuing the questions due to low membership numbers. Because of the resulting data gaps, it is useful to supplement data from national election surveys with data from cross-national surveys. Judiciously combining such data yields a long-term picture of party membership development from the perspective of individual supporters.

Using self-reported membership data avoids some of the measurement problems of party-reported data, but it has its own set of measurement discrepancies. Most importantly, self-reports have a systematically positive bias. This is partly due to selection bias in survey participation: more engaged citizens are more likely to complete surveys. In addition, some respondents may incorrectly identify themselves as members, for instance because they confuse formal enrollment with informal party support or party voting, or because lapsed dues-payers still think of themselves as members. For whatever reason, systematic comparisons between survey data and party data show that surveys usually produce higher enrollment estimates.[4] The magnitude of these differences varies across countries, but within countries the effect seems to be relatively consistent over time. As a result, longitudinal party data and survey data show broadly similar patterns of enrollment change, even if they report different enrollment levels and a somewhat different timing for the changes (Mair and van Biezen 2001; Scarrow and Gezgor 2010).

Survey-reported membership also is affected by discrepancies caused by variations in question wording. Cross-national surveys generally use consistent wording within each survey wave, but questions vary across the surveys, and across waves of the same survey. These differences, compounded by normal margins of error for survey instruments, can introduce additional measurement noise into self-reported party membership figures. One way to reduce the impact of question-wording effects is to only compare data that were generated using identical (or at least, quite similar) questions.

Surveys have asked three main varieties of the party membership question:

1. **The Narrow Member Question** asks, "Are you a member of a political party?," and offers a yes/no response option, sometimes followed by an option to designate the party to which the person belongs.
2. **The Broad Member Question** asks, "Are you a member of a political party *or group* (emphasis added)?" This question may more accurately capture the membership of those who belong to groups that function as parties but which avoid using the party label, and instead give themselves designations such as "movement" or "rally". On the other hand, it also may garner positive responses from those who belong to non-party political groups, be these local citizen action groups or international organizations such as Greenpeace.

3. **The Active Member Question** asks respondents whether they are an active party member, an inactive party member, or not a member.

Comparisons from countries in which different combinations of these questions have been asked suggest that these wording differences matter: the "active member" option generates the fewest positive responses, followed by positive answers to the "narrow member" question (Ponce and Scarrow 2011). The largest group results from combining respondents who describe themselves as being either an active *or* an inactive member.[5] Because these different questions yield different estimates of party membership, changes in question wording can produce seemingly radical behavioral shifts. For instance, in 2002 the New Zealand election study switched from using the Active Membership Question to the Broad Membership Question.[6] This wording change may account for much of the dramatic plunge in self-reported membership, which fell from 19 percent of respondents in the 1999 national election survey who were party members (active *or* inactive), to 4 percent who reported as members in its 2002 counterpart. New Zealand's party-reported membership also fell during this period, but at a more moderate rate (Edwards 2003, ch. 6).[7] This extreme example illustrates why it is important to base cross-survey comparisons on data that are gathered using very similar membership questions and response coding. With this caveat, data from national election and cross-national surveys can provide useful complements to party-reported membership figures. They are particularly useful for studying change over time, because survey series which use consistent questions do not suffer from the measurement changes that affect much party data. Because of this, survey data should be consulted when trying to pinpoint the timing of enrollment changes.

The following investigation combines party data with self-reported membership data from national election surveys and from cross-national surveys. The cross-national data come from two sources, the World Values Survey (WVS) and the European Social Survey (ESS). The ESS included the Narrow Member Question in its first five biennial waves (2002–10). All the European countries included in the current study are included in at least some of the ESS waves.[8] The WVS included a party membership question in its first five waves, starting in 1979/80, but these waves used two different membership questions. For the sake of consistency, the figures presented here use only the waves that use the Broad Member question ("political party or group").[9] Judiciously combining data from these surveys makes it possible to construct pictures of self-reported membership that span up to four decades. The timing and slope of enrollment decline shown in these pictures reveals which factors are the most plausible sources of these declines.

DECLINING MEMBERSHIP ENROLLMENT: ONGOING LOSSES OR PUNCTUATED EQUILIBRIUM?

As explained at the beginning of this chapter, different macro-level explanations for party enrollment generate different predictions about the speed and timing of this drop. The big distinctions are between the explanations that predict sharp and sudden drops to a new equilibrium, and those that predict slow and gradual declines. How do national patterns of party membership change fit into these patterns?

Figures 4.5–4.7 show long-term trends in the self-reported membership numbers found in public opinion surveys. Because of the potential impact of question-wording differences, the survey data line uses markers to indicate the survey sources. As a check on the survey data, these figures also include party-reported data (expressed as a percentage of the electorate) and a slope derived from party data. Reassuringly, party data and survey data generally show similar trajectories, even when they show different timing for the changes. These figures divide the countries into three groups, roughly clustered based on the timing and pace of overall enrollment changes. In all of the figures, the vertical black line indicates the introduction of public funding for national extra-parliamentary party organizations.[10]

Figure 4.5 displays the countries in which the survey data show ongoing and gradual membership decline starting in the 1970s or 1980s. This decline seems to have leveled off in three of the countries (Denmark, Finland, and Sweden) by the first decade of the twenty-first century. In the UK and Norway, both survey and party data showed enrollment still declining through the end of the series. While we lack more recent survey data for Italy, it is notable that the survey data in this country show a much flatter decline in party membership than do the party data, largely because the self-reported membership was lower to begin with.[11] In all six countries, slow and ongoing declines are consistent with generational explanations that highlight cultural (supply-side) changes. On the other hand, the evidence for a subsidy-related change is more mixed. In four countries, public subsidies were indeed introduced soon before the decline began, but in Denmark and the UK most of the membership decline occurred prior to their introduction.

Figure 4.6 shows countries in which decline started at least a decade later than in the countries shown in Figure 4.5. It started in the late 1980s and 1990s in Austria, Germany, the Netherlands, New Zealand, and Switzerland.[12] It started in the twenty-first century in the low-enrollment parties in Portugal and Spain. Here, too, the data only partially support the idea that public subsidies caused a demand-side shift that affected enrollment. Public subsidies cannot be the culprit in New Zealand or Switzerland, which had yet to introduce these. In Germany and the Netherlands, party

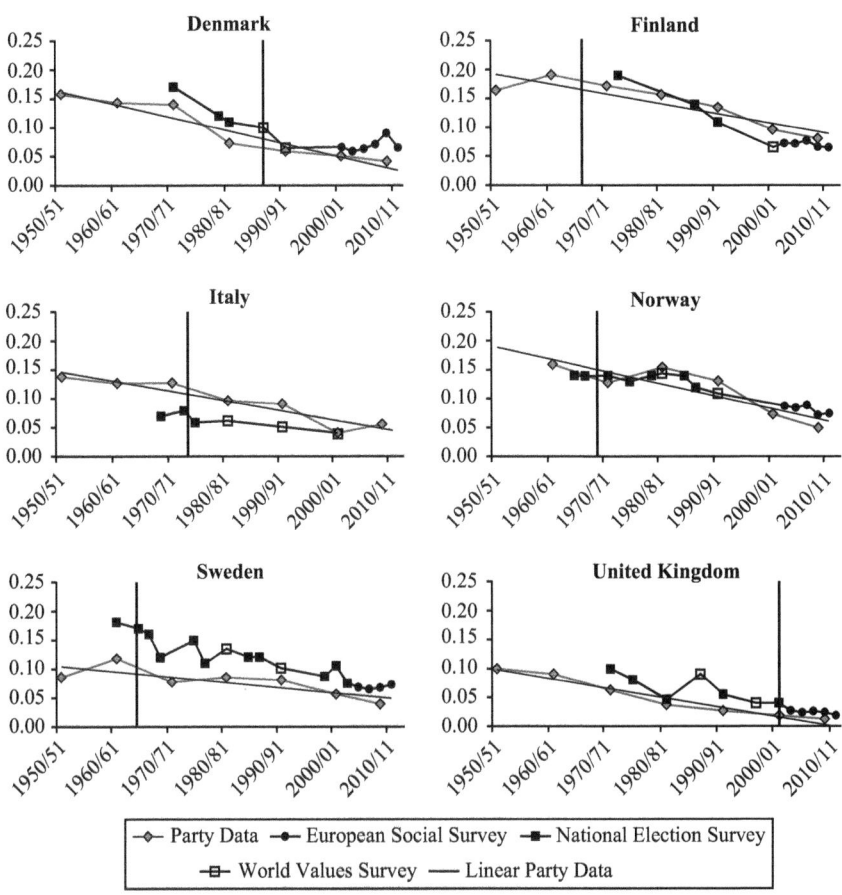

FIGURE 4.5 Party membership density: long term decline (member/electorate ratio) Solid line: introduction of public funding for national parties

Sources: Figures 4.5–4.7: Party data from Tables A4.1 and A4.2. National Election surveys from Scarrow 2000, Dutch National Election Studies; World Values Survey 1981–2008 integrated data file; European Social Survey Rounds 2002, 2004, 2006, 2008, 2010. Party funding data from Scarrow 2011 and International IDEA Political Finance Database, 2013

membership stabilized or even temporarily rose (Germany) soon after subsidies were introduced. In Austria, too, party subsidies are not a compelling explanation for enrollment changes, because they were introduced at least fifteen years prior to the big slides in membership shown in both the party and the survey data. In all four countries, the drops occurred at least two decades after televised campaigning had reduced the importance of grassroots campaign organizations. The timing of losses in these cases seems more consistent with the argument that political changes in the 1990s weakened the appeal of traditional cleavage-based parties. In Spain and

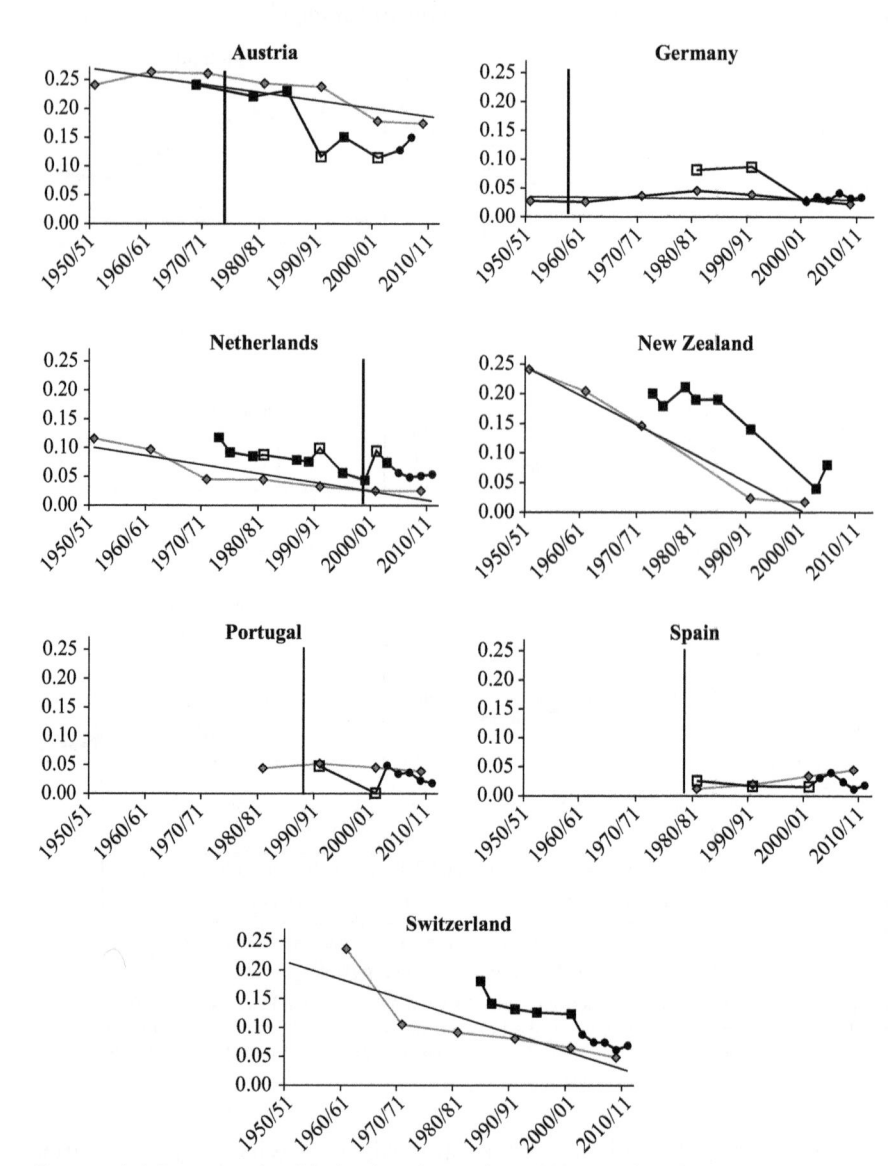

FIGURE 4.6 Party membership density: change since 1990s (member/electorate ratio)
Sources and labels: as for Figure 4.5

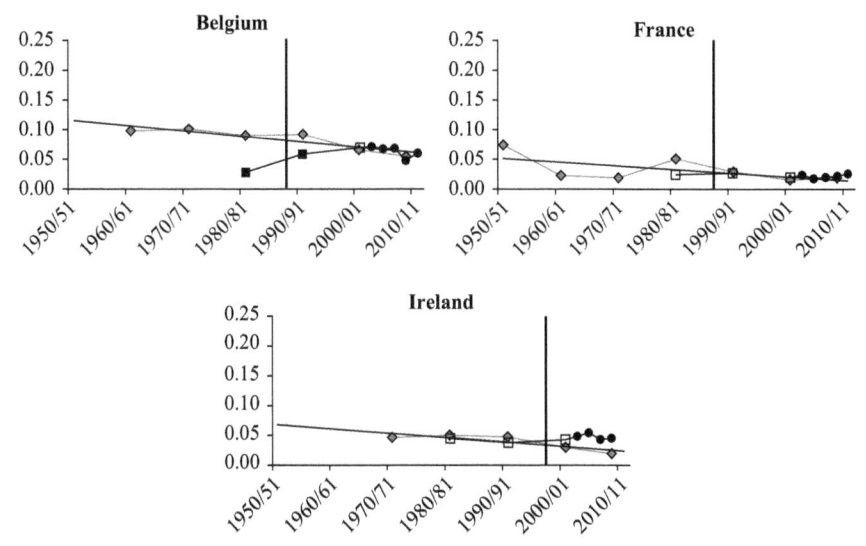

FIGURE 4.7 Party membership density: relative stability (member/electorate ratio)
Sources and labels: as for Figure 4.5

Portugal, the early availability of public subsidies for parties is a more plausible explanation of why parties in these new democracies failed to build stronger membership organizations in the first place. Even so, subsidies cannot explain the parties' losses in membership in the first years of the twenty-first century.[13]

Figure 4.7 shows countries in which enrollments have been relatively stable, or have changed much more slowly. This group includes Belgium, France, and Ireland. Enrollment in these countries seems to defy predictions of uniform decline, probably because overall membership in these countries was always relatively small. All three countries did experience the macro-factors that have been linked to changes in party membership, including greater use of mass media in campaigns, cultural changes, and the introduction of party subsidies, but their enrollment patterns showed no consistent long-term trends.

The varied national trajectories shown in Figures 4.5–4.7 suggest that it may be misleading to emphasize the cross-national commonality of trends in party membership decline: there are great variations in both the slope and timing of such losses. Some countries have even resisted such trends altogether, including places where parties never enrolled many members to begin with. Explanations that highlight the impact of public subsidies to extra-parliamentary parties tend to overlook the weak temporal connection between subsidy introduction and enrollment decline. It may be argued that the introduction of subsidies is too blunt a measure to test the impact of these subsidies, because it ignores big variations in the sizes of subsidies. At the least, however, these figures show that the relation between party subsidies and membership decline has not been a simple mechanism. They echo other studies which also failed to find clear links between public subsidies and party membership size (for instance, Bonander 2009; Hofnung 1996).

Similarly, other system-level demand-side explanations for membership decline find only weak support in the patterns presented in these figures. For instance, by the 1970s parties in all these countries had already switched to more professional and media-centered campaigns, and were putting less emphasis on labor-intensive local campaign efforts. Such switches might help account for the patterns of long-term decline shown in Figure 4.5, but they cannot explain the countries shown in Figure 4.6 that did not experience membership drops until the 1990s or later, nor do they explain the absence of decline in the countries shown in Figure 4.7.

Another caveat is that long-term changes may have had multiple causes. For instance, political forces may be a prime culprit for membership losses that started in some parties in the 1990s, and which continued in others during this decade. The end of the Cold War undercut the relevance of political appeals tinged with anti-Communism. Equally, the unique appeal of Labour and Social Democratic parties faded in this decade, when some parties of the left began embracing the tenets of market liberalism. The 1990s brought the end of formal links between trade unions and political parties in Norway and Sweden, and it witnessed new strains in relations between trade unions and governing left parties in countries such as Germany and the United Kingdom. Growing distrust of politicians and parties of all political stripes was another, and possibly related, widespread pattern in this decade (Norris 1999; Poguntke and Scarrow 1996). These relatively abrupt shifts in political moods and circumstances may help to explain the widespread enrollment drops of the 1990s. If so, the prime suspects seem to be supply-side factors more than demand-side ones: the political "products" that traditional parties were offering became much less attractive to their consumers, resulting in growing electoral volatility and a declining ability to motivate and a mobilize supporters. This explanation would not negate the impact of demand-side forces. Instead, parties' changing resource needs and their shift to alternative funding sources may reflect how parties reacted when faced with the decay of their organized membership base. However, if some of what is happening is due to politically determined supply-side effects, rather than to demand-side forces, it is more likely that parties might respond to the losses by seeking to alter the calculations of potential members.

Equally important, the apparent variation in national experiences suggests that we should be cautious when generalizing about factors which have affected party enrollment. Similar environmental changes do not necessarily lead to similar organizational outcomes, not least because political parties are not helpless victims in the face of social and institutional change (Hellman 2011). As tempting as it is to look for overarching causes for party membership decline, the data suggest that it may be more useful to investigate the causes of cross-party and cross-national *differences*. Of particular interest are the contrasts between countries with traditionally low and traditionally high enrollments. The sources of these differences may provide clues about the circumstances which make membership organizing more appealing to parties (demand-side forces), and more attractive to potential enrollees (supply-side forces).

CROSS-NATIONAL DIFFERENCES

As Figures 4.1–4.3 showed, the countries in this study can be roughly divided into three groups on the basis of their reported membership strength in the 1950s and 1960s. In one group, reported party memberships routinely exceeded 15 percent of the eligible electorate (Austria, Denmark, Finland, Italy, New Zealand, Norway, and Switzerland). In a second group, memberships were traditionally between 8 and 15 percent of the electorate (Belgium, Italy, the Netherlands, Sweden, and the UK). A third group included countries which reported mid-century party enrollments of less than 8 percent of the electorate (Australia, Canada, France, Germany, and Ireland).[14] The differences between these groups have diminished, but the countries which report the highest membership density figures today are the same ones that did so a half-century ago.

There are three main explanations for these initial and enduring differences. The first one emphasizes the importance of cross-party and cross-national definitional differences. Second, demand-side explanations identify institutional reasons that make members more valuable to party organizers in some countries than in others. Third, supply-side explanations suggest cultural factors that affect supply-side calculations about joining.

Definitional Explanations

A big reason why some countries report enduringly high party enrollments is that one or more big parties include both direct and indirect members in their membership figures (Austria, New Zealand, and Norway through the mid-1990s). This is an appropriate measure to use for some comparisons, given that individual members of affiliated organizations may perceive themselves to be party members. This seemed to be the case in Norway, where self-reported membership levels closely track party-reported data, and dropped at the same time that the party abolished indirect membership (see Figure 4.5). However, reports combining both types of membership reflect very different situations than those which report just one type. This inclusion goes a long way towards explaining why some countries show consistently high enrollment figures. When membership figures for these countries can be calculated based solely on individual memberships, their enrollments look similar to those of their direct membership counterparts, with M/E ratios of .07 or less. In other words, a big reason why some high enrollment countries looked different is that they were counting different types of members.

Demand-Side Explanations

Institutional differences can affect demand-side calculations, thereby producing long-term cross-national differences in organizing levels. For instance, electoral systems create different incentives for parties and candidates to invest in building up party organization (Aldrich 1995; Schlesinger 1991). Candidates should be more likely to promote party structures under electoral systems that foster party-centered competition rather than personalized contests, and in systems without strong intra-party competition. Table 4.2 supports this argument, showing a striking relationship between electoral systems and levels of party enrollment in the 1960s—a date that is chosen because it is close to the apogee of membership, where we would expect the effects to be clearest. At this point the lowest overall party enrollments were found in countries in which local electioneering was unequally profitable for parties because there were uncompetitive districts, or in which candidates from the same party competed against each other to win nomination or election. Conversely, list-system proportional representation was associated with higher levels of enrollment. Only New Zealand, the UK, and Germany did not fit neatly into this table, with UK membership enrollments being higher than expected (partly due to the over-reporting of membership already described), and German memberships being lower. Given the stability of electoral systems, this demand-side explanation cannot explain changes in the M/E ratio, but it may help to explain why environmental changes had more impact in some systems than in others.

Demand-side explanations also help to account for high enrollments in Austria, one of the countries with the traditionally highest memberships. Here the internal structure of the center-right Austrian People's Party (ÖVP)

TABLE 4.2 *Party membership density and electoral systems: 1960s*

	Personal Votes: SMD, STV, ATV	Mixed Member Proportional	Party List Votes
M/E >.15	New Zealand*		Austria* Denmark Finland Norway* Switzerland
M/E .08–.15	UK		Belgium Italy Netherlands Sweden
M/E <.08	Australia* Canada France Ireland	Germany	

*Membership figures include indirect memberships>
Source: Table A4.2.

boosted the demand for members. The party's affiliated Leagues have operated as competing internal factions, and ones with strong incentives to recruit in order to boost their conference voting rights. This is one case in which demand-side recruiting pressures may have been stimulated by intra-party competition at least as much as by external electoral pressures.

Supply-Side Explanations

Parties in some countries have used state resources or campaign contributions to offer members selective benefits. Patronage and other selective benefits can boost or sustain the membership supply by increasing the benefits associated with enlistment. For instance, patronage probably helped to boost partisan affiliations in post-World War II Austria. This country's two largest parties overcame traditional conflicts by using partisan proportionality (*proporz*) as the main principle for dividing state resources. As a result, it was widely perceived that party membership could help an individual to receive state-linked benefits such as public housing, civil service appointments, and university scholarships. This meant that there were practical reasons for party supporters to become formal affiliates, at least for certain life stages. Austrian parties' extensive use of patronage began declining in the 1990s, partly because parties were trying to reach beyond their traditional constituencies, and partly because of fading public toleration for partisan patronage practices (Müller 1993; Treib 2012). In post-war Italy, too, parties also used patronage-linked incentives to boost their memberships. Both the Christian Democrats and the Communists built up large membership organizations in the 1950s and sustained these through the 1980s. They, and to a lesser extent the Socialists, used municipal resources as recruitment incentives. All three parties saw their electoral support plummet in the early 1990s when Italian popular opinion rebelled against the perceived corruption of the established political parties (di Mascio 2012; Leonardi and Wertman 1989). As both examples suggest, although patronage benefits can boost enlistment, offering such benefits can incur electoral costs if public opinion turns against them.

PARTY MEMBERSHIP TRENDS: WHAT WE LEARN BY GETTING THE NUMBERS RIGHT

This close examination of party and survey reports of party membership sheds some useful light on the geographic and numeric extent of party membership decline, and on possible explanations for these changes. To begin with, it shows the relatively small amount of change over the past fifty years. Outside of a few countries where parties maintained affiliated memberships, party members have only occasionally constituted even as much as 10 percent of the electorate. Few of the so-called "mass" parties have been "massive" by any standard. This does not mean that the decline is irrelevant. It also does not mean that small membership organizations are politically unimportant. However, it does suggest that we should not judge the importance of grassroots organizations solely in terms of membership numbers, because most of these organizations have usually been relatively small. More generally, the decline of party membership needs to be measured against this real baseline rather than against an imagined ideal of past organizational intensity. Little is gained by lamenting the passing of a non-existent universal golden age of democratic party organizing. Even where membership numbers really have declined, numbers alone do not tell us about changes in who is participating within the parties, or about the extent to which members control party decisions. Second, it is important to acknowledge that the general pattern of declining overall party membership hides a great deal of variation at the national and party level, both in terms of timing, and in terms of the extent of change. These patterns suggest that we need to focus less on the macro-factors that are said to be driving common patterns of membership decline, and to focus more on forces affecting individual parties and countries.

One way to do this is to give more attention to the flip side of the story of membership change, investigating why some parties have experienced recent membership growth. For instance, the British Labour Party boosted its membership from about 280,000 in 1992 to over 400,000 in 1997, coinciding with the surge in electoral popularity and political mobilization that brought Tony Blair to office in a Labour landslide election in 1997 (Webb 2000, 193). In France, the UMP membership grew from around 100,000 to over 300,000 in the early 2000s, a change that was partly due to giving members a greater say in the selection of the party's presidential candidate (Ivaldi 2007, 264). The French Socialists experienced a similar growth in 2005 and 2006, with enrollment spurred by a special low membership rate and by the prospect of participating in an intra-party ballot to select the party's presidential candidate. In the year prior to the ballot, PS membership grew from 127,000 to 217,000 (Dolez and Laurent 2007, 138). Moreover, many parties founded since the 1970s have succeeded in attracting and retaining members, including Green parties, nationalist parties, and more centrist challengers to established parties. Their membership density may not replicate that which is often (and often falsely) attributed to mass parties in their hey-day, but it is nevertheless notable that some newer parties have successfully adopted the membership-based organizing model, enrolling dues-paying members and giving them central roles in party affairs.

These examples suggest that parties may still have the capacity to make party membership attractive to some supporters, whatever the cultural and institutional forces that are pushing in the other direction. In recent years many parties have been experimenting with ways to boost this appeal. One of their preferred strategies has been to expand the political incentives for membership with the deliberate aim of attracting the attention of those who are especially interested in party affairs. The second section of this book investigates this phenomenon more closely, weighing changes in both the demand-side and supply-side incentives that affect party recruiting. Chapter 5 examines evidence of what parties get from having members, and why contemporary parties might be interested in retaining or developing membership organizations. Chapter 6 explores the membership calculus from the perspective of current and prospective members, asking what membership benefits seem to be most valued by the members themselves. Finally, Chapters 7 and 8 consider recent party efforts to reduce the costs and increase the benefits of membership, and ask whether any of these reforms seem to be altering how citizens participate in partisan politics. Together these chapters argue that crises of legitimacy have persuaded some parties to pursue new types of organizational relations with their supporters. The results are profoundly transforming how parties function as channels of representation.

NOTES

1. The figures upon which these are based are shown in Appendices A4.1 and A4.2 at the end of this chapter. They aggregate membership for all parties with at least 5% of seats in the legislature, and for some smaller ones, as data is available.
2. Paying for subsidized or fictitious memberships was also a way that the beneficiaries of public contracts could legally direct money of questionable origins into party coffers (Nassmacher 2009: 203).
3. The pool of potential members did not increase as much as the pool of eligible voters, because some parties previously admitted members who were younger than the voting age.
4. Austria is one notable exception to the pattern of survey data yielding higher reports of party membership. In Austria the self-reported ESS and WVS data are markedly *lower* than party-reported data, though national election data generate levels similar to party data. Italy is another exception.
5. A fourth option is the Historical Member Question. This question avoids some of the confusion of other phrasing by asking whether the respondent is currently a party member, was previously a party member, or has never been a party member. The advantage of this wording is that it gives lapsed dues-payers a response option other than non-membership. In practice, however, it has seldom been asked.
6. In 2008 it asked the Narrow Membership Question.
7. In 1999 and before respondents were asked about their membership in "a political party, organization or movement"; in subsequent polls the equivalent question asked exclusively about political party membership.
8. The party membership question was not included in the 6th wave. The ESS has not included Australia, Canada, or New Zealand.
9. For 1979/80, 1989/90, and 1998/2000.
10. Australia, Canada, and Greece are missing from these figures due to the scarcity of longitudinal survey data based on similar membership questions.
11. This may reflect the Type 2 measurement problem (deliberate overstating) described earlier.
12. As noted elsewhere, the big drop in M/E ratio in Swiss party data between 1960 and the 1970s is due to the expansion of the electorate to admit women. Part of the drop in membership reported in the Swiss national election surveys is due to a change in question wording. Whereas most Swiss election studies used a Narrow Membership question (with a follow-up to ask whether self-reported members described themselves as active or inactive), in 1999 and 2007 responses showed only those who identified themselves as active party members.
13. As noted, record cleaning explains the timing of the reported loss in Portugal's largest parties, though it does not explain why the earlier losses occurred.
14. This excludes Greece, Portugal, and Spain, which were democracies for only part of the post-1950 period.

TABLE A4.1 *Total party enrollment (by approximate year)*

	1950	1960	1970	1980	1990	2000	2008
Australia			265,000	234,000	239,200		
Austria	1,041,000	1,262,000	1,308,000	1,321,000	1,335,000	1,031,000	1,055,000
Belgium		478,000	495,000	671,000	644,000	481,000	426,000
Denmark	597,000	599,000	489,000	276,000	232,000	205,000	166,000
Finland	396,000	485,000	531,000	607,000	543,000	410,000	347,000
France	1,259,000	589,000	644,000	1,089,000	1,100,000	615,000	813,000
Germany	1,126,845	1,018,000	1,299,000	1,955,000	1,873,000	1,780,000	1,423,000
Greece				225,000	510,000	600,000	560,000
Ireland		59,000	82,000	114,000	120,000	86,000	63,000
Italy	3,698,000	4,280,000	4,620,000	4,078,000	4,150,000	1,974,000	2,623,000
Netherlands	630,000	730,000	369,000	431,000	355,000	294,000	304,000
New Zealand	288,000	264,000	228,000	167,000	50,000	49,000	
Norway		324,00	399,000	461,000	420,000	242,000	172,000
Portugal				337,000	418,000	384,000	317,210
Spain				323,000	612,000	1,131,000	1,531,000
Sweden	400,000	580,500	437,000	508,000	506,000	366,000	267,000
Switzerland		367,000	357,000	367,000	360,000	293,000	233,800
United Kingdom	3,436,000	3,065,000	2,424,000	1,693,156	1,137,000	840,000	535,000

Sources: pre-1980 Scarrow 2000, except Sweden. Sweden Rustow 1955 for 1950; Therborn 1988 for 1948 and 1960; for 1960 Katz and Mair 1995a, with Therborn estimate for Socialists; for 1970 Katz and Mair 1995a using 1967 data on direct membership in Socialists 1980 sources: Austria, France, Italy, New Zealand, and Switzerland from Scarrow 2000, rest from Mair and van Biezen 2001. 1990–2008 sources: van Biezen et al. 2012, except New Zealand 2000, from Edwards 2003: 368.
Years: Figures are closest available membership figures within three years of decennial year except Austria 1950 = 1956; Ireland 1960 = 1967; Ireland 1980 = 1986; New Zealand 1950 = 1954.

TABLE A4.2 *Membership density (members/electorate)*

	1950	1960	1970	1980	1990	2000	2008
Australia			.037	.026	.022		
Austria	.239	.262	.259	.242	.237	.177	.173
Belgium		.098	.10	.09	.092	.066	.055
Denmark	.157	.143	.14	.073	.059	.051	.041
Finland	.164	.191	.172	.157	.135	.097	.081
France	.075	.022	.019	.036	.03	.016	.019
Germany	.029	.027	.037	.045	.039	.029	.023
Greece				.032	.063	.068	.066
Ireland			.046	.05	.047	.031	.02
Italy	.139	.127	.128	.097	.091	.041	.056
Netherlands	.114	.095	.044	.043	.032	.025	.025
New Zealand	.238	.202	.146	.082	.023	.017	
Norway		.16	.128	.154	.131	.073	.05
Portugal				.043	.051	.044	.038
Spain				.012	.021	.034	.044
Sweden	.085	.117	.077	.084	.08	.055	.039
Switzerland		.234	.104	.091	.08	.064	.048
United Kingdom	.10	.09	.062	.038	.026	.019	.012

Sources: Table A4.1 for membership totals. Electorate based on first national election in each decade, from Mackie and Rose 1991, and from Interparliamentary Union Parline Database: <www.ipu.org/parline>.

Part II

Party Membership: The Uncertain Future

5

What Do Party Members Contribute?

What do parties gain from having members, and how much do they lose if they move beyond party members in numerical terms—for instance, if memberships decline to an extent that imperils local party networks? From a broader societal perspective, these losses would be most relevant if they weaken the bonds of interest and accountability that link citizens to those who govern, and if they aggravate inequalities in political participation. Yet from the perspective of electorally motivated political parties, this impact must be measured in much narrower terms: to what extent do membership losses undermine parties' electoral chances and their long-term political prospects? To answer these questions, we need to consider what it is that party members do for their parties, and whether parties could easily find substitutes for these contributions.

This chapter will use survey data and information on party finance to sketch a picture of what parties forfeit when they cannot, or can no longer, enlist significant numbers of formal party members. Illuminating the demand-side ledger of the party membership equation will help reveal the circumstances that might motivate parties to expand their recruiting efforts.

WHAT CAN MEMBERS DO FOR THEIR PARTIES?

Members' potential contributions to party success can be roughly divided into seven main types of activities (Katz 1990; Lawson 1980; Scarrow 1996, 40–6). These can be further subdivided according to whether members provide the benefits primarily by working within party structures, or whether the benefits derive from members' activities and interactions outside the formal party sphere.

Activities Primarily Inside Party Organization

1. Providing volunteer labor.
2. Providing financial support.
3. Standing as candidates for public office.
4. Transmitting ideas and preferences into party debates.

Activities Primarily Outside Party Organization

1. Providing electoral support.
2. Communicating party ideas.
3. Enhancing party legitimacy.

The variety of tasks on both lists suggests that parties could still have good reasons to value members even if, as is often asserted, party members have become much less useful as campaigners or donors. A second message of these lists is that parties can benefit from members who are largely inactive within the party, for instance because they help to carry party ideas into the community. Parties can gain enhanced legitimacy even from members who never attend a party meeting or volunteer for a campaign. As a result, they have reasons to recruit members who live in communities without active party branches, or who prefer not to get involved in a local party.

These lists of members' *potential* contributions tell us where to look when trying to assess the impact of membership decline, but they tell us little about what today's parties are *actually* losing when they suffer membership losses. For that, we need to know more about what party members have contributed in the past, and whether they have been unique or primary providers of such benefits. This chapter uses survey and financial data to answer these questions. It constructs a picture of party members' contributions focused on four of the areas listed: volunteer support, financial support, electoral support, and ambassadorial outreach. The areas are chosen because they are ones that can be best tracked using available data. Subsequent chapters will look more closely at members' roles in policy formation and in enhancing party legitimacy.

The survey data used in this chapter come from recent waves of two cross-national surveys, the International Social Survey Program and the European Social Survey. Party finance reports and studies based on these reports provide information about the changing importance of members' contributions to party organizational success. None of these sources provide complete coverage for all nineteen democracies that are at the center of this volume, but jointly they offer a reasonably complete picture of what (if anything) party members do differently from other citizens, and to what extent those activities might still be valued by the parties that enroll them.

PARTY MEMBERS AS PARTY VOLUNTEERS

Volunteer labor is sometimes portrayed as the most valuable resource that members provide for their parties. Party members can help candidates and parties accomplish the labor-intensive side of local organizing and electoral campaigns. One demand-side explanation for the demise of membership-based organizing is that parties' need for volunteer labor dropped when parties began professionalizing and centralizing campaigns. Meanwhile, national television advertisements and leader-led tours and rallies became the dominant face of contemporary parliamentary election campaigns. In the process, campaigning became less labor-intensive and more capital-intensive. Yet although these changes in campaign style are undeniable, they have not necessarily made grassroots campaigning altogether obsolete. Indeed, recent studies in diverse institutional and political settings have found that grassroots campaigns and contacting efforts provide parties and candidates with an electoral edge even in a mass media age (for instance, Carty and Eagles 1999; Johnston and Pattie 2003; Karp et al. 2008; Tavits 2012). The extra boost provided by good local organization may be relatively minor, but in many situations small mobilization advantages are enough to change election outcomes. When elections are close, parties can potentially reap important benefits from grassroots campaigning. How many of the campaign volunteers are members is a different question. Even in parties with large memberships, the pool of potential volunteers extends well beyond the formal membership.

Few recent studies have asked detailed questions about volunteering in national election campaigns, so we have very little information about who is actually providing various kinds of support. One of the rare studies that did ask this question, an investigation of constituency campaigning in the UK general election of 2010, found that non-member supporters played important roles in local efforts (Fisher et al. 2014). This study suggests that local parties could respond to membership losses by turning to non-members for help with specific tasks. Although we lack comparable local-level studies for other countries, we can form a more general picture of member vs. non-member contributions by comparing responses about political participation in cross-national surveys. The 2010 European Social Survey provides a recent window on such activity. It includes reports from fourteen of the nineteen countries in this study.[1] The questions asked respondents about their activities within the past twelve months in various organizations, including within party organizations. From these questions we can learn something about reported engagement in three types of activities which are directly or indirectly associated with party members' contributions: working within a political party; working within a civic group other than a party (potential partisan ambassadorial work); and wearing a campaign badge.[2]

Because of the small number of party members in each country, it does not make sense to further disaggregate the data to the party level; nevertheless, the data do show some intriguing cross-national patterns and outliers.

The top bar in each country cluster in Figure 5.1 shows the percentage of party members who have recently done volunteer work in a party. In most countries at least one-third of party members reported having worked in a party within the past twelve months. In Germany and Spain that figure exceeded 60 percent; only in Sweden and the UK was it below 30 percent. These participation rates suggest that, at some levels of the party, capital has not entirely displaced labor in party organizing work: there are still volunteer jobs for party members. In light of the findings of party member surveys, discussed in more detail in Chapter 7, it is not surprising that in most countries only a minority of party members reported doing party work. Indeed, from this perspective the activity levels reported in Figure 5.1 might appear high, except that the question in this figure sets a very low bar for activity, and includes those who may have engaged in only one or two activities during the past twelve months.

Because the question asks about work done within the previous year, we might expect to find the highest participation levels in the countries which

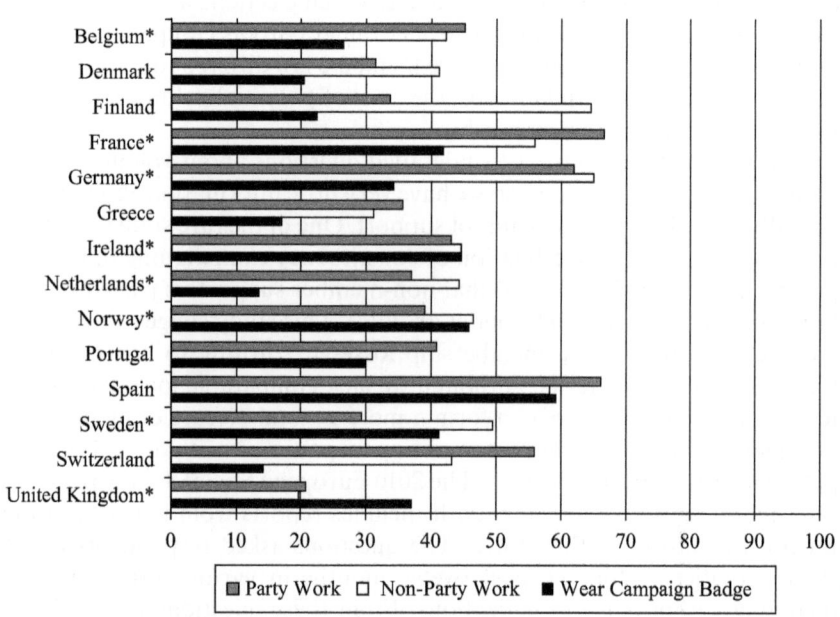

FIGURE 5.1 Party member activity (prior 12 months)
% participation

* held national elections within 12 months prior to data collection.

Source: Norwegian Social Science Data Service, *European Social Survey Round 5* (2010–11)

recently held national elections (indicated with an asterix in Figure 5.1). However, that was not the case. Indeed, the lowest participation rates were found in the UK, which held a hotly contested national election in the survey year. The interesting and unexpected non-relationship between national elections and levels of party work could have many explanations. For instance, if we were to examine a longer series we might see within-country levels rising and falling in response to national election cycles, even while cross-national differences remained. Alternately, we might find that levels of party volunteering also respond to local or regional elections, thus diluting the impact of national elections on these figures. The current data raise but cannot answer the important questions of why partisans are more active in some countries than others, and of whether campaigning parties are able to mobilize normally inactive members. For present purposes, however, the main message is that parties appear to be calling on their members to engage in political activity, and that many members are heeding the call, at least occasionally.

Even if many members work within their parties, this is not the whole story of party volunteering. As preceding chapters have made clear, party members constitute only a small proportion of parties' adult supporters. Thus, it is also relevant to ask about the importance of members' contributions relative to those provided by other supporters: to what extent do members constitute the core of parties' volunteer workforce? This question is answered in Figure 5.2, which displays party members' share among those who engaged in each of the three activities. These data confirm the importance of party members as party volunteers. The top bar in this figure shows that in most countries in the ESS survey, party members constituted more than half of those who reported working within a party. The two exceptions were the UK and Spain, where non-members provided large majorities of the self-identified party workers. As expected, members are much more likely than non-members to work within their parties, and parties rely disproportionately upon them, although non-members also contribute.

Figures 5.1 and 5.2 show slightly different participation patterns for one type of low-intensity political activity: wearing a campaign sticker or badge. Although this type of campaign propaganda is not used everywhere, the data suggest that respondents are thinking of some kind of campaign propaganda when they read this question, given that usage reports were highest in the countries which had held national elections within the past year. Yet even in these countries, party members were less likely to do this activity than to work in the party in some capacity. In contrast, non-members were more likely to display the party symbol than to do party work. As a result, non-members constituted a much bigger portion of the contributors to this activity.

106   *Beyond Party Members*

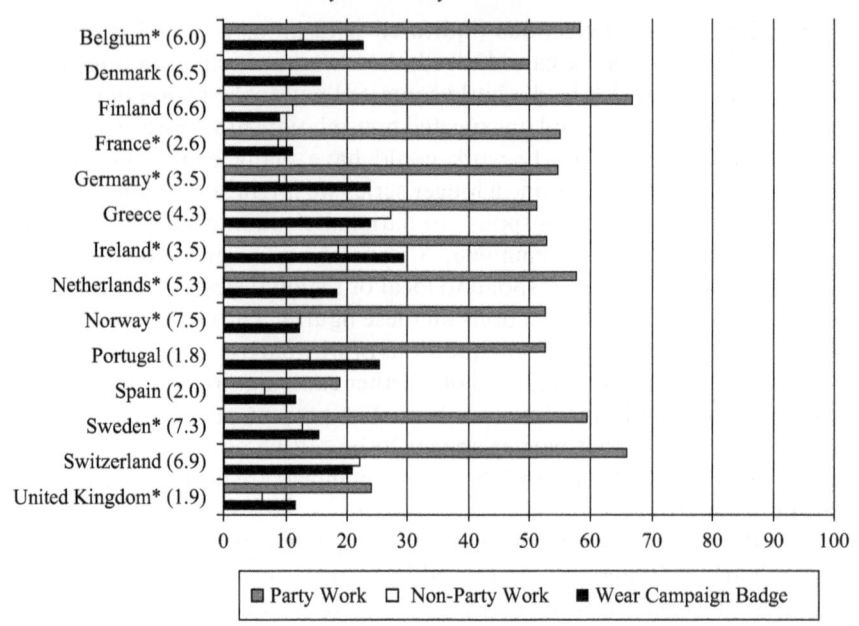

FIGURE 5.2 Member impact: % of participants who are party members
(in brackets: survey-reported % party members)

* held national elections within 12 months prior to data collection.

Source: see Figure 5.1

We can amplify this picture of members' role relative to that of other supporters by looking at several questions about civic and political activities asked in the 2004 round of the International Social Survey Program (ISSP). One question asked respondents whether they had attended a political meeting or rally within the past year.[3] Although the question does not refer exclusively to party events, we would expect active members to report engaging in such activities, because monthly meetings and campaign rallies are at the heart of traditional party life. Figure 5.3 shows one way to look at these data, by comparing behavior patterns of members and non-members. The total length of the bar (grey plus black sections) represents the percentage of members who reported attending political events in the past year. The grey part of the bar shows the percentage of non-members who reported attendance. The black portion, the "member bonus," is the extent to which members' attendance rate exceeded that of non-members. Even though the question does not ask specifically about party events, this figure shows a consistently large gap between the behavior of current party members and others. In most countries, more than one-quarter of party members reported having attended at least one political event in the past

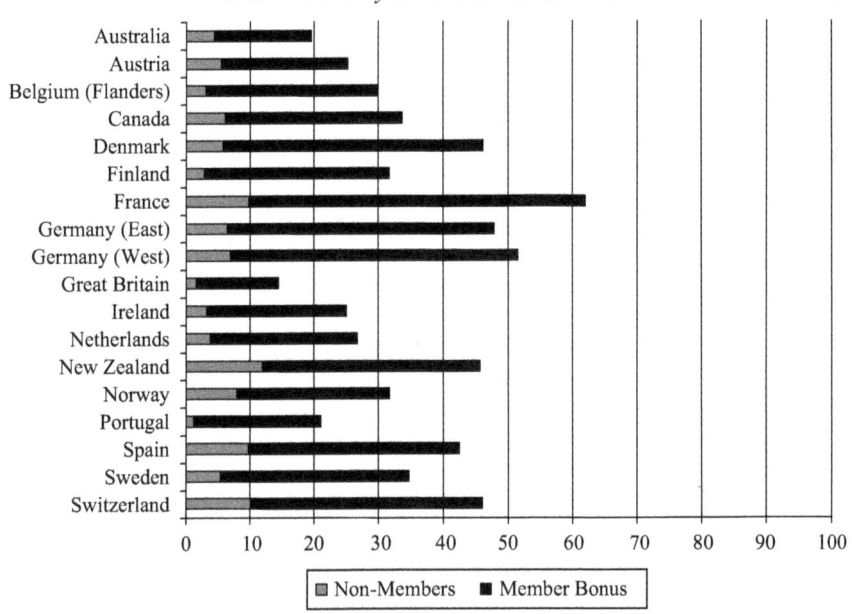

Figure 5.3 Event attenders: participation levels
(member % = non member + member bonus)

Source: International Social Survey Program 2004

year. In contrast, in all but one country, 10 percent or fewer of non-members report attending such events. As expected, party members are more likely than non-members to engage in traditional partisan behavior.

Figure 5.4 gives a different view of the same activities. Like Figure 5.2, it shows the relative importance of party members' contributions by displaying their share of those who engaged in this activity. (For comparison, the numbers in brackets report the share of all respondents who attended political events.) The figure shows that in most countries members comprised less than half of the audience at political meetings; put differently, in thirteen countries non-members dominated attendance at these meetings.

As a group, Figures 5.1 through 5.4 have twin messages. First, if parties are seeking to activate supporters to work within traditional party channels, party members are still the ones who are most likely to respond to their appeals. Parties thus have good reasons to invest in recruiting and retaining members in order to carry out traditional party work. The second, complementary, message is that non-members already play a big role in some traditional political activities. Given that there are so many more non-members than members, there could be high pay-offs for parties which can figure out how to boost the mobilization levels of supporters who are not traditional party members.

108   *Beyond Party Members*

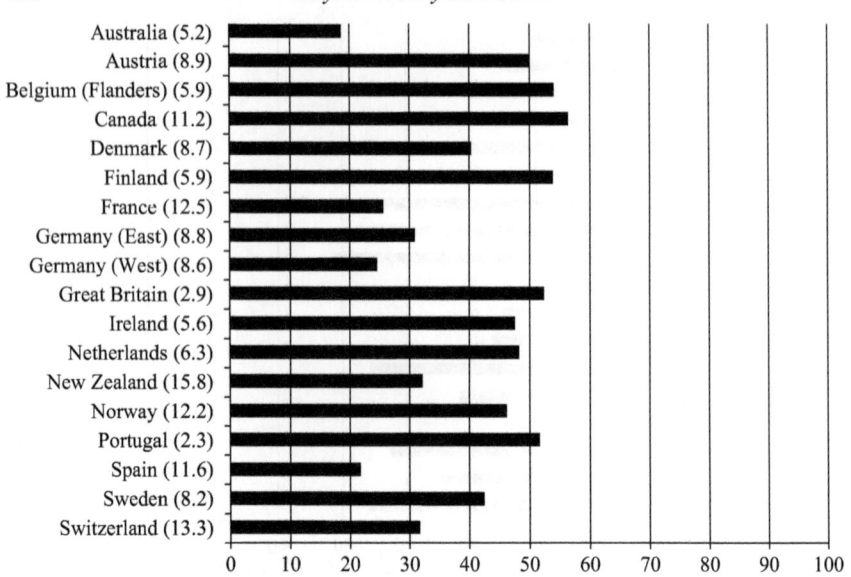

Country	Value
Australia (5.2)	~18
Austria (8.9)	~50
Belgium (Flanders) (5.9)	~53
Canada (11.2)	~56
Denmark (8.7)	~40
Finland (5.9)	~53
France (12.5)	~25
Germany (East) (8.8)	~30
Germany (West) (8.6)	~24
Great Britain (2.9)	~52
Ireland (5.6)	~47
Netherlands (6.3)	~48
New Zealand (15.8)	~32
Norway (12.2)	~45
Portugal (2.3)	~51
Spain (11.6)	~22
Sweden (8.2)	~42
Switzerland (13.3)	~32

FIGURE 5.4 Event attenders: % of participants who are party members
(in brackets: % of all respondents who attended a political rally or meeting in past year)
Source: International Social Survey Program 2004

To what extent do these reportedly high levels of non-member mobilization constitute a shift in the ways that parties derive grassroots support? Are they a response to waning memberships, or have parties always enlisted campaign help outside the ranks of traditional party members? Cross-national surveys like the ESS have not asked about partisan activity for long enough to provide a comparable measure of change, but we can get some sense of practices in this area by comparing older and recent election studies in countries whose surveys have regularly included questions about both party membership and campaign participation. For instance, evidence from Dutch national election studies suggests that the high involvement of non-members is nothing new in the Netherlands (see Figure 5.5).[4] The solid black line represents the percentage of members who volunteer for campaigns, while the dashed line depicts the percentage of non-member volunteers. The gap between these lines shows that party members were consistently more likely than non-members to participate in campaigns. For a while in the 1980s the size of this gap narrowed, but it subsequently returned to previous levels. Like the horizontal bars in Figure 5.3, the vertical bar in Figure 5.5 indicates party members' share of those who actively campaigned. This figure gives a much different impression of members' relative importance. As a group they constituted only a small portion of those who were at least slightly engaged in the campaign. This proportion ranges

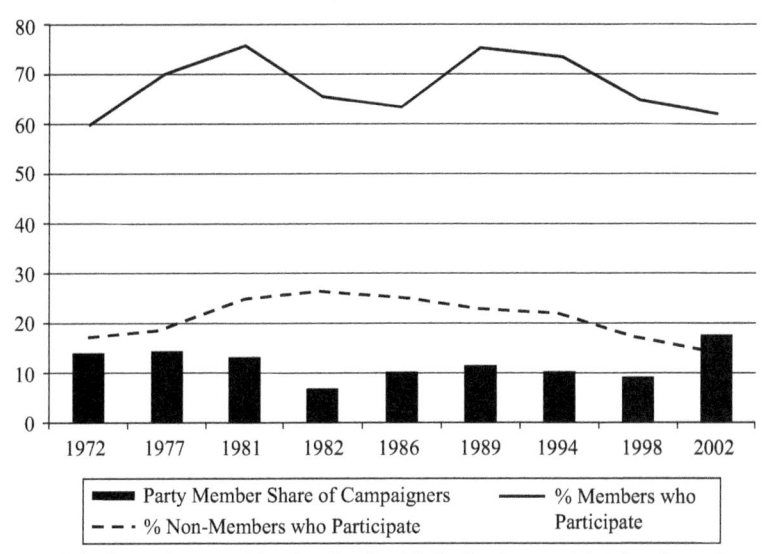

FIGURE 5.5 Campaign participation in the Netherlands: participation in at least one activity

Source: Dutch Parliamentary Election Study, cumulative data-set 1971–2006

from just under 7 percent in 1982 to almost 18 percent in 2002. The fact that there is no secular trend in their share of total volunteers suggests that election-specific political factors are more important than long-term demographic or social forces in affecting non-member political engagement.

While we cannot generalize from this evidence to other countries or to other activities, it does suggest that it is worth further investigating the role of non-members in party mobilization efforts. Their contributions have received little attention in party-centered accounts of grassroots campaigning, but there is good reason to suspect that campaigns may always have mobilized many supporters who remained outside the formal organizations. Whatever the case in the past, today's parties clearly have good reason to employ mobilization strategies that enlist the help of non-member volunteers. The challenge for them will be to identify and connect with the non-member supporters who are likely volunteers.

PARTY MEMBERS AS FINANCIAL SUPPORTERS

Party members were once the backbone of some parties' financial plans. Indeed, in Duverger's romantic vision, members' regular dues payments were crucial to the success of large membership parties. In his memorable phrase, "this invention of the mass party is comparable with that of National Defence Bonds in 1914: before then Treasury Bonds were issued in large denominations and taken up by a few great banks which loaned to the state: in 1914 came the brilliant idea of issuing many more small bonds to be taken up by as many members of the public as possible. In the same way, it is characteristic of the mass party that it appeals to the public" (1954, 64). According to this account, member-based financing enabled parties of the left to compete with parties sponsored by a few plutocrats. This depiction of member-based party finance in classic mass parties is widely accepted, and often forms an implicit justification for linking the obsolescence of party membership with the advent of public subsidies for political parties. In these arguments, the general conjunction of rising public subsidies and declining party memberships is no mere coincidence. Subsidies compensate parties for the membership dues and other funds they lose when memberships dwindle; they also may encourage parties to be complacent about membership losses (Bartolini 1983, 209). From this perspective, data showing that members provide far less than 50 percent of revenues for most contemporary parties are evidence of the displacement of membership-finance by state funding (Hopkin 2004; van Biezen and Kopecký 2001; van Biezen 2004).

The figures in Chapter 4 already have raised doubts about one part of this story, showing the weak temporal connection between the introduction of public subsidies and party membership decline (see also Pierre et al. 2000 for another skeptical conclusion). Historical and contemporary accounts of party finance strategies raise further doubts about another part of this story, the one that argues that many parties once depended heavily on member revenues. Depictions of member-based mass-party finance appear to have only a slim basis in fact. Prior to the 1950s only a few parties relied on membership dues and small donations for even half of national party revenues. Among these were the German Social Democrats, the Austrian Socialists, and the Dutch Labor Party. These are important and well-known cases, but they were not representative examples of party funding strategies.

The reasons for this should be fairly clear by now. Most notably, and as Chapter 3 has shown, prior to the 1950s there were few parties of either the left or right with large direct memberships. On the right, parties that had large memberships tended to have unsystematic dues collection processes, and a large part of dues revenues stayed at the local party level. Their national organizations were almost always more reliant on large donations from individuals and firms than they were on income from dues. Parties on the left were much more likely than others to collect regular dues payments from members. Indeed, such parties often emphasized their financial dependence on the workers' pennies. Despite this, at the national party level, most socialist and social democratic parties relied more heavily on funding from trade unions (sometimes paid in the form of membership affiliation fees) than from individual members.

As a result, at the beginning of the 1960s party finance scholar Arnold Heidenheimer could write: "The average income from individual dues of major parties in Western countries which do have a membership base and attempt to collect dues is probably somewhere around twenty per cent of their normal non-electoral-year expenditures," though he noted that this varied from 10 to 50 percent (1963, 793). Heidenheimer's figures may even have overstated the impact of member financing, because his estimates were based on sketchy and unaudited party reports. Other studies confirmed his picture of the relatively modest role of membership contributions in party financing through the mid-century.[5]

How did the introduction of generous public subsidies for parties affect this pattern? By the beginning of the twenty-first century, public subsidies had become the major funding source for political parties in most of the countries in this study. However, public subsidies did not necessarily make members' financial contributions obsolete. To begin with, many national parties may now be receiving larger dues payments per member than they did in the 1950s. Over the past half-century many parties have adopted more formal dues schedules and stricter payment expectations. Many have implemented centralized and automated dues collection. These twin changes have increased the amounts collected and raised the reliability of dues as a revenue stream. Finally, and as will be shown later, parties have tended to raise their minimum dues rates faster than the rate of inflation. In some cases these changes may have offset the financial consequences of declining membership numbers.

Political conditions also can alter the perceived value of member-based funding, regardless of the sums involved. Today's parties face an anti-party political environment, and one in which government budgets are under strain. In this context, it is politically difficult to increase party subsidies. Indeed, it is imaginable that some governments could find it expedient to reduce party subsidies when they are forced to make cuts to more popular programs. In 2011 the Canadian Conservative government did just this, adopting legislation that phased out per-vote subsidies for political parties (though retaining tax subsidies which were designed to encourage individual donations). Even without actual cuts in subsidies, the perceived value of member-generated funds may increase in an era of government austerity, both because such funds are self-generated (i.e. not coming from potentially "suspect" sources such as big donors or the state), and because they have more growth potential than public subsidies.

Thus, although many studies have highlighted the diminished importance of party members' financial roles, it is worth taking a second look at their monetary contributions. The following section investigates how contemporary parties have been fundraising from members and other individual supporters, and analyzes the impact of their contributions on party accounts. These perspectives yield a more differentiated picture of how party strategists are trying to derive financial benefits from party members, a picture that varies as much by country as by party family.

The Changing Importance of Members' Financial Contributions

Available recent figures confirm that party members are (still) not a mainstay of party finance. Table 5.1 presents country-level estimates from various sources of dues and/or member contributions as a source of total party revenue (in other words, combined revenue for local, regional, and national party levels). The data come mostly from the late 1990s and early 2000s, though a few of the estimates go back to the late 1980s. The figures themselves are not strictly comparable, because the years differ, as does their proximity to national elections (which often affects party income), and because there are big cross-country differences in what parties must or do report. Yet even allowing for such variations, the magnitude of the differences suggests that the underlying discrepancies are real. At the low end, members were estimated to contribute only 1 percent of overall party revenues (in Spain); at the

TABLE 5.1 *Total party revenues: average % from membership dues (late 1980s through early 2000s)*

	1	2	3
Austria	27	41	
Belgium			2–9[a]
Denmark	36	63	20
Finland	3	4	
France			9–10
Germany	31	20	
Ireland	33		
Italy	17	49	15–20
Netherlands	75		35–61
Norway	34	10	
Portugal			1
Spain		1	15[b]
Sweden	7	8	
Switzerland			2–60
UK	36		

Sources: 1. Krouwel 1999; 2. Casas-Zamora 2005; 3. Nassmacher 2009 except. [a] Weekers and Maddens: 35; [b] van Biezen 2000: 335.

high end, they were estimated to contribute over 50 percent (in the Netherlands). Within countries, the revenue share provided by party member contributions can also vary widely across parties. According to Karl-Heinz Nassmacher, the most extreme cross-party variations are found in Switzerland, a country which does not provide public subsidies to extra-parliamentary parties. Here, members provided at least two-thirds of funds for Socialist Party headquarters, but only 2 percent for the Liberal Party (Nassmacher 2009, 213). Other ways of tallying party funding also show cross-party and cross-national variations. Around the turn of the twenty-first century, membership funds provided a median 20 percent of central party revenues for the parties in established parliamentary democracies with the largest memberships (Socialist/Social Democratic and Christian Democratic parties), but much less for other parties (Nassmacher 2009, 207–13).

These estimates suggest that party members may still have a small but significant role in funding some parties. Members were not the most important revenue source for any of the parties studied here, but as Heidenheimer (1963) noted half a century ago, that was seldom the case. The introduction of direct public subsidies for political parties has undoubtedly changed patterns of party revenue. However, as Figure 5.6 shows, in most countries the central parties have never relied on members for even one-quarter of revenues. Subsidies may have slightly reduced this ratio, but in most countries the bigger shift associated with subsidies—and with simultaneous funding restrictions—was to reduce the funding role of wealthy individuals, corporations, or trade unions.

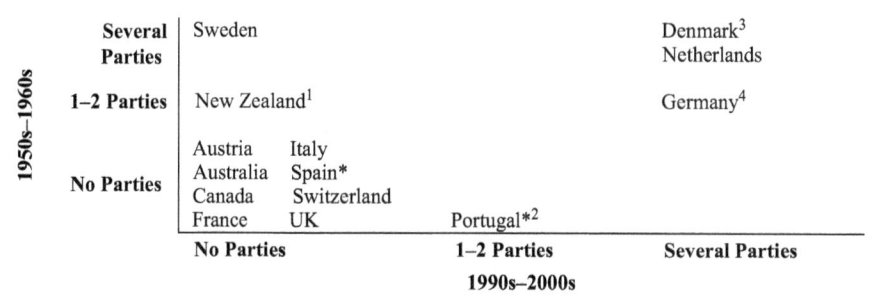

		No Parties	**1–2 Parties**	**Several Parties**
1950s–1960s	**Several Parties**	Sweden		Denmark[3] Netherlands
	1–2 Parties	New Zealand[1]		Germany[4]
	No Parties	Austria Italy Australia Spain* Canada Switzerland France UK	Portugal*[2]	
		No Parties	**1–2 Parties**	**Several Parties**
			1990s–2000s	

FIGURE 5.6 Changing importance of member-based financing: number of parties for which membership fees provided at least 25% of central party income

* Not a democracy in the 1950s–1960s.
[1] Possibly National Party (Edwards 2003).
[2] The Portuguese Communist Party is the one party that received at least 25% of its income from dues in the 1990s.
[3] In 2000s Socialist People's Party, Unity List Red Green, Christian Democrats.
[4] SPD in the 1950s; SPD, CDU, CSU in the 2000s.

Sources: Edwards 2003; Heidenheimer 1963; Casas-Zamora 2005; Krouwel 1999; Nassmacher 2001, 2009

In a few countries member-based financing remained relatively important throughout the period (the Netherlands and Denmark), or even grew in importance (Germany). In the Netherlands, party membership was a main source of central party revenue in the 1950s, and that pattern continued into the twenty-first century. This is even more notable because several contemporary Dutch parties did not exist in the 1950s, meaning that their financial reliance on members is not a legacy of past practices. The Netherlands was one of the last European democracies to introduce direct public subsidies for basic party work (in 1999, though it had financed the work of party foundations and youth organizations for much longer). These subsidies remain relatively modest: a 2008 report estimated direct public subsidies in the Netherlands at €0.93 per capita, far below most of its European neighbors (for instance, Germany at €5.79 per capita and Belgium at €1.89 per capita) (Tweede Kamer der Staten-Generaal 2011, 21). Even relatively modest public subsidies could change the share of revenues provided by members. However, in the Dutch case this effect has been mitigated by collection rules that factor in the number of each party's dues-paying members. In other words, the subsidy legislation was designed to ensure that parties have a financial incentive to recruit.

Germany is the real outlier, being the one country in Figure 5.6 in which the largest parties became *more* dependent on membership revenues since the 1950s. This occurred despite Germany's early introduction of generous public subsidies. There are several explanations for this change. One institutional element that affected all German parties was the legal requirement that parties should receive no more than half of their revenues from public subsidies. This made it potentially costly for them to neglect non-public revenue sources.[6] Second, in the 1960s and 1970s the main German parties all introduced new dues payment systems, thus making it easier for parties to collect funds from members. Finally, several of the country's oft-changing formulas for allocating German public subsidies have paid a premium for revenues collected from individuals, whether as dues payments or small donations.[7] These payout rules increase parties' incentive to raise funds from a broad base of supporters, instead of just relying on a few major sponsors.[8]

As the Dutch and German cases suggest, party finance data provide little support for the hypothesis that public subsidies *necessarily* reduce the financial value of membership. Indeed, public subsidy formulas can be written in ways that amplify the value of members' financial contributions. The figures in Chapter 4 showed that there was no consistent pattern of membership decline occurring soon after party subsidies were introduced. The party finance data further undermine the argument that subsidies are responsible for membership decline, because they suggest that in many parties the introduction of subsidies did not dramatically change the extent of party reliance on members' dues and donations.

What Do Party Members Contribute?

Put differently, when assessing the changing importance of party members' contributions to party finance, we should not dwell excessively on public subsidies. As Kevin Casas-Zamora concluded, with or without public funding for political parties, "members' financial dominance in modern parties is no more than a remembrance of things past" (2005, 48). It is probably safe to go further than this: for many, or even most, parties in parliamentary democracies, "members' financial dominance" is a *mis-remembrance* of things past. However, being a minor source of party funding is not the same as being insignificant. Moreover, it is striking that in many parties members continue to provide a steady stream of income, one that may be valued for its reliability even if it is not the dominant revenue source. As the next section will show, the small but enduring importance of member funding is not accidental, but instead results from parties' deliberate efforts to stabilize financial support from their members.

The Message from Membership Dues

Parties face a potential tradeoff between making party membership maximally accessible (which implies low or no minimum dues rates) and making it financially profitable for the party (which implies higher minimum dues rates). This tradeoff is one that parties must repeatedly revisit as inflation erodes the real income generated by existing dues structures.[9] Parties which are primarily concerned about maintaining or boosting membership numbers may be reluctant to raise dues rates too often, even in inflationary periods, fearing that such increases would reduce renewal rates. Parties with a more revenue-oriented view of membership are more likely to take this risk. Indeed, parties which are truly revenue-oriented might increase basic dues rates faster than the inflation rate. Doing so could help them offset the financial impact of membership losses. The question, then, is what strategies have parties pursued in adjusting dues rates: have dues increases lagged inflation, as we would expect in parties that prioritize membership retention, or have they matched or even exceeded inflation, as we would expect in parties that view membership through a more financial lens?

Table 5.2 answers this question by summarizing changes in minimum dues rates in twenty-six parties in eight countries.[10] It shows 2011 dues figures in euros, and inflation-adjusted percentage changes for three periods: during the high-inflation period from the start of the 1970s to the end of the 1980s; during the lower-inflation, membership-loss period from the end of the 1980s to 2011; and across the whole period. This table includes all the parties in the Katz and Mair *Data Handbook* (1995a) for which minimum dues levels are listed for the 1970s and/or 1980s. Because some of the missing cases are parties that did not set national minimum dues levels in

TABLE 5.2 *Minimum regular dues rates, 1970–2011*

COUNTRY	PARTY	Annual Rate € 2011	% Real Change 1970–1989	% Real Change 1989–2011	% Real Change 1970–2011
Austria	Freedom Party		19.3		
	Socialist	60.00	59.0	9.4	74.0
Germany	Christian Democratic Union	60.00	142.5	37.2	266.4
	Christian Social Union	62.00	93.9	95.2	278.6
	Free Democrats	96.00	142.3	20.9	192.9
	Social Democrats	60.00	61.6	37.2	144.1
Belgium	Ecolo	25.00		–35.2	
	Greens	10.00		–13.7	
Denmark	Center Democrats		–54.8		
	Christian People's	50.48	13.1	61.0	82.1
	Social Democrats	47.12	75.3	–9.1	59.3
	Socialist People's	2.31	205.3	–71.4	–12.6
Ireland	Fianna Fáil		117.1		
Netherlands	D66	60.00	–60.3	454.0	120.0
	Green Left	10.00	–79.4	–48.7	–89.4
	Labor	24.00	–2.5	23.2	20.1
	PSP	20.00	–40.4	–23.0	–54.2
Norway	Christian Democrats	29.04		40.5	
	Conservative	51.63	67.3	66.6	178.7
	Labour Party	32.27	–23.1	56.2	20.1
	Liberal	38.72		10.2	
	Progress	38.72	–25.6	87.4	39.3
	Socialist		33.8		
	Socialist Left	38.72	123.1	–37.5	39.3
UK	Labour	49.11		139.3	
	Liberal	14.37		180.1	

Minimum suggested dues rates for regular members (not including special rates for youth, senior citizens, unemployed, etc.) Non-Euro currencies converted to Euros at rate of Dec. 31, 2011.
Sources: Figures 1970 and 1989 from Katz and Mair 1995a; 2011 from party web pages.
Inflation adjustments for all countries except Germany based on World Bank Consumer Price Index; 2011 figures calculated with 2010 prices. West Germany 1970–1989; United Germany 1989–2011 using 1991 inflation figures; *Statistische Bundesamt 2011*.

earlier periods, this table over-represents the parties which were concerned about revenue-maximizing in the earlier period. Yet though the sample is not random, it has some breadth, including parties from eight countries and all the large political families. These comparisons show that in the two sub-periods (1970–89, 1989–2011) most parties raised their minimum dues rates faster than the rate of inflation. In the latter period, fifteen out of the twenty-two parties did so. Most increases were greater than 20 percent. These real hikes, coupled with the introduction of procedures that facilitated dues collection, help explain why declining membership numbers did not produce an exactly proportionate decline in the financial importance of party membership.

The fact that most of these parties have raised dues rates faster than inflation suggests that many parties have paid attention to the revenues generated by dues. The rates may be set with an eye towards accessibility, but apparently they are not regarded as entirely symbolic. Table 5.3 presents average minimum standard dues rates in 2011 for the sixty-nine parties which published these on their web pages, grouped by party family. In general, it costs relatively little to become a member at the basic rate. The median rate for the more established party families varied between €21 and €28 per year, while the mean rate varied between €27 and €34. As might be expected of parties which have emphasized members' financial importance, average basic dues rates were highest among socialist parties, but this was a substantively slight difference.

Cross-national differences were somewhat larger. Among countries for which rates were available for at least two parties, the top average minimum rate (Germany) was almost ten times as high as the lowest average (Canada) (see Table 5.4, arranged from highest to lowest average minimums). These differences suggest that there are underlying national differences in how parties evaluate the financial importance of membership. Yet these differences are not easily explained by differences in party finance laws or in public subsidies for parties. Thus, minimum dues rates were lowest in Canada, a country with low caps or outright prohibitions on most types of donations, and with low public subsidies. Furthermore, they were highest in Germany, even though this country has no caps and few restrictions on individual or corporate donations, and even though it has quite generous public subsidies.[11]

Paying dues is the most obvious way in which members contribute to their parties' financial fortunes, but it is not the only way. Some party members may volunteer as fundraisers, for instance by selling lottery and

TABLE 5.3 *Average minimum dues by party family, 2011 (€)*

	Mean	Median
Center-Right	33.27	27.70
Christian Democrat	29.18	22.50
Green	26.91	25.00
Liberal	34.44	20.89
Socialist	30.68	28.10
All Parties	28.34	20.89

Party families classified based on transnational party federation membership.
N = 69
Source: Party web pages.

TABLE 5.4 *Average minimum dues by country, 2011 (€)*

		Number of Parties Included
Switzerland	68.98	1
Germany	59.20	5
Netherlands	39.02	9
Norway	38.10	6
France	37.50	4
Austria	35.00	1
Denmark	31.63	5
Finland	27.50	6
United Kingdom	24.93	4
Sweden	22.54	4
Ireland	16.67	3
Italy	16.67	3
Portugal	15.00	1
Belgium	14.94	9
Greece	10.00	1
New Zealand	8.85	4
Canada	5.98	3

Source: party web pages.

raffle tickets and by organizing bazaars and other social events. Anecdotal accounts suggest that such activities used to be an important source of funding for local parties and local candidates in at least a few countries (for instance, in the UK, Canada, and New Zealand; Pinto-Duschinsky 1981; Edwards 2003, ch. 7; Koop 2011). This kind of activity may still be important locally, but precisely because it is local, it is hard to track.

Party members also may contribute funds above and beyond their dues payments. Canadian parties have traditionally set very low dues rates, and have put more emphasis on fundraising from members and other supporters. Canadian parties' interest in encouraging such individual donors was boosted by legal changes introduced in 2003, which banned corporate and trade union contributions to parties, and which set relatively low limits on individual donations. These changes, made in responses to finance scandals, have given Canadian parties increasing reasons to view party members as prime targets for party fundraising efforts.

Parties in other countries may begin to feel similar pressures to raise funds from party members and other small donors, especially if they undergo their own waves of party finance scandals. Anecdotally we know that some parties have been able to temporarily boost revenues by creating member-based clubs of financial supporters who make above-average donations. This strategy helped British Labour Party fundraising in the 1990s when it was in opposition. It also helped to wipe out the New Zealand

Labour Party debt in the 1970s, when it, too, was in opposition (Edwards 2003, ch. 7).

More generally, surveys suggest that if parties want to expand grassroots donations, they should cultivate party members. Figure 5.7 shows that in all the countries in the 2004 ISSP Surveys, at least one-quarter of party members reported donating to a political or social cause within the past twelve months; in eleven of the seventeen countries more than 40 percent did so.[12] Data from ESS 2002 (the only year the survey asked about donations) confirm this picture, showing that even when controlling for other factors that might encourage both membership and donations, such as income and age, party members are more likely than other supporters to make such donations (Ponce and Scarrow 2011). Yet even if members are more likely to donate to causes, including political parties, some non-member supporters will give as well. Here again we see the twin pattern of greater engagement by party members, but much larger numbers of potentially engaged non-members. Figure 5.8 once again makes clear that differences in group size may trump differences in engagement levels: there were only five countries in which party members represented at least 20 percent of all those who gave to social and political causes. These levels, like the overall levels of fundraising engagement (numbers in brackets in Figure 5.8), show

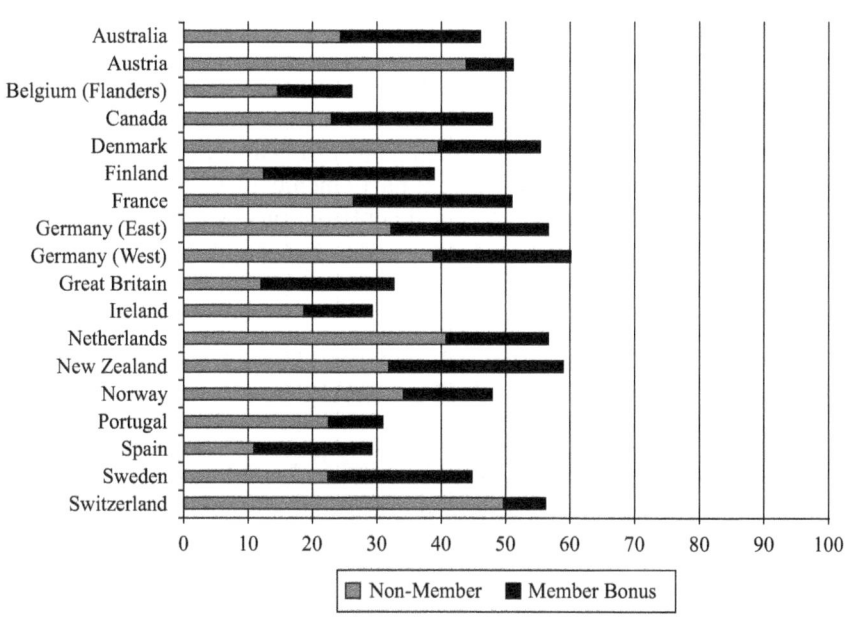

FIGURE 5.7 Donors and fundraisers: participation levels (member % = non member + member bonus)

Source: ISSP 2004

120   *Beyond Party Members*

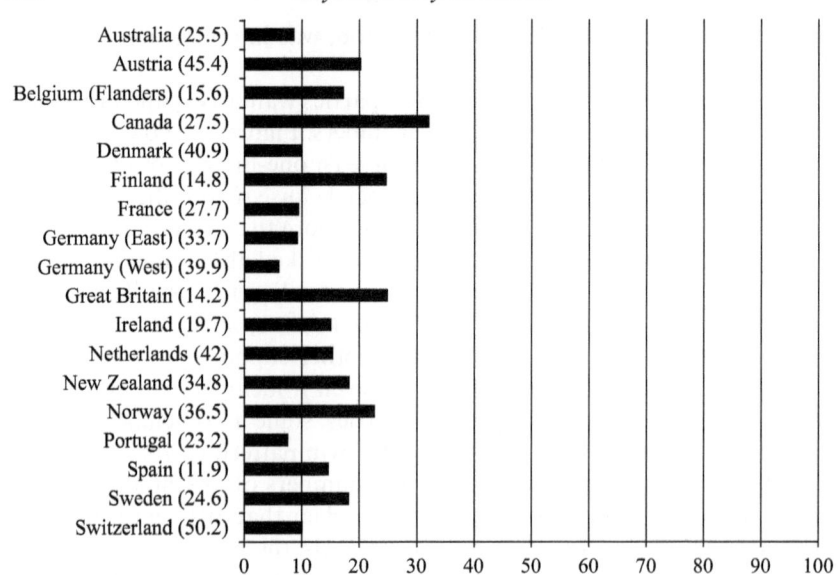

Australia (25.5)
Austria (45.4)
Belgium (Flanders) (15.6)
Canada (27.5)
Denmark (40.9)
Finland (14.8)
France (27.7)
Germany (East) (33.7)
Germany (West) (39.9)
Great Britain (14.2)
Ireland (19.7)
Netherlands (42)
New Zealand (34.8)
Norway (36.5)
Portugal (23.2)
Spain (11.9)
Sweden (24.6)
Switzerland (50.2)

FIGURE 5.8 Donors and fundraisers: % of participants who are party members (in brackets: % of all respondents who donated or fundraised for a political or social cause in past year)

Source: ISSP 2004

intriguing cross-national variations. Whether the source of these differences in individual philanthropy are more institutional or cultural, these figures suggest that parties should direct their fundraising appeals to a group that includes, but is not limited to, current party members. Chapter 6 will look more closely at parties' efforts to boost contributions by both groups.

VOTING FOR THE PARTY: TURNOUT AND PARTY LOYALTY

Another way that parties can benefit from members is through their electoral loyalty. In situations of declining turnout and increasing electoral volatility, members who are loyal and who make the effort to vote could potentially serve as valuable anchors of partisan support. Figure 5.9 shows self-reported turnout levels. These are higher than actual turnout in the countries, as is normal for survey data. However, there is a pronounced member/non-member difference in the data: party members are consistently more likely to self-report voting than other citizens.[13]

What Do Party Members Contribute?

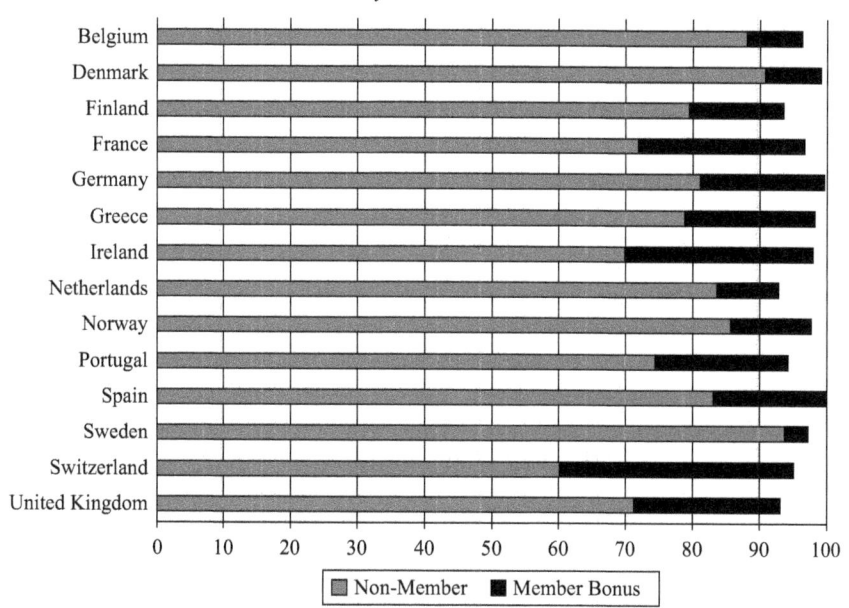

FIGURE 5.9 Voters: % eligible voters who participated in last election (member % = non member + member bonus)
Source: ESS 2010

This difference is most pronounced in countries with lower turnouts. In all countries included in this figure, almost all party members claim to have voted in the most recent national elections; what varies is how many of their compatriots did likewise. For instance in Switzerland, with a survey-reported overall rate of 63 percent participation in the previous national election, 95 percent of party members reported voting, compared with only 60 percent of non-members. In Ireland the difference was 98 percent to 70 percent; in the UK the difference was 93 percent to 71 percent. In comparison, in high-turnout Sweden the member/non-member difference was minimal: 97 percent compared to 94 percent. The value of members' electoral loyalty clearly grows as turnout declines. Because of this, participation disparities are likely to have their greatest impact in low turnout elections, such as European Parliament elections and municipal elections.

Of course, party membership is not necessarily the sole cause of this turnout difference. We know that the resource factors which encourage party membership also encourage electoral participation: age, education, and income certainly play a role in both joining and voting (Whiteley 2011; Gezgor and Scarrow 2010). However, from the point of view of political party organizers, the causes of the differences are less important than the fact that members are the citizens who are most likely to respond to campaign mobilization efforts.

PARTY MEMBERS AS COMMUNICATORS: AMBASSADORS TO THE COMMUNITY

Another way that members can help their party's cause is by carrying its message into the community. Members can reinforce national media communications by disseminating party ideas and arguments to their friends and colleagues. Beginning in the 1970s, researchers began to popularize the idea that candidates and campaigns could benefit or suffer from the (un)willingness of supporters to stand up for their party (Noelle-Neumann 1980). This potential impact has grown in recent years thanks to the expanded size of individuals' digital networks.

Survey data suggest that contemporary party members continue to play important roles as party envoys. They make use of on-line and face-to-face opportunities to discuss politics and to try to persuade others. The lowest sets of bars in Figure 5.1 show the proportion of party members who claimed to have worked in one or more non-party organizations in the past twelve months. In eleven of the fourteen ESS countries, more than 40 percent of party members reported this type of engagement outside the party sphere. Such community engagement outside of party networks should give party members opportunities to communicate partisan messages. Other data suggest that they may actually use these opportunities. For instance, the 2004 ISSP survey found that party members were particularly likely to discuss politics with friends, and to try to persuade others. Figure 5.10 shows that in most countries at least two-thirds of party members reported participating in such discussions (lower bar); at least half of them said they tried to persuade others about political issues (upper bar).[14] Other citizens also engaged in such low-intensity political participation, but party members were universally more likely to share their political views with others. The difference between the groups was even stronger in the higher-intensity activity of contacting the media to share a political opinion.[15] Few citizens engaged in this activity, but party members were again over-represented among those who did so. In most countries members were two or three times more likely than non-members to contact the media (see Figure 5.11). The fact that party members are so over-represented among political message-carriers is important, because these are contributions that members can make even if they are not tightly connected with their local parties. Again, however, given that party members are a small share of the whole population, they comprise only a small share of all those who are discussing, persuading, and sharing their views with the media (see Figure 5.12 and Figure 5.13)

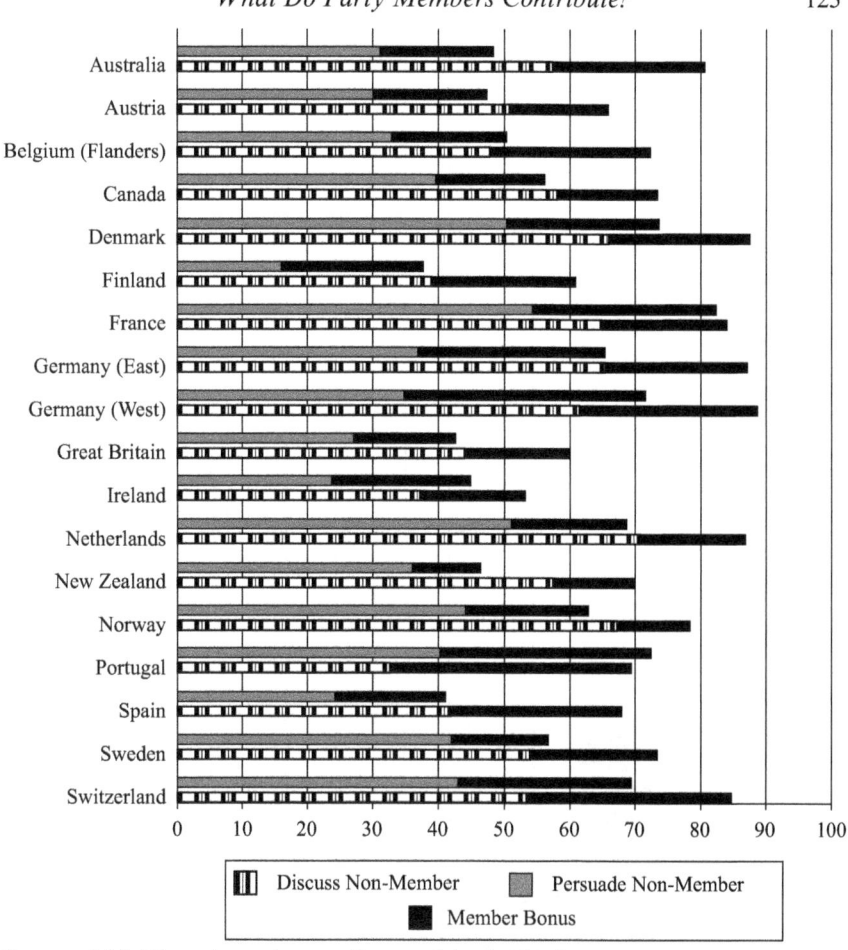

FIGURE 5.10 Discussing and persuading: participation levels
% engaging in behavior sometimes or often
(member % = non Member + member Bonus)

Source: ISSP 2004

CONCLUSION: PARTY MEMBERS AS A PARTIALLY REPLACEABLE RESOURCE

This chapter has looked at ways that members contribute to contemporary political parties, investigating whether party members provide enough help to make it worthwhile for parties to continue to invest in recruiting and retaining them. It also has considered the extent to which non-members do or could supply similar benefits. The result is a decidedly mixed picture.

On the one hand, and contrary to prevailing views, some national parties apparently receive more funds from party members than they once did,

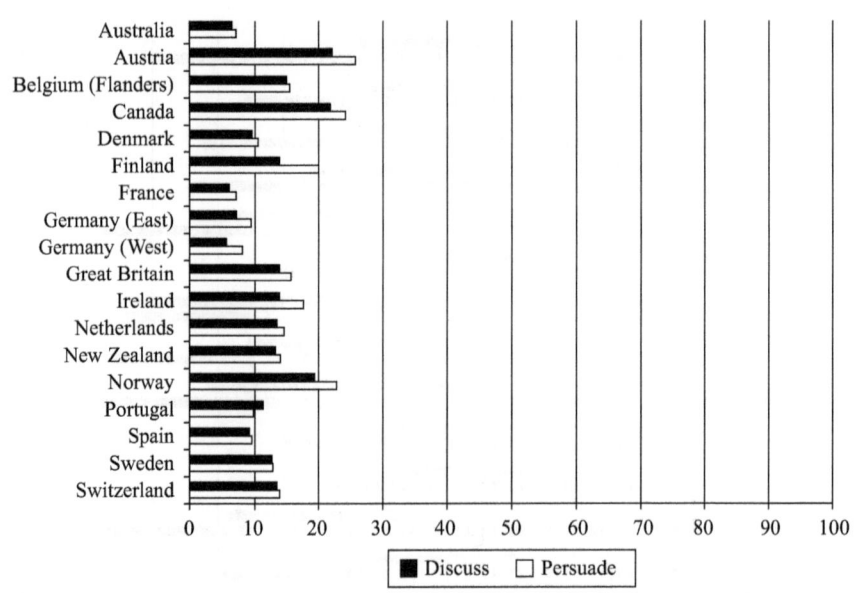

FIGURE 5.11 Discussing and persuading: % of participants who are party members
Source: ISSP 2004

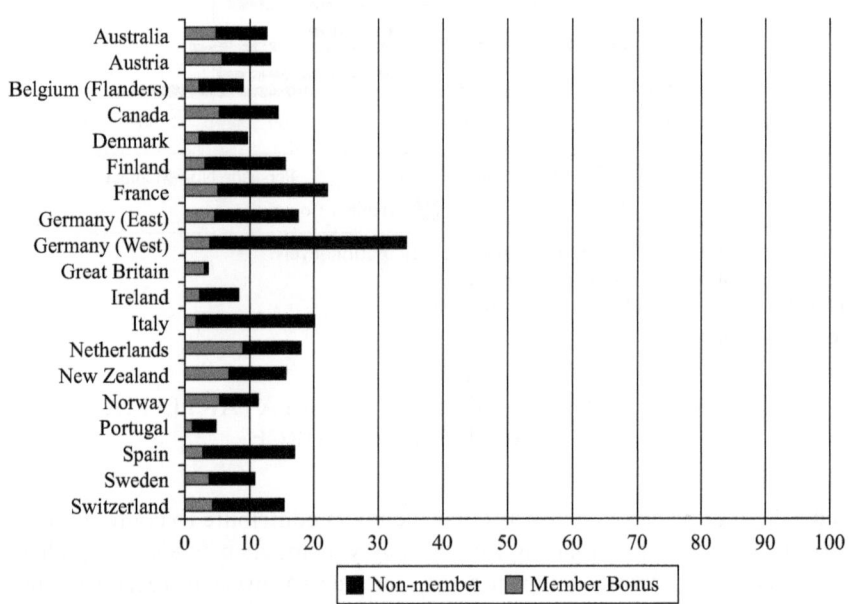

FIGURE 5.12 Media contacters: participation levels
(member % = non member + member bonus)
Source: ISSP 2004

What Do Party Members Contribute?

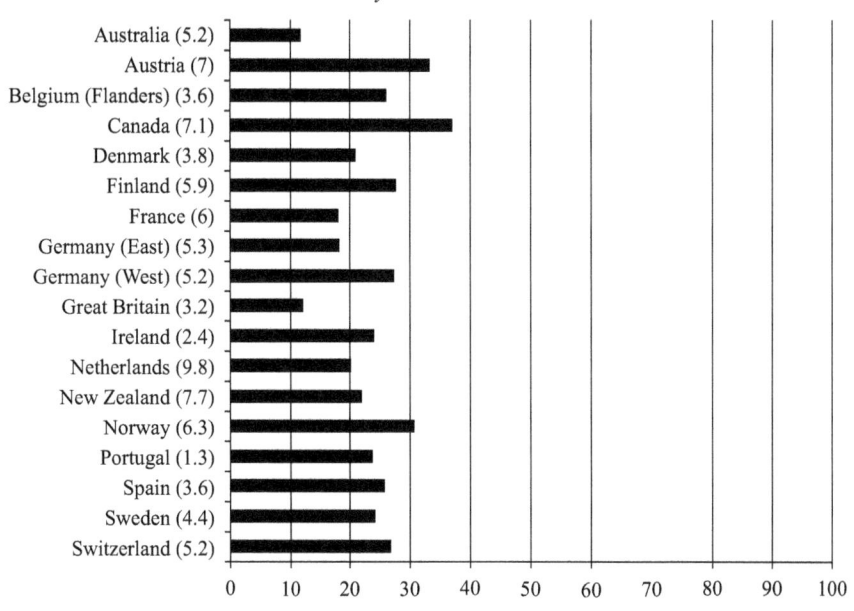

FIGURE 5.13 Media contacters: % of participants who are party members
(in brackets: share of all responders who contacted or appeared in media in past year)

thanks in part to the centralization and automation of membership procedures. Members are not the dominant funding source for any of the parties studied here, but for many parties their dues and donations provide non-trivial financial benefits. Party members also remain the most important source of party volunteers in all but a few countries. They were far more likely than non-members to act as opinion multipliers by contributing to informal political discussions, whether among friends or by contacting local media. They also were far more likely to vote, a distinction that is most pronounced where turnouts are lowest. In all these ways, party members aided their parties to an extent that far exceeded their population share.

On the other hand, party work was not the exclusive preserve of party members, with non-members providing at least one-third of party workers in the ESS subset of countries—and providing over three-quarters of party workers in the UK and Spain. Because party members make up such a small portion of the population, non-member supporters represent a very promising source of potential workers, donors, and partisan opinion leaders, if only parties can figure out how to mobilize them for these tasks.

Given these activity patterns, parties have good reason to pursue two-pronged strategies when trying to mobilize grassroots supporters. There still are many reasons for parties to retain formal membership organizations. In order to nurture such organizations, parties need to retain the loyalty of those who are already enrolled, but also must identify and reach out to potential members. However, as party memberships decline, parties have growing reasons to strengthen contacts with all those whom they may be able to activate for partisan purposes, whether or not they ever become formal members. Given these two separate but important reservoirs of potentially active supporters, it makes sense for parties to supplement and reform traditional modes of party memberships in order to form closer links with the active non-joiners.

Because contemporary parties have good reasons to recruit various types of affiliates, the next chapters examine what parties have been doing to enhance the appeal of traditional party membership, and to create stronger ties with supporters who remain outside traditional structures. Many parties are reaching out to both groups by establishing new categories of affiliation. In the process, they have been creating multi-speed membership organizations, ones in which supporters either simultaneously or serially maintain multiple links to their preferred party, each conferring different obligations and privileges.

NOTES

1. All the European countries except Austria and Italy.
2. The questions asked whether the respondent had done any of the following within the past 12 months: "worked within a political party or action group," "worked in another organization or association," or "worn or displayed a campaign badge/sticker."
3. The question asked whether the respondent had "attended a political meeting or rally" in the past year.
4. The series stops in 2002, after which the question format changed. The list of activities presented to the respondents varied across the surveys. They generally included some version of the following: "displayed window-posters or campaign boards," "distributed folders and the like," "engaged in conversations to gain votes for the party," "contributed money to a party's election campaign," and "attended election rallies and the like."
5. For instance, Australia: Hughes 1963; Canada: Amr and Lisowski 2001; France: Drysch 1993; Germany: Duebber and Braunthal 1963; Italy: Passigli 1963; UK: Pinto-Duschinsky 1981.
6. One of these sources was contributions from SPD elected representatives (party taxes).
7. For instance, in 2012 this premium covered dues and donations from individuals up to €3,300 per person per year.
8. They also have an incentive to use accounting methods that boost the amounts that fall into this category. For instance, from 1982 to 2002, the parties' annual

financial reports included a category labeled "dues and other similar regular payments." The latter covered "party taxes" paid by public office-holders, a category of funding that some describe as covert funding by the state, in that the money comes from public salaries. A 2002 law changed the reporting categories as of 2003, separating the two categories of payment.

9. They could circumvent this by making dues rates automatically inflation-adjusted, but few parties have adopted this alternative.
10. Minimum dues rates tell only part of the story about the connection between membership and party revenues. Many parties have income-related suggested dues rates, so minimum dues apply to only a small portion of members (though parties have no way of enforcing these differentiated rates). In addition, many members pay less than the minimum "regular" rate in parties that have reduced minimum rates for senior citizens and young people. As a result, the actual revenue that a given party generates from dues cannot be simply inferred on the basis of membership size and minimum dues rates. Even so, the minimum dues rate is a signal to potential members about the party's financial expectations.
11. One institutional explanation for this would be German party finance legislation that rewards parties for small contributions, including membership dues.
12. All parties in these countries require members to pay annual dues. Thus, it is likely that some respondents interpret this question as referring to dues payments. However, 50–70 percent of respondents who call themselves "party members" do not list themselves as "party donors." This large gap suggests that many respondents interpret this question as referring to donations other than dues. Others may describe themselves as "members" even if their dues payment has lapsed.
13. It is possible that some of the gap between non-members and members may be due to members' greater susceptibility to social desirability pressures in regards to questions about voting, however, there is no way to determine this from the data used here. Even if this explains some of the gap, it is unlikely to account for all of it.
14. The questions asked: "When you get together with your friends, relatives or fellow workers how often do you discuss politics?" and "When you hold a strong opinion about politics, how often do you try to persuade your friends, relatives or fellow workers to share your views?"
15. The question asked whether respondents in the last year had "contacted or appeared in the media to express your views."

6

Multi-Speed Membership Parties

Parties can pursue three main strategies aimed at increasing the numbers of their affiliated grassroots supporters. First, they can boost the rewards associated with traditional membership. Second, they can reduce the costs of joining. Successful changes of either or both types would elevate the supply of traditional members. Their impact depends in part on the slope of the membership curve—how sensitive are potential members to changes in the costs or benefits? A third strategy is to change the slope altogether by redefining what enrollment means. In pursuit of this third strategy, parties might attempt to build stronger links with non-member supporters, particularly with those who already are providing membership-like contributions to party efforts. Parties that adopt all three strategies would be pursuing a multi-speed approach to party membership, one that seeks to bolster traditional membership while at the same time creating new affiliation options for supporters who may or may not eventually acquire traditional membership.

The current chapter examines the extent to which contemporary parties are responding to membership losses and electoral setbacks by rethinking their approaches to grassroots organizing. It looks particularly at party efforts to make traditional membership more accessible by diversifying affiliation options, and by reducing the costs of joining. Subsequent chapters will investigate parties' efforts to enhance the appeal of partisan affiliation by boosting the benefits available to those who link with their preferred party in either traditional or new ways.

How do we know what parties are doing to recruit members and other supporters? Some parties discuss their organizational initiatives in public forums such as party conferences and party strategy documents. However, these discussions are of limited value for figuring out what is really happening, because they do not reveal which policies were implemented, or with how much enthusiasm they were pursued. Instead of relying on discussions of this sort, this and subsequent chapters make use of a different type of documentary evidence: national party web pages. Web pages are parties' public faces. A party web page is a type of graphic manifesto, one that is likely to be seen by many more people than is a party's traditional manifesto. By now, web pages have become a standard tool for party communication. Their availability and ready accessibility make them a highly useful new resource for the comparative study of party organizational practices. They are particularly well-suited for learning about party strategies for recruiting and activating members and potential members, because those who visit party web sites constitute a prime target for such appeals. For this reason, party web pages tend to give a clear idea of the participation and affiliation options that each party offers to its supporters.

The web page evidence discussed comes from a 2011 survey of web pages that covered 109 parties in all nineteen of the countries included in the current study.[1] The survey included only national parties which held seats in the lower chambers of the national legislatures, and excluded most regional parties (with exceptions in Belgium, and for some regional parties with large parliamentary delegations, including the German CSU, the UK Scottish Nationalist Party, and the Italian Northern League). The survey examined the information that parties provided about traditional membership, including what the pages said about why to join, the costs of joining, and the procedural options for acquiring traditional membership. It also looked at the information the pages provided about other affiliation and support options, and at member-only resources available on these pages. As will be shown, although the medium itself leads to some standardization in terms of format, in terms of content these web pages are by no means cookie-cutter replicas of each other. Of particular interest are variations in the prominence they gave to different affiliation options, and in the ease of on-line affiliation. These differences reflect and reveal parties' diverging priorities regarding the uses of traditional party members and other supporters.

REDUCING AFFILIATION COSTS

One way to make traditional party membership more attractive is to reduce the costs of joining and renewing. Membership can impose several types of externalities, including financial, procedural, and reputational costs. Procedural costs are the time and effort required for an individual to get herself enrolled. Reputational costs relate to the ways that others view partisan participation. Parties have experimented with ways to lower all three types of costs.

Financial Costs

Dues rates are the most visible membership cost. Parties can lower them by introducing outright reductions for some or all members, or by letting dues rates lag behind inflation. As the previous chapter showed, most of the parties for which data are available have raised minimum dues rates faster than inflation, but their minimum rates remain quite modest (see Table 5.4). Moreover, most parties offer discounted dues rates to some groups. In 2011, forty-one of the sixty-nine parties (59 percent) which set minimum dues rates offered below-minimum rates to some groups. The most common beneficiaries were students or all young people (whom they want to attract as first-time members), and senior citizens (whom they want to retain). In most cases these concessionary rates were less than half of the minimum "normal" rate; in a few cases membership was free for at least one year to those in the designated groups. Even in an age when parties distribute most of their membership communications electronically, and therefore do not have high unit costs for printing or postage, members recruited under these reduced-rate dues schemes may cost their parties more than they pay.

A few parties have temporarily or permanently offered special low rates that explicitly target new members. In 2011, fourteen of the sixty-nine parties (20 percent) with national dues rates offered new member discounts. Two Finnish parties offered all new members free membership for their first year. In 2009 and 2010 the British Labour Party experimented with a first-year membership fee of 1 pence for new members under the age of 27. Such schemes may yield temporary successes, but unless parties work to incorporate these new members and convince them of the value of long-term membership, they may have low rates of renewal after the special rate expires.

The widespread use of concessionary dues rates for certain groups suggests that parties are concerned that cost might deter some potential members. If that is true, offering reduced dues rates for everyone would seem to be a good course for parties which want to boost membership levels. However, such a strategy would be financially costly to the parties, and the previous chapter has demonstrated that many parties seem to look to members to generate a modest but steady revenue stream. Reducing membership dues for targeted groups (youth, unemployed, seniors) is a compromise aimed at those who are considered to be most price sensitive, and who may be accustomed to receiving discounts on other services.

Procedural Costs

Parties have been comparatively more active in reducing procedural costs than in reducing financial costs. Most importantly, in recent years parties on both the left and right have embraced new technologies that make it much easier for first-time members to enroll, and for existing members to renew their memberships.

To understand how much has changed in this regard, it is worth recalling how members used to join and stay current in their membership. At the beginning of the 1960s, the most common way to join a party was by contacting a local party branch or local party leader. In parties with formal membership procedures, local parties accepted application forms, and local party volunteers collected dues. In parties with less formal procedures, joining might be based on some type of interaction with the local party, such as showing up at meetings or rallies, or donating to the local party's annual gala. Local party leaders could and did reject applicants for political or personal reasons. Because local parties played such a leading role in membership enrollment, membership accessibility was determined by the visibility and activity level of local branches. In regions where a party had few active branches, it could be difficult for would-be members to join. Inactive branches also were likely to be lax in pursuing membership renewals.

This model began changing in the 1960s and 1970s, as parties adopted country-wide enrollment procedures, and as they established central databases to track party membership. Such systems gave national parties a more accurate count of their members. Some of them enabled national parties to contact individual members directly with renewal notices, without the mediation of local or regional party structures. Centralized record keeping literally "formalized" enrollment practices: even in parties that once had fairly casual membership rules, would-be members now completed a form as part of the application process. At first, however, local parties generally retained the primary (and often, the sole) responsibility for accepting membership applications. In order to join, would-be members had to find their way to a local party.

This has changed dramatically since the 1990s because of the growing importance of national party websites. Those who are interested in learning more about party membership can reach a national party's web page at any hour of the day. They do not need to visit a local party office to find out how to join. Even in those parties where local branches retain the main responsibility for membership administration, the national party websites usually help interested visitors to take the first steps towards enrollment: 95 percent of the national party web sites explicitly invited supporters to join the party, sporting tabs with labels such as "join now," "become a member," or "membership." Seventy-five percent of parties placed these invitations on their home page; in the rest, information about membership was usually easily located under more general headings that encourage active participation ("support us," "get active"). One of the very few parties that did not mention membership on its websites was the Dutch Party for Freedom of Geert Wilders—an unsurprising omission, given that this party had only one member (its leader). The web pages of the Greek and Portuguese Communist Parties also omitted information on how to join the party, although both parties did enroll small and select memberships. Two examples illustrate the wide spectrum of procedural costs. At the high end was the Spanish People's Party, whose web page only enabled potential members to get as far as downloading a PDF of the long paper form. To complete this, they needed to have endorsing signatures and party membership numbers from two current party members, as well as a photocopy of their identification papers. The form was to be submitted at the local party headquarters. At the other end of the spectrum was the Norwegian Left Socialist Party, which allowed supporters to immediately join by using their mobile phone to complete a very short form and send payment.

Although almost all of the websites gave recruiting information, Figure 6.1 shows important differences among the parties in regards to how much of the enrollment process could be accomplished during a single website visit. In some cases, prospective members could complete all formalities in one visit by filling out a form and simultaneously paying their dues on-line. Over two-thirds (72 percent) of parties fell into this most open category. Among the rest, the most common practice was to ask would-be members to complete and submit an on-line form, with the promise that someone from the appropriate level of the party would get back to them with more details.[2] In a few cases, the web page offered only a printable form that could be mailed back or brought to a local party office.

Another way in which some parties have enhanced membership accessibility is by reducing or eliminating formal probationary periods. Probationary membership used to be characteristic of ideological parties and ones with strong community identity. Under strict probationary schemes, candidate-members were expected to prove their commitment to party aims through months or even years of partisan activity. Moving to full membership status was not automatic, and usually required the endorsement of local party leaders. In 2011 the leadership-dominated Italian Lega Norda was the only party in this set that clearly had a true probationary model, one in which supporters had to separately apply for full membership after paying dues for at least a year.[3] As will be explained in more detail in Chapter 8, several other parties placed temporary restrictions on new members' intra-party political rights. However, in these parties members automatically acquire full membership rights after a defined period, meaning that members faced no additional procedural costs.

A third type of procedural barrier to membership requires prospective members to obtain the endorsement of one or more existing members. This requirement is supposed to ensure that new members back party goals, or that they meet other membership qualifications (such as trade union membership

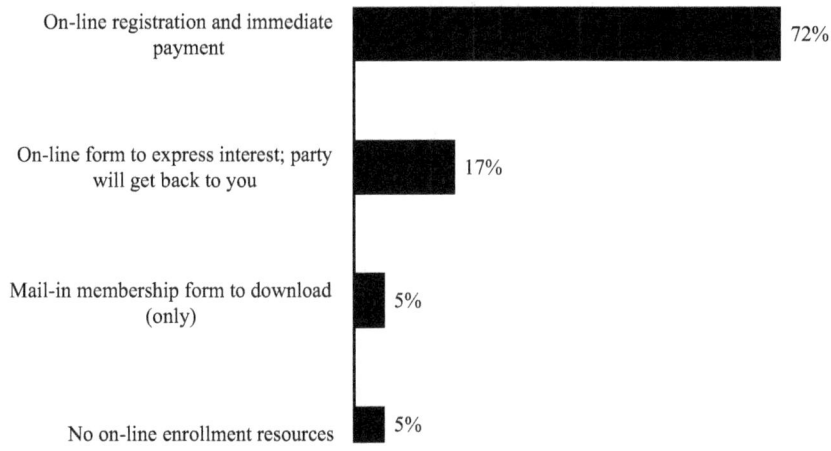

Option	Percentage
On-line registration and immediate payment	72%
On-line form to express interest; party will get back to you	17%
Mail-in membership form to download (only)	5%
No on-line enrollment resources	5%

FIGURE 6.1 Membership accessibility: ease of joining 19 parliamentary democracies (n = 109)

Source: Party Web Page Survey, Spring 2011

or good moral character). Such a requirement prevents the spontaneous self-recruitment that web-based enrollment encourages. Current websites cannot tell us the extent to which parties once required such recommendations. However, this rule is clearly rare today: in parties that posted their registration forms on-line, only a handful included spaces for the names of recommenders.[4]

Finally, changes in financial technologies since the 1960s have greatly reduced the procedural costs of membership renewal. In many parties, particularly on the left, members used to receive weekly or monthly visits from neighborhood dues collectors. These collectors played a community-building function as well as a financial role. By the 1970s such labor-intensive practices were disappearing. Automated dues payment is now the most common collection method, whether by credit card or bank order. Even if such payments do not automatically renew from year to year, members may receive an e-mail reminder that directs them to an on-line renewal site. The new payment procedures make it easy for even minimally engaged supporters to retain their membership whether or not they have any contact with a local party branch.

In short, new technologies have made it considerably easier for supporters to join parties and to stay in good standing. The parties studied here have almost universally embraced web-based membership solicitation, thereby significantly reducing the procedural costs of joining a party. Supporters can now easily join, whether or not they live in an area with an active and visible party branch. Virtual accessibility may be increasingly important in parties with shrinking memberships, ones in which active branch parties may be fewer and further between. Even if renewal rates may be higher when individuals are contacted by a neighbor who encourages them to renew, parties may benefit if they do not have to rely exclusively on volunteers to initiate recruiting efforts or to collect payments for membership renewal. Overall, the automated systems are easier for the parties to manage, and they also reduce the procedural costs imposed on individuals who want to acquire or renew membership. In this respect, parties on the left and the right have converged towards models of membership that are simultaneously more formal (with specified dues levels, application forms, central membership registries) and more accessible.

Reputational Costs

Parties can also try to reduce less easily quantified membership costs, such as economic liabilities and social stigmas that might be associated with partisan affiliation. On the economic side, some supporters may view party membership as incompatible with their job situations. Countries vary as to which professions discourage acts of public partisanship. For instance, in countries with an avowedly non-partisan press, journalists may be expected to eschew party affiliation; in contrast, active partisanship may be tolerated or even expected in countries with a more openly politicized press. Similarly, in countries in which the state is viewed as a non-partisan and technocratic actor, high-ranking public employees may be discouraged or even prevented from affiliating with parties (the flip side of countries in which political patronage appointments are common). A wider issue may be work environments where pressures from peers or from bosses discourage open support for particular parties. For instance, employers in banks and law firms may look askance at supporters of the left or far-right. Similarly, membership in a center-right party may raise eyebrows in some unionized work places.

Parties have few options for combating career norms or requirements that explicitly discourage partisan affiliation. They may, however, be able to do more to combat perceptions that membership in particular parties is incompatible with certain careers. To this end, some Christian Democratic parties have reached out to unionized industrial workers by establishing sub-organizations to promote workers' interests. For similar reasons, some social democratic parties created sub-organizations to appeal to the self-employed. Yet such initiatives are unlikely to completely alter perceptions about which types of professions or confessions are (and are not) associated with cleavage parties that once based their appeals on their links with specific economic or religious interests.

More recently, as popular trust of parties has eroded (Dalton and Weldon 2005), and as party membership has declined, it has become less likely that party members of *any* stripe will encounter partisan solidarity at work: instead, members are more likely to encounter hostility to all parties. Such environments increase the reputational costs of joining any political party. It is not easy for parties to combat general perceptions that traditional party life is old-fashioned and unappealing, or that parties themselves are suspect. In order to recruit and retain members, parties may need to do more than offer new benefits or lower the costs of joining; they may need to change the image of what it means to be an active and engaged partisan. This is one reason why some parties have been experimenting with new forms of partisan affiliation and partisan action, ones that may be considered more novel and interesting, or at least carry fewer negative associations, than traditional party membership.

INTRODUCING NEW FORMS OF AFFILIATION

The approaches described so far involve tinkering with long-established models to make traditional membership easier and cheaper to obtain and to renew. Another approach to declining party membership is to rethink membership altogether. An increasing number of membership-based parties are doing just this, augmenting traditional membership structures by creating new ways for supporters to affiliate. This is the origin of the multi-speed membership parties described in Chapter 2.

Figure 6.2 reproduces a figure from this earlier chapter, illustrating how new affiliation categories enable supporters to link to the party in multiple ways. They may choose to become trial members, light members, cyber-members, sustainers, followers, or audience for party news media. These categories are neither exclusive nor hierarchical. Supporters may use some of these new options to supplement old-style membership, or they may affiliate in one or more of these new ways instead of acquiring traditional membership. Individuals may oscillate between categories, for instance paying membership dues only in election years, but permanently staying on the list to receive their party's e-newsletter. In this sense of combining both traditional and new forms, multi-speed parties differ from the cyber-parties described by Margetts (2006), because they offer a diversification of the partisan experience that goes beyond the exploitation of new technologies.

The new affiliation categories introduced by multi-speed parties differ from traditional memberships in that their costs are low (including procedural and reputational costs), and they do not require long-term

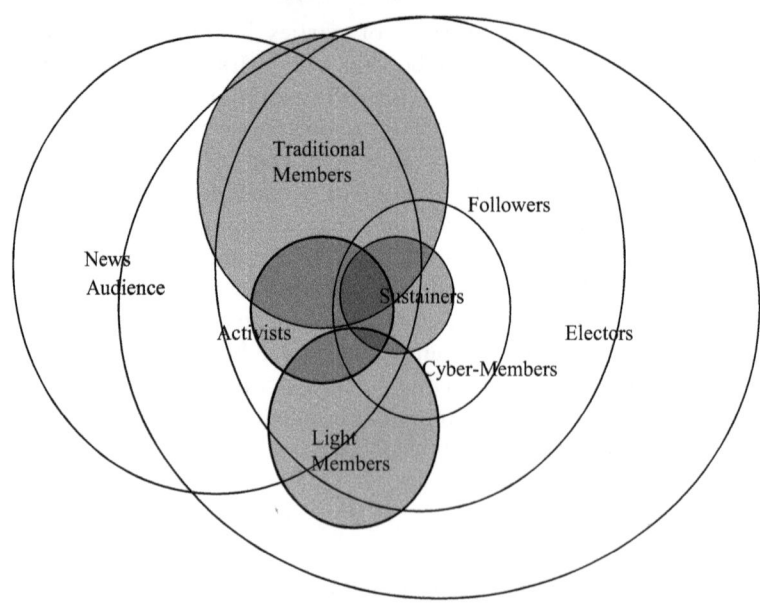

FIGURE 6.2 Party affiliation: the multi-speed model

commitments. Instead, they offer immediate opportunities for participation and communication, be this spur-of-the-moment involvement or ongoing input. In return, parties gain contact information from their supporters which they can use for one-way and two-way communication to nurture partisan interest and engagement.

Parties have emphasized the new affiliation options with greater or lesser zeal. In many cases, these changes do not result from thoroughly considered organizing strategies, but rather come as a bandwagon response to trends in technology and marketing. Precisely because of this, parties may adopt new layers of affiliation without much thought about the possible political implications of the new structures. There is not a single template for these efforts, but most steps in the direction of multi-speed organization share three common characteristics: they are centralized, they are digital, and they are highly accessible.

Centralized

The new support categories create direct contact between a national party and its potential supporters. Centralization of newer affiliation modes is characteristic even in parties in which local or regional parties still retain primary responsibility for traditional membership recruiting and enrollment.

Digital

Most of the new affiliation categories are based on electronic media. They can be as formal as statutorily recognized cyber-branches, which are the non-geographic equivalents of traditional local branches. More common electronic affiliation options include registration to receive party-generated content in the form of e-newsletters, blogs, Facebook or Twitter messages, or text messages. These connections are not recognized in party statutes. They incur no obligation and confer no rights. However, they do provide those who affiliate with some of the benefits traditionally associated with membership. In return, affiliates provide their parties with contact information that otherwise might be given by members alone; such information can be particularly useful to parties seeking to run data-driven campaigns. Maintaining websites and running social media platforms can be modestly expensive, because interactive media require the ongoing attention of personnel with specialized skills. New parties and small parties may find it difficult to hire personnel to adequately maintain and support these contact modes. However, for parties that can afford the start-up and maintenance costs, digital communications methods offer big economies of scale compared to most other mass media: parties can enlist large numbers of digital affiliates without charging them any fees, and can maintain frequent contact with them, because the marginal costs of e-communications with new affiliates is close to zero. This is a big difference from most traditional membership models.

Accessible

Parties' new affiliation schemes are readily accessible and are low-cost or free to join. Becoming a party Facebook friend, Twitter follower, or blog reader generally requires nothing more than basic registration. These affiliations are open to party members and non-members alike. For some types of affiliation, such as official party friend or registered sympathizer, applicants may be asked to provide additional information, including their residential address, so that local parties can contact them. They may be required to pay a reduced affiliation fee to obtain light membership status. Interested supporters can spontaneously and independently sign up for these various types of affiliations, most of which are compatible with traditional dues-paying membership.

These three traits of the new affiliation modes—centralized, digital, accessible—reduce the costs for party supporters to link with a party, and for parties to connect with them on an ongoing basis. Because most of these new options are digitally based, we can once again look to parties' web pages to assess how much parties have been investing in the various affiliation modes shown by the multi-speed diagram in Figure 6.2.

Light Membership

These are relatively new schemes that create a second class of traditional membership, one that carries reduced obligations and reduced rights. Party arguments in favor of creating these new options stress that they can make party life more attractive for those with qualms about acquiring traditional party membership. Although these second-class membership schemes have sometimes gained positive media attention for parties which promote them, in 2011 only fourteen of the 109 parties (13 percent) actually offered such an option. In some cases, this was constructed as a time-limited deal, intended as a prelude to traditional membership. For instance, two German and two Dutch parties[5] offered *trial* or *guest* memberships. These were one-year, reduced-fee options that carried reduced benefits. In the other cases, parties offered long-term light membership options with names such as *friends, sympathizers,* and *cooperators*.[6] In most cases, these affiliates had reduced rights as well as reduced obligations, although some parties permitted them to participate in important party decisions.[7]

Cyber Membership

Cyber membership may parallel the rights and duties of traditional membership, or it may be much more loosely structured. At the more formal end are a handful of parties such as the Spanish PSOE which changed its statutes in 2008 to recognize "cyber-militantes" as a distinct group of party members. The Portuguese Socialist Party also changed its statutes in 2012 to give greater formal recognition to basic units which were organized on-line rather than by traditional geographic principles. Other parties have created on-line communities and on-line action groups, many of which recruit both traditional members and non-member supporters. These groups foster on-line discussion and encourage supporters to spread the party message through electronic media. Party experiments with such on-line communities have had names such as the "nettivists" of the Norwegian Labor Party, the on-line "circles" of the Italian Democratic Party, and the Action Network of the UK Liberal Democrats. This is an area of rapid change, and one in which there is still much experimentation.

The possibilities and limitations of cyber membership were vividly demonstrated in the second decade of the twenty-first century by two new parties, the German Pirates Party and the Italian Five Star Movement. These parties were not included in the 2011 web page survey, because they did not then hold seats in the national legislature. Yet their attempts to build internet-based organizational structures deserve to be mentioned here, not least because these efforts received a great deal of media attention, and thus were heavily scrutinized by other parties as well. The German Pirates Party was founded in 2006 as part of a backlash against restrictions on internet file sharing and on digital privacy. It captured much wider attention in 2009, when it won over 2 percent of the vote in that year's federal election. Befitting its original interest, the party made on-line forums the central focus of its popular organization. Members and non-members alike could contribute to the party's Wiki forum and blogs, and could participate in its many on-line working groups (discussion forums). The party's experiment in on-line membership democracy, its "Liquid Feedback" board, could be read by all, but only members were eligible to vote on the issues discussed there. These tools facilitated debate and participation, but the party's avowedly non-hierarchical and open structures proved unwieldy once the party won representation in several state legislatures (Lewitzki 2011; Niedermayer 2012; Totz 2012).

Like the Pirates Party, the Italian Five Star Movement based its membership around on-line forums, but its membership requirements were much looser and decentralized. The movement functioned like a party, in that it selected candidates and contested elections, but its members were formally described as "Friends of Beppe Grillo" (Grillo was the party leader), not as party members. Would-be members first joined one of the party's many on-line discussion groups, and then petitioned members of their forum to admit them to membership; once admitted, they had the right to vote in their forum (Hartleb 2013; Passarelli and Tuorto 2013).

Both parties were populist movements that experienced rapid growth in public support, not least because their active on-line communities enhanced parties' claims to have strong popular backing. Having a primarily on-line organization facilitated rapid membership expansion. Once the parties began winning seats in regional and national legislatures, however, office-holders in both parties found it difficult to maintain the support and enthusiasm of their loosely organized supporters. For the Pirates, some of the problems were a result of their radically open and non-hierarchical structures of cyber democracy; for the Five Star Movement, some of the tensions were due to the contradictions between having a strong national party leader and having statutes which granted members a strong role in overseeing local party leaders. These parties represent extreme cases of new parties building primarily or exclusively cyber memberships. Their rapid growth illustrates the great potential for parties to use non-geographic, topic-based, networks to stimulate political debate and participation. Their difficulties in sustaining initial momentum, and in capitalizing on electoral success, also suggest some of the

Financial Sustainers

By 2011 about two-thirds of the parties were using their web pages to nurture a different type of connection, that of being a financial supporter.[8] However, web pages varied greatly in terms of the prominence of their financial solicitations, and in the ease with which web-page visitors could make a spontaneous gift. At one end of the spectrum were the eight parties, primarily in Scandinavia, that gave potential donors the very easy option of donating via text message (see Figure 6.3). The potential pay-off for these types of small donations is more than financial, because text-message donations enable supporters to spontaneously express solidarity and to (literally) buy in to the party's campaign. In addition, the parties that receive such donations also obtain donors' contact information, enabling them to easily follow up with these self-identified supporters.

More party web pages solicited one-time donations by other media, such as credit card, or intermediary payers (such as PayPal). Most also gave instructions for those wishing to use more traditional payment options. At the other end of the fundraising spectrum were the nine parties which appealed for donations but did not provide options for immediate payment; instead, they advised potential donors to set up standing orders on bank accounts, or to contact the party for details on how to give.

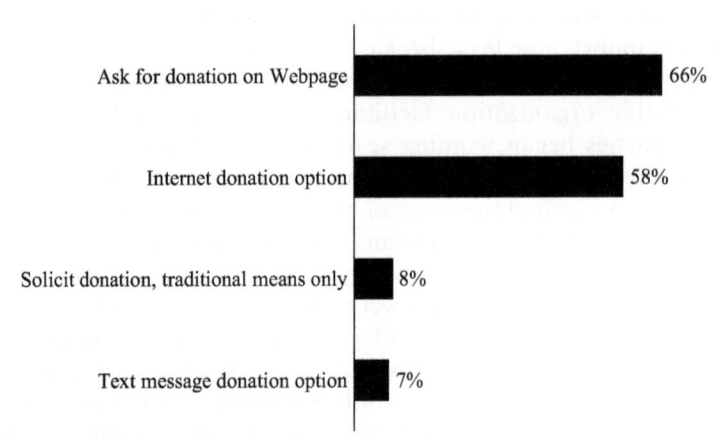

Ask for donation on Webpage	66%
Internet donation option	58%
Solicit donation, traditional means only	8%
Text message donation option	7%

FIGURE 6.3 Sustainers: party web pages and fundraising
19 parliamentary democracies
(n = 109)

Source: see Figure 6.1

Why do parties differ so much in how they appeal to potential donors? Some of the differences are probably dictated by national factors, including differential rates of credit-card usage, legal restrictions on donations, and the extent of alternative funding sources. Yet system-level factors do not explain cross-party differences in funding solicitations. When only some parties in each country solicit on-line donations, this may indicate that such efforts may not (yet) be lucrative enough to encourage imitation. (On the other hand, even where all parties within a country are soliciting on-line donations, they are not necessarily generating large sums.)

Followers and Friends

Parties' efforts to cultivate new types of affiliates are most evident in their employment of new social networking media. Political parties, like other associations and businesses, quickly recognized the potential value of these new communications platforms. Parties and party leaders adapted to the new possibilities with varying alacrity, and with varying interest in promoting two-way communication.

In 2011 Facebook was the most ubiquitous of the new social media sites. As Figure 5.3 showed, by then 83 percent of the 109 parties had placed links to a party or leader's Facebook page on their national web pages, and many exhorted readers to show their partisan colors by "liking" the party's Facebook page. An organizational "like" is costless and can be done spontaneously, but even so it creates a lasting connection. Parties can send targeted (and free) messages to their self-identified fans, and through them, to their fans' wider networks.

Although party Facebook pages were ubiquitous by 2011, they were not equally popular. At that point only seventy of the parties covered in this book had readily identifiable party Facebook pages (as opposed to party leader pages). Of these, only one listed more than 100,000 "likes" (the British Conservative Party, whose fan-base had grown prior to the 2010 election). In contrast, sixty-three parties listed fewer than 10,000 "likes." Such popularity differences cannot be explained away as the product of differential national rates of Facebook usage. Although national usage rates did differ, by 2011 there were millions of users in each of these countries, meaning that parties had large potential audiences (see Table 6.1). More telling was the fact that in each country parties as a group had far fewer Facebook friends than traditional members. This relationship held even when party "likers" were nationally standardized in terms of overall Facebook users.[9] These low numbers are a bit surprising, given the low cost of Facebook affiliation, and given that there is more of a bias toward permanency with "likes" than with party membership: parties

TABLE 6.1 *Party Facebook popularity, spring 2011*

	Party Members as % of Electorate	FB Users as % of Electorate	Party FB "Likers" as % of Electorate	Party FB "Likers"/FB Users
Australia		67.6	0.2	0.2
Austria	17.3	34.5	1.7	5.1
Belgium	5.5	46.3	0.5	1.1
Canada		66.7	0.1	0.2
Denmark	4.1	63.8	1.1	1.8
Finland	8.1	47.1	1.0	2.1
France	1.9	44.3	0.2	0.4
Germany	2.3	17.6	0.1	0.7
Greece	6.6	34.5	0.7	2.0
Ireland	2.0	54.8	0.5	0.9
Italy	5.6	35.9	0.2	0.5
Netherlands	2.5	22.5	0.3	1.4
New Zealand		34.3	2.1	6.0
Norway	5.0	74.7	1.3	1.7
Portugal	3.8	30.1	0.2	0.6
Spain	4.4	31.4	0.2	0.5
Sweden	3.9	57.7	0.9	1.6
Switzerland	4.8	53.7	0.2	0.4
UK	1.2	62.8	0.8	1.2

Sources: Party membership and electorate from van Biezen et al. 2012; Facebook membership from Internet World Stats 2011; Internet World Stats http://www.internetworldstats.com/europa.htm; accessed Apr. 2011.

will remove members for non-payment, but Facebook "likers" need to take the initiative to remove themselves. One explanation, not investigated here, is that supporters are more likely to create a cyber link (a "like") with a political personality such as the party leader, rather than with the party itself. Even if this were true, the very low figures for party Facebook affiliates are somewhat surprising, especially given that liking the organization and liking the party leader are costless and completely compatible.

Figure 6.4 graphically depicts the weak relation between party membership and Facebook likes in the fifty-three parties for which both types of data were available for roughly the same period. As of spring 2011, only seven parties had more Facebook likers than traditional party members; five of these parties were small, with fewer than 25,000 members. These exceptions aside, few parties had established their Facebook pages as hubs of on-line communities that rivaled the numerical reach of their traditional membership networks. However, to the extent that Facebook friends were non-members, they did represent an expansion of parties' ability to communicate with registered supporters. That expansion may have

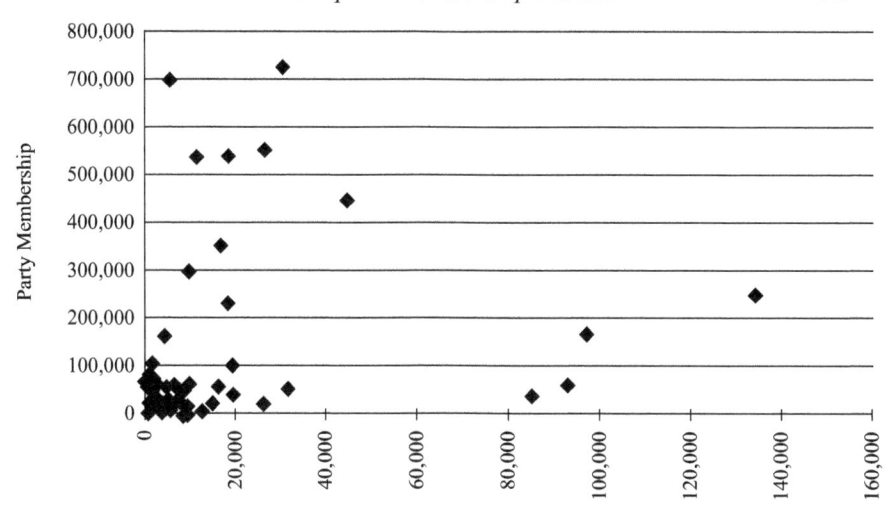

FIGURE 6.4 Party membership and party Facebook friends, 2011 (n = 53)

been particularly valuable if, as seems likely, these Facebook friends were younger than the traditional membership.

In this period parties and party leaders were also experimenting with using Twitter feeds and similar micro-blog services to stay in touch with a self-registered audience (see Figure 6.5). These messages might comment on current events, provide details about campaign schedules, or exhort supporters to spread the party perspective. In spring 2011, three-quarters of the parties advertised Twitter feeds on the home pages of the websites, and more than half posted links to political blogs written by party leaders.

News Audience

Some supporters may want to receive communications that are more in-depth than Twitter messages or Facebook posts. For these supporters, most parties offer free subscriptions to on-line magazines, newsletters, news feeds, and party videos. Recipients must give the parties their contact information in order to receive these services.

In creating these multiple communication channels, many parties are returning to their former role as news providers. Through the 1960s many parties, particularly parties of the left, produced their own newspapers or were supported by avowedly partisan newspapers. Party members and

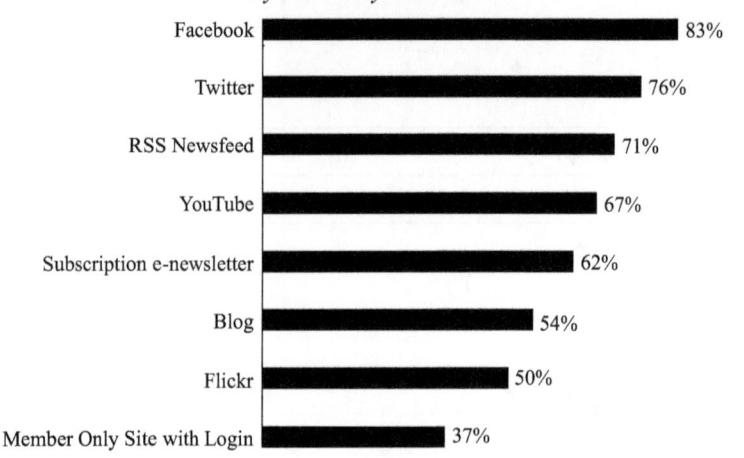

Platform	Percentage
Facebook	83%
Twitter	76%
RSS Newsfeed	71%
YouTube	67%
Subscription e-newsletter	62%
Blog	54%
Flickr	50%
Member Only Site with Login	37%

FIGURE 6.5 Followers: parties advertising digital communication options: 19 parliamentary democracies
(n = 109)

Source: see Figure 6.1

other supporters were encouraged to purchase these papers and to get their news from them. Such traditions were strongest and have endured longest in countries which have provided public subsidies for partisan newspapers, including Austria, Finland, Italy, Norway, and Sweden (Murschetz 1998). Elsewhere, partisan newspapers generally had smaller audiences, but they reached at least parties' core supporters. These party and party-associated newspapers presented readers with a partisan interpretation of current politics, and they connected readers with the inner life of their favored party. As early as the 1960s, party-sponsored newspapers were falling victim to the consolidation of media markets and declining readership. By the end of the twentieth century this model had waned even in a country like Finland, which still provided state subsidies for partisan newspapers (Picard and Grönlund 2003, 118). While this demise was partly due to the changing economics of print journalism, it also had something to do with party electoral strategies. As parties abandoned cleavage identities in pursuit of wider electorates, they became more interested in projecting their messages in national news media than in narrowcasting messages to the party faithful. Some parties compensated for the declining reach of party newspapers by producing in-house membership magazines or newsletters, but these were expensive to print and costly to mail. In the absence of national party media, local parties became the main sources of privileged political information for members, which might be provided by speakers and forums at local party meetings. Inactive members missed out on these types of selective information benefits.

The rise of the internet radically altered the economics of news distribution, and lured many parties into resuming or assuming active roles as news providers and interpreters. Some who assess the impact of internet technologies on party practices have lamented the missed opportunities for democratic participation, labeling top-down communication styles as a "normalization" strategy that reinforces traditional hierarchies (for instance, Gibson and Ward 2009). This diagnosis overlooks the fact that by the end of the twentieth century few parties were engaging in much direct communication of this sort. They had instead been conveying their messages through non-party media. Their increasing use of web pages, e-newsletters, and other top-down communication channels for self-selected audiences returns them to a narrowcasting and direct communication role that most parties had long ago abandoned. The most active parties post news and commentaries on the home pages of their websites, host blogs, have free e-newsletters, offer Twitter feeds from party leaders and party Facebook pages, and post links to politically relevant video clips. Some parties update their video clips often enough to create what they label the "party television channel," a site to which supporters can permanently link to find party-curated news videos. Parties can adopt different strategies for controlling access to these resources, making access broad to encourage maximum but loose affiliation, or restricting some or all of its dues-paying members, to boost the rewards of traditional membership.

This reappearance of parties as news providers, and the expansion of parties' affiliated audiences, potentially results in a big increase in the number of party supporters who are actively spreading the party message. Through these efforts in digital messaging, parties not only reach their registered supporters; they also encourage them to serve as *digital ambassadors*. Supporters are urged to share a blog post with friends, forward a party e-newsletter, or post a link to a party video on their Facebook page. When news affiliates assume these roles, they are taking on important mobilizing tasks previously associated primarily with traditional party members: political discussion and persuasion.

ASSESSING THE CUMULATIVE IMPACT

What has been the cumulative impact of change in these separate areas, and can we discern any patterns among the parties that have been at the forefront of adopting new ways of interacting with members and other supporters? One way to answer these questions is to take another look at the information from party web pages, scoring them based on the extent to which they are developing multi-speed characteristics.

Multi-speed membership parties are distinguished by their multi-faceted efforts to engage with supporters who have varied interests, and who are unevenly willing to make long-term commitments. Party web pages offer sufficient information to compare the diversity and flexibility of party efforts to build five types of affiliation categories: traditional members, light members, sustainers, news audience, and followers. Each of these areas is scored on a 0–2 scale based on the range of tools they use to attract these types of affiliates, as measured by the options a non-member would see if she visited the national party's web pages.[10] For instance, traditional membership is scored based on whether the party offers member-only web pages as a member benefit, whether it offers a new member discount, and whether it offers a youth member discount. This category gets a score of zero if none of these options were located on the web pages; it is scored one if one of these options is available; it is scored two if two or three of them are available. Light membership is similarly assessed in terms of the number of alternative affiliation options. Sustainers are scored based on the ease of immediate donation. News audience is rated based on the number of news platforms. Finally, followers are scored based on the variety of social media platforms which are advertised on the web page. (The full coding scheme is found in the appendix to this chapter.) Table 6.2 presents country averages for each category, and for a 0–10 combined score for all categories. These are arranged from lowest to highest aggregate score. This table shows clear national differences in the extent to which parties are exploring new affiliation options. This suggests that the national competitive context plays a large role in shaping these types of organizational decisions. The UK parties score at the top end in the aggregate score, and are well above the mean in each of the areas. In contrast, whereas Greece and Portugal are both at the low end in terms of the aggregate score, each of them is above the mean on at least one of the five sub-dimensions (though not on the same ones). This table again shows how few parties have created "light membership" options. Parties that offer such alternatives offer *either* trial memberships (time limited), or registered sympathizer categories (indefinite); as of 2011 no parties offered both options.

There are several possible explanations for the large cross-national differences in party efforts to spur digital affiliation. For instance, they may reflect the important of institutional contexts, such as electoral system incentives. Differences in the level or structure of public funding for parties might also matter, particularly because well-funded parties may be able to afford to hire staff to manage digital technologies. Given the diversity of electoral systems and party funding levels among the high-scoring countries, neither of these explanations look very promising. Alternatively, the

Multi-Speed Membership Parties 147

TABLE 6.2 *Multi-speed attributes: country averages*

	Traditional Members	Light Members	Sustainers	Followers	News Audience	Multi-Speed Score
Portugal	0.2	0.0	0.0	1.6	1.8	3.2
Greece	0.3	0.3	1.0	1.0	1.0	3.5
Belgium	1.0	0.1	0.2	1.6	1.5	4.4
Italy	0.6	0.2	0.4	1.6	1.8	4.6
Finland	0.6	0.0	0.9	1.8	1.5	4.8
Canada	0.0	0.0	2.0	2.0	1.0	5.0
Netherlands	0.6	0.2	1.4	1.6	1.2	5.0
Ireland	0.8	0.3	2.0	1.5	0.8	5.3
Austria	0.6	0.0	1.4	1.8	1.6	5.4
Sweden	1.1	0.0	1.1	2.0	1.1	5.4
France	1.0	0.2	2.0	1.2	1.2	5.5
Netherlands	0.6	0.2	1.6	1.8	1.5	5.7
Norway	1.7	0.3	0.9	1.7	1.1	5.7
Germany	1.0	0.3	2.0	1.7	1.0	6.0
Spain	1.0	1.0	0.0	2.0	2.0	6.0
Switzerland	0.5	0.5	1.8	1.7	1.5	6.0
Denmark	1.4	0.0	1.5	1.8	1.5	6.1
Australia	0.7	0.0	2.0	2.0	1.7	6.3
UK	2.0	0.8	2.0	2.0	1.5	8.3
Overall averages	0.9	0.2	1.2	1.7	1.4	5.3

Coding: 0–2 scales except Multi-speed scale of 0–10. For details, see Appendix A6.
Source: Party web page survey, spring 2011.

differences might be more a reflection of the power of political contagion than of institutional incentives, with parties not wanting to be left behind once a competitor adopts a new technology. To test the power of this explanation we would need to know more about when parties embraced the new techniques: a diagnosis of contagion is easiest to support when one party adopts a technique, its electoral fortunes improve, and then rivals imitate its organizational innovations.

Ideology seems much less important as a source of cross-party differences. The cross-national variation shown in Table 6.2 is far greater than the party-family differences shown in Table 6.3. This table averages the same scores by party family, again arranged from lowest to highest overall score.[11] Green/Alternative parties score highest in three of the five areas, as we might expect given their reputation as parties which promote participation, and which have catered to younger audiences. However, their average scores are not that different from those for social democratic parties. Despite the eye-catching organizational innovations of newer and smaller parties such as the German Pirates, as a group the (generally smaller) "other" parties have been least likely to experiment with new forms of outreach to supporters. Another possible explanation for these organizational variations,

TABLE 6.3 *Multi-speed attributes: party-family averages*

	Traditional Member	Light Members	Sustainers	Followers	News Audience	Multi-Speed Score
Other	0.6	0.1	1.1	1.4	1.3	4.5
Center-Right	1.0	0.2	1.1	1.7	1.4	5.4
Liberal	0.9	0.2	1.1	1.9	1.2	5.4
Social Dem.	0.8	0.3	1.5	1.9	1.6	6.0
Greens	1.2	0.3	1.7	1.7	1.2	6.2
Overall averages	0.9	0.2	1.2	1.7	1.4	5.3

Coding: see Appendix A6 and Endnote 11.
Source: Party web page survey, spring 2011.

not tested here, is that they reflect resource differences. Such differences may be closely related to electoral size, especially in countries which pay parties public subsidies based on their electoral success. Although newer and smaller parties may be more open to organizational experiments than are their more established rivals, especially parties in government, they may not have the resources required to employ a broad range of digital outreach platforms.

Multi-speed parties were earlier described as characterized by three features: being centralized, digital, and accessible. Thus another way to assess the extent of party developments is to calculate an index of on-line accessibility. Tables 6.4 and 6.5 do this, using an index that describes how much the web pages facilitate three types of supporter activities: joining, donating, and volunteering. Membership access describes how far a prospective member can get in the enrollment process by visiting the party website, ranging from just getting information about how to join to being able to complete and submit an on-line membership form. Donation access describes how much help a prospective donor gets from visiting the party web page, ranging from getting no directions on how or where to give, to being able to donate immediately via text message or on-line. Volunteering access describes the extent to which the party web pages encourage personal political involvement, ranging from no discussion of this topic, to mentioning specific on-line or off-line projects for individuals, to inviting prospective volunteers to identify themselves to the party. (Full details of the coding are in the appendix to this chapter.)

Combining the score for these three items produces a 0–9 scale of digital accessibility. Compared with the multi-speed attributes shown in Tables 6.2 and 6.3, the on-line accessibility dimensions shown in Tables 6.4 and 6.5 may be less constrained by resources, because they represent more static choices, and do not require the same level of resources to maintain and manage as blogs, newsletters, or limited-time trial memberships. On the other hand, we might expect larger cross-national differences, particularly

TABLE 6.4 *On-line accessibility index: country averages*

	Membership Accessibility	Donation Accessibility	Volunteering Accessibility	Combined Accessibility Score	N
Portugal	1.4	0.0	0.0	1.4	5
Greece	0.8	1.0	0.3	2.0	4
Italy	2.0	0.4	0.4	2.8	5
Austria	1.8	1.4	0.0	3.2	4
Belgium	2.8	0.0	0.4	3.2	10
Spain	2.5	0.0	1.0	3.5	2
Finland	2.6	0.5	0.5	3.6	8
Switzerland	2.7	1.2	0.2	4.0	6
Sweden	3.0	0.9	0.4	4.3	7
Norway	3.0	0.9	0.6	4.4	7
Germany	2.3	2.0	0.5	4.8	6
France	3.0	2.0	0.0	5.0	6
New Zealand	3.0	1.2	1.0	5.2	5
Denmark	2.8	1.8	1.0	5.5	8
Netherlands	2.5	1.5	1.5	5.5	10
Ireland	2.8	2.5	0.8	6.0	4
Australia	2.3	2.0	2.7	7.0	3
Canada	2.8	2.0	2.3	7.0	4
UK	3.0	2.0	2.5	7.5	4

Index = 0–9. For explanation, see Appendix A6.

because institutional contexts are likely to affect parties' approaches to fund raising and their use of election volunteers.

Table 6.4 shows party averages by country, again ranging from low to high. Once again, there are large national differences, and once again, the UK parties are at the top and those in Portugal and Greece are at the bottom. Because on-line giving is a component of this index as well as the multi-speed index, differences in party finance laws and party subsidy schemes may explain some of the similarities in the cross-national rankings. There are, however, differences in the order of the countries

TABLE 6.5 *On-line accessibility index: party-family averages*

Party Family	Membership Accessibility	Donation Accessibility	Volunteering Accessibility	Combined Accessibility Score	N
Other	2.2	1.1	0.7	3.9	31
Center-Right	2.5	1.0	0.7	4.2	27
Social Dem.	2.6	1.4	0.8	4.8	20
Liberal	2.9	1.1	0.9	4.9	18
Greens	2.8	1.5	0.8	5.1	13

Sources: See Appendix A6 and note 11.

in between. Once again, the differences across party families are much less extreme than the cross-national differences. And once again, there are big within-family variations. For instance, the UK Labour Party was at the high end among socialist parties. Its web-page visitors could complete an on-line membership application, fill out a form to indicate interest in volunteering, and make an on-line credit card donation. In contrast, the web page of the Portuguese Socialist Party provided a membership form that could be downloaded and mailed in, but did not provide for joining on-line (perhaps because prospective members needed to provide the names and membership numbers of two current members who endorsed their application). The web page did not ask for on-line donations, and it had no mechanisms to enlist supporters as volunteers. Strikingly, the three top-scoring countries earn this place because of their parties' greater interest in using on-line tools to recruit volunteers; it is probably no coincidence that all three countries use single-member district systems to elect the lower houses of their national legislatures, systems that elevate the importance of constituency-level campaigning. Accessibility index scores varied more widely across party families than did the multi-speed index. In particular, parties of the center-right (mainly conservatives and Christian Democrats) and "other parties" (which includes new populist parties) have, on average, taken fewer steps in the direction of digital accessibility.

To what extent could the party-family differences shown in Tables 6.3 and 6.5 reflect the impact of different inherited traditions concerning the roles of members in establishing party legitimacy? The second chapter's discussion of narratives of legitimacy argued that parties cast members in different roles, such as "fans" or "stakeholders," and that members' rights and responsibilities vary according to party conceptions of their roles. This discussion also posited that such traditions might constrain experiments with new types of affiliation options: parties which view members primarily as fans should be least concerned to police the boundaries of membership, while those which view members as part of a cleavage community, or of an ideological movement, might be more likely to preserve control over admission to the party. These tables offer limited support for these hypotheses. As they predict, Green/Alternative parties (political process parties) and Liberal parties (generally, subscriber democracy parties), are the high scorers for on-line accessibility, and Green/Alternative parties also score highest in terms of offering a variety of affiliation options. On the other hand, and contrary to predictions, Social Democratic parties (cleavage representation parties) also score relatively high for on-line accessibility and affiliation options. This may be evidence that some of these cleavage parties are experiencing an important shift in organizational orientation, towards a "stakeholder" view of party membership that is more concerned with attracting affiliates than with ensuring the homogeneity of those who join. Finally, the low scores of the "other" parties are also in line with predictions, at least to the extent that they reflect the practices of ideologically nationalist or cleavage-oriented ethnic parties: such parties should be interested in limiting membership access to maintain a homogenous identity. However, the lower scores could also just reflect the fact that most of these parties are smaller, and thus have fewer resources to devote to organizational efforts. In order to understand more about relations between party membership traditions and the limits (and implications) of organizational changes, we would need more longitudinal data on parties' varied efforts to cultivate affiliated (identified, contactable) supporters.

The multi-speed index and the index of on-line accessibility are two tools to capture and compare the ongoing evolution of parties' outreach efforts. These or similar measures could usefully supplement more traditional evidence in the study of party organizational development, such as membership numbers and party rules. Any specific scales probably would need to be altered to reflect new technologies and new practices; nevertheless, systematic analysis of parties' web pages should provide a good tool for comparing parties' organizational priorities as long as these web pages remain prime portals for party contact with self-identified supporters.

EXPANDING OPTIONS FOR PARTISAN AFFILIATION

In the face of declining memberships and growing public distrust of established political options, many parties have been experimenting with ways to reduce membership costs and to make it easier for their supporters to connect with them. The resulting initiatives have helped to create new organizational outlets which enable supporters to link to their parties in multiple ways. Not coincidentally, many of these initiatives are aimed at younger citizens, members of the cohorts who are proving most resistant to traditional party membership appeals.

For the most part, parties have presented these new affiliation options as complements, or gateways, to traditional membership. Parties which already have established membership traditions are not seeking to replace their networks of geographically organized, dues-paying, members with exclusively on-line organization. Nevertheless, the growing array of digital affiliation options potentially changes how parties relate to supporters, and which supporters they are trying to mobilize. This shift may be particularly noticeable in parties that once emphasized cleavage mobilization. Through electronic outreach strategies, parties are going beyond traditional efforts to mobilize members of specific groups. They are reaching out to wider swathes of potential supporters, offering them new affiliation options.

As Chapter 8 will show, cultivating new and overlapping connections raises questions about how to accommodate traditional party members and new affiliates into party narratives concerning leadership accountability and party ownership. For instance, parties must continually revisit choices about which types of affiliates (if any) are eligible to participate in party decisions. When those in newer affiliation categories gain rights to advise or to participate in intra-party votes, this potentially dilutes the influence of traditional members—at least if traditional members previously had any rights in this area. Before examining these possible tradeoffs and conflicts, the next chapters first take a broader look at the benefit side of the membership equation, asking what parties have being doing—and what they could do—to make traditional membership seem more desirable.

NOTES

1. Collected between Feb. and May 2011.
2. This practice was particularly likely among the parties in which regional or local parties set different dues rates.
3. Some of the small former Communist parties may also have retained this practice, but it was not clear from the explanations on party web pages.
4. Among those that did were the forms of the Spanish People's Party and the Portuguese Socialists.
5. The German Christian Democratic Union and Social Democratic Party, and the Dutch Christian Democratic Appeal and Green Left.
6. Belgium's Francophone Green Party, the French Green Party, the British Conservative and Labour Parties, the Spanish Popular and Socialist Parties, Greek New Democracy, New Zealand's ACT, and the Swiss Social Democrats and Free Democrats.
7. See Ch. 7 for more details.
8. Among the few parties that did not mention donations on their web pages were all the Portuguese and Spanish parties, all but one of the Italian parties, and all but two of the Belgian parties.
9. Of course, many Facebook users may be too young to be eligible voters, but this is probably true in all countries.
10. Parties may be making efforts that are not clearly advertised, and there is undoubtedly measurement error in the survey that has missed certain party efforts. However, if these efforts are difficult to locate on the web pages, they are unlikely to catch the eye of casual visitors who might be willing to consider

acquiring some type of affiliation. Cyber-members are not included here, because it would be necessary to consult party statutes, not just web pages, to find out whether parties offer cyber-branch alternatives for traditional members.

11. Parties were assigned to party family families based on their membership in transnational party federations (if any). The center-right category combines members of both the Centrist Democrat International and the International Democratic Union. Members of other groups and no groups were assigned to the "other" category.

APPENDIX A6

MULTI-SPEED INDEX

Each item scored:

0. None of the following
1. One of the following
2. Two or more of the following

Traditional Members

–Member only pages
–New member discount
–Youth discount

Light Members

–Registered sympathizers
–Trial members

Sustainers

–Ask for donation
–Accept on-line donation, PayPal or credit card
–Accept text message donation

Followers: advertise these options for following party or party leader

–Facebook
–Twitter
–Delicious
–Blog

News Audience

–Subscription news letter
–RSS feed
–Phone alert

ON-LINE ACCESSIBILITY INDEX

Sum of scores for three items:

Membership

0. Applying for membership isn't obviously discussed.
1. Can't start application process on-line on national party web page. Includes parties which redirect to provincial party web pages.
2. Can print PDF of form or send e-mail to ask for more information.
3. Can complete on-line membership form

Donations

0. No directions on how to give
1. Gives address for mailing check or bank account number. No immediate giving option.
2. Can make on-line donation or give by text message.
3. Gives both on-line and text message donation options.

Volunteering

0. None.
1. Mentions on-line *or* off-line action opportunities.
2. Mentions *both* on-line and off-line action opportunities.
3. Offers on-line volunteer sign-up form or website gives directions on where/whom to e-mail to sign up as a party volunteer.

7

Making Party Membership Rewarding
Social and Material Benefits

If parties want to inspire supporters to form closer links, they must make party membership seem rewarding, whether that reward is altruistic or something much more tangible. Even if they make it very easy for supporters to enroll in the party and renew membership dues, such steps are unlikely to stem the slide in traditional membership unless parties give supporters good reasons to join in the first place. Yet offering new types of membership incentives is a potentially costly proposition, one that can have political as well as financial implications. In parties, as in other organizations, new efforts to attract members can alter the organization's character, because different types of incentives attract members with varied priorities (as described in a classic work by Clark and Wilson 1961). This tradeoff is particularly acute in political parties, because some of the most potent incentives that they can offer are political incentives, and these are intimately connected with a party's purpose and identity.

THE BENEFITS OF MEMBERSHIP: WHAT CAN PARTIES OFFER?

The distinctive business of political parties in electoral democracies is to contest elections in order to influence and implement policies. They campaign by promoting programs and plans which they say will be benefit some section of society. If such collective political goods were all that parties offered to prospective members, it would be no surprise to learn that party membership is declining; the only puzzle would be why so many people once joined.

A traditional way to resolve the apparent paradox of party membership is to point to other benefits which are reserved for formal affiliates. Peter Clark and James Q. Wilson labeled these types of organizational incentives selective benefits. They divided such benefits into three categories: solidary (social), material, and political (purposive) (1961). Wilson further distinguished between benefits available to all group members (inclusive benefits), and those available to only a few members (exclusive benefits) (Wilson 1973, 37). He argued that some political benefits (selective ones) could be attained through the process of participation, not merely through the achievement of the substantive goal (see Laux 2011a for a further elaboration).

Patrick Seyd and Paul Whiteley developed these categories of benefits in their general incentives model, adding psychological components of altruism and solidarity. They argued that such psychological elements were crucial for explaining the supply of party membership: even though parties' primary products are collective goods, there are selective satisfactions to be earned by helping parties get into the position to be able to provide such goods.[1] Seyd and Whiteley also pointed out that psychological incentives could be negative as well as positive: partisan participation might be fueled by a desire to improve the world, but it also could be inspired by aspirations such as the hope of unseating a disliked governing party or politician (1992; Whiteley et al. 1994; Whiteley and Seyd 2002; see Hansen 2002, ch. 2, for a good overview of these models).

Table 7.1 draws from these categories to map various types of benefits that have been said to inspire partisan participation. For purposes of the discussion that follows, the exact labeling of the categories is less important than the structures they provide for systematically examining different types of rewards that parties have used, and might use, to attract and retain members. One important distinction is between benefits available to all supporters (collective, column I), and those available to party members alone (selective, columns II and III). Another choice for parties is whether to emphasize providing benefits to all members (inclusive, column II), as opposed to benefits that are available only to some members (exclusive,

TABLE 7.1 *Benefits for party members and supporters*

	I Collective: Members & Others	II Selective and Inclusive: All Members	III Selective & Exclusive: Some Members
Social & Psychological	1. **Group identity**	2. **Leisure Activities** **Make a difference**	3. **Status**
Material	4. **Policy benefits**	5. **Services:** credit cards, consumer discounts **Education & training**	6. **Patronage** **Career opportunities:** networking
Political	7. **Positive:** advance a cause **Negative:** oust current government or combat political threat	8. **Influence:** party decisions **Information** **Self-actualization**	9. **Influence:** Party & Government decisions **Office:** party, public, or quasi-public jobs

column III). The rows in Table 7.1 distinguish between the nature of the rewards that parties grant, be these social and psychological, material, or purpose-oriented. The following discussion uses these categories in evaluating factors that affect contemporary parties' capacities to provide or even increase benefits they offer to potential members. Central evidence in this investigation comes from surveys of party members, which give clues about the actual appeal of specific types of benefits. Together, these sections help answer the question of what, if anything, parties could do to recruit more members.

WHAT MOTIVATES MEMBERS?

One way to find out why people join and remain in political parties is to ask them. In the past twenty years a number of surveys of party members have done just that. Of course, responses to such survey questions cannot be taken at face value. People may not know why they joined, and even if they did, they might find it socially unacceptable to mention certain motives, such as the hope of winning elective office or receiving patronage opportunities. Nevertheless, members' responses shed light on the stories that they tell themselves and their friends and family about what makes party membership worthwhile.

Researchers have posed questions about membership motives in different ways, which hinders precise cross-party comparisons. Yet despite these differences, in surveys of over forty parties in eleven countries party members show surprising consistency in identifying the factors that are most important for inspiring and sustaining their engagement.[2]

The Limited Appeal of Selective Material or Social Incentives

In the membership surveys, few respondents connected membership with selective material or social benefits. Even when respondents could name multiple reasons for joining, they seldom mentioned socializing (generally 15 percent or fewer). Fewer still mentioned careerist reasons. One of the highest responses of the latter sort were the 14 percent of Canadian party members who mentioned general career help as "very" or "somewhat important" to their decision to join (Young and Cross 2002, 558). Younger party members were different in this regard, perhaps because young people are more focused on building careers than those at other life stages. A large minority of young party members from seven countries named career aspirations as motivating their decision to join. Some said they hoped to build

Making Membership Rewarding 159

a career in politics, others mentioned building a professional network and acquiring marketable skills (Bruter and Harrison 2009; Young and Cross 2007). With this exception, members seldom link party membership with aspirations for material or social benefits.

The Importance of Collective Political Incentives

In contrast, party members consistently placed political reasons at the top of their lists when they were asked to explain why they enlisted. This held for parties across the political spectrum in Canada, Denmark, Germany, Ireland, Italy, the Netherlands, Norway, and the UK. For instance, more than half the members of all nine Danish parties mentioned ideology among the four main reasons they joined; 46 percent mentioned general "support for the party" (Pedersen et al. 2004, 370). Similarly, 45 percent of Irish Fine Gael members named support for the party's policies as a reason to join, while 34 percent said they joined to support the party in general (Gallagher and Marsh 2004). In a 2000 survey, 58 percent of Norwegian party members listed political reasons for joining their parties, up from 50 percent in a similar survey conducted in 1991 (Heidar and Saglie 2003, 774). In Canada, 84 percent of members named support for party policies as an important reason for joining (Young and Cross 2002, 557). In the Netherlands, 80 percent of members named "expressing sympathy for this party" as a reason why they joined (Holsteyn et al. 2000).

As we might expect, negative collective political incentives were most frequently mentioned as motives for joining anti-system parties and parties that had spent many years out of government. For instance, in Denmark members of the far-right and far-left parties were most likely to name opposition to other parties as a main motive for joining (Hansen 2002, 96). In the early 1990s, members of the British Labour Party (long in opposition at that point) were much more likely to mention joining due to their opposition to then Prime Minister Margaret Thatcher than Conservatives were to mention anti-trade union or anti-Labour Party motives[3] (Seyd and Whiteley 1992, 74; Whiteley et al. 1994, 96). Members of the Italian far-right National Alliance also named opposition to the left as the most common motive for joining the party (Ignazi and Bardi 2006, 48).

The Importance of Self-Starters

Another common finding from the party member surveys is the prevalence of self-recruitment. Among the surveys which asked this question,[4] many reported having approached the party about membership, not vice versa. This described one-third of the British Conservative Party members, about half of Canadian Liberals and Irish Fine Gael members, and over two-thirds of the responding members in the British Labour Party and Canadian Alliance surveys. Similarly, in the 2009 German party member survey only 2 percent of respondents reported joining because someone else recruited them (Laux 2011a, 76).[5]

Party members' self-identified reasons for joining give clues about which of the parties' current membership incentives are most effective, and about which might be strengthened in order to recruit new members and to retain current members. The consistency of the picture across party ideologies and political systems suggests strong similarities among those who take up membership in any type of political party. Above all, party members highlight political reasons to explain why they joined, and why anyone else might want to do so.[6]

Party member surveys tell us why party members say they joined a political party, showing which arguments in favor of party membership are most persuasive and most socially acceptable. Against this background it is worth turning the tables to examine how parties depict the benefits of party membership: what do the parties themselves say about why supporters ought to enlist, and what do these messages tell us about parties' views of what members can do for their parties?

THE PARTIES' APPEALS: WHY JOIN?

Party websites offer an interesting glimpse into the arguments that parties make to those who may be considering membership. As the previous chapter showed, by 2011 most party web pages provided links that enabled prospective members to initiate, and in many cases to complete, enrollment. Many of the web pages gave prominent placement to these links, and had tabs exhorting readers to "become a member!" or "join us!"

Despite the visibility of the appeals and the accessibility of the procedures, surprisingly few parties offered many—or even any—arguments to persuade supporters to take this step. A 2012 follow-up survey of party web pages found that for almost 40 percent of the web pages that had a membership link ("join now!") on the home page or elsewhere, this link led directly to a membership form, without any intermediate discussion of why a supporter might want to join (see Table 7.2). An additional 11 percent of the web pages listed reasons to join, but gave only very general arguments, such as "support your principles," or "we need members." In other words, only half the websites gave visitors specific reasons to enlist. Among those that did, the most commonly mentioned membership benefits were opportunities to participate, to influence policies, and

Making Membership Rewarding

TABLE 7.2 *Reasons to join (multiple responses possible)*

Responses listed under "become a member" pages

	Number	%
Do not mention reasons to join	43	39.4
Only reasons are to "show support"	12	11.0
Show support for party or principles	48	44.0
Participate	36	33.0
Influence	29	26.6
Get information & education	22	20.2
Internal votes	19	17.4
Member-only intranet	7	6.4
Become a candidate	6	5.5
Meet nice people, have fun	5	4.6
Enjoy consumer benefits or gifts	3	2.8
Oppose what is happening or who is governing	2	1.8

Source: Party web pages Feb. 2012. N = 109.

to get political information. Only two parties listed negative membership incentives (in both cases, to defeat an incumbent party). None of the web pages engaged in extensive marketing to enhance the appeal of membership, for instance by presenting profiles of exemplary members, or videos showing local party volunteers having fun or making a difference.

One of the clear findings from these surveys is that many parties are using web pages to make it easier for supporters to join, but surprisingly few are using them to *promote* membership. It should come as no surprise that parties are losing members if they do not send strong and consistent messages about why supporters might want to join.

Having examined what members and parties say about the benefits of membership, it is now time to turn to more behavioral evidence to see which benefits members actually use. Boosting these benefits seems likely to appeal to those who already have an affinity for the party, and could therefore help retain existing members. The next sections thus examine each of the benefit types described in Table 7.1, looking for evidence of their popularity, and assessing parties' options to increase each type of benefit.

CHANGING THE SOCIAL AND PSYCHOLOGICAL BENEFITS OF MEMBERSHIP

Parties in established democracies face a waning ability to provide traditional social benefits. This decline is both relative and absolute. Party-provided socializing has become less attractive as other leisure alternatives have increased. Even if this were not the case, as local party organizations have weakened, they have become less able to provide social opportunities. In response, some parties have been attempting to change local organizational culture to make party life more appealing to new members. They also have been trying to create stronger national-level and on-line partisan communities. Initiatives of these types have been widespread, but so far they have not fundamentally transformed the social experience of party affiliation.

Collective Social Benefits (Cell 1): Identity and Community

One potent collective benefit that some political parties offer to their supporters is the reinforcement of group identity. This benefit is most pronounced in cleavage-based parties. In the early twentieth century, religious parties in Belgium, the Netherlands and Austria, and social democratic and labor parties more generally, offered members and their families a wide variety of organizational outlets for all facets of daily life. They established women's organizations, youth organizations, sports clubs, and social welfare collectives, all of which were connected with the wider political movement (whether or not with the party itself). These extra-party networks reinforced members' links with a partisan-charged social group identity, and in some cases were more prominent than the local party branches. They cultivated group identity, a collective social benefit that was offered to members and non-members alike.

In today's parliamentary democracies, only a handful of political parties make group identity their main appeal. The non-party organizational networks of most cleavage parties have declined at least as rapidly as parties' membership organizations. With a few exceptions, milieu organizations survive only in limited form.[7] Even where they persist, parties have become much less interested in fostering links with leisure-oriented subgroups whose political aims are indirect, and which focus on fostering identity politics.

The decline in leisure provision is partly due to greater competition in this area from a host of other sources, ranging from television and films to vacation travel deals. But it is also due to parties' shift from cleavage to catch-all electoral strategies. Parties seeking a broad electoral appeal have less to gain from organizational strategies that are based on cultivating class or ethnic identities. This generalization does not apply to parties with more targeted appeals. Ethnic and nationalistic parties continue to foster communities that extend beyond the bounds of formal party membership. For instance, starting in 1996 Italy's Northern League began mobilizing sympathizers and members at annual regional festivals of "Padanian" (Northern Italian) identity. Similarly, the National Front in France has built up a cult of the national heroine Joan of Arc, celebrating her day (May 1) with parades and rallies. Similar traditions persist in the socialist and labor parties which continue to celebrate May 1 as *their* day. Such parties still proclaim allegiance to workers' interests, and they still participate in events that reaffirm this identity, even if these rallies tend to be much smaller than in earlier decades.

These examples of milieu-building organizational activities illustrate how parties can use collective identity benefits to attract members and other supporters. The relative scarcity of such examples is because few contemporary parties rely heavily on this strategy. Shifting away from identity politics is one way for a party to broaden its electoral appeal; this can also increase the party's coalition options. However, at an organizational level, this strategy may diminish the value of party membership by stripping it of some of its symbolic significance. Joining a party that emphasizes its ties to a specific group or ideology is a way for an individual to affirm and reinforce his or her membership in a select community. Such symbolism wanes as parties drift closer to becoming consumer organizations, ones that respond to citizens' demands rather than integrating those citizens into a community of shared interests.

Selective Social Benefits (Cells 2 and 3): Friends and Social Status

One reason that people join and become active in local party branches is because they enjoy the company and collegiality of fellow party members. Some may also view local parties as good venues for meeting like-minded citizens (and even potential spouses).[8] The pleasures of socializing with other partisans are available to all supporters, but are most likely to be enjoyed by the active members who attend meetings and work on campaigns. In contrast, by definition only select members can enjoy the some of the more exclusive status benefits that parties offer, such as the privilege of being invited to small group meetings with political celebrities: these would not confer intra-organizational status if they were equally available to all members.

The social value of party membership may be difficult for outsiders to appreciate. Non-members are as likely to be deterred as attracted by the thought of attending local party meetings, events which may (correctly or not) conjure up images of dingy meeting rooms and formally minuted discussions. In some parties, national organizers have tried to combat these perceptions, for instance by exhorting local party leaders to make meetings more lively and welcoming. Yet it is probably unfair to blame intransigent old-timers for the non-spontaneous and non-passionate nature of routine party work. Local party life is constrained by the political tasks assigned to these organizations. Laws and party statutes often dictate precise procedures for performing these tasks. Conducting party business under formal rules probably reduces conflicts and provides good training for those who later serve in local government or party committees, but it may enforce a procedural dullness that deters those who are passionate about specific issues.

Whatever the format of their meetings, it would be difficult for local parties to reinvigorate their branches purely on the basis of social appeals. Few (if any) contemporary political parties enjoy reputations for being great local social clubs, though some young members do prize the social opportunities they offer (Bruter and Harrison 2009, 35). However, it seems unlikely that today's parties could significantly boost recruiting merely by persuading non-members that party activities are enjoyable. On the other hand, social benefits and personal ties may be quite important in persuading existing members to renew or to get active. If so, parties may be able to boost membership retention by making greater efforts to quickly integrate new members into party social networks.

Self-reported behavior of party members suggests that one promising approach to doing so would be for local parties to do more to cultivate intra-party participation. Most party member surveys find that anywhere from one-third to one-half of party members were completely detached from their local parties, never attending party meetings or other activities. Only a handful report attending meetings as often as once a month (see Table 7.3). These participation estimates are probably high, because inactive members are least likely to respond to such surveys. Such activity levels are consistent with self-reported reasons for joining or staying in a party, which placed little importance on social benefits.

Collegiality is an inclusive selective benefit, one which is available to all members who choose to participate in party activities. In contrast, organizational status is an exclusive social benefit. Those who make visible and significant contributions of time or money may acquire such status, sometimes reinforced by the award of titular positions (chairperson, honorary chairperson, etc.). As with socializing opportunities, local parties with declining party memberships are less able to confer status benefits: becoming chair of a local party is a dubious honor if no one else is available to do the job. As local party networks become smaller and organizationally flatter, holding intra-party office may involve less honor than it used to do; it also may require more work if there are few other volunteers to help out.

In short, parties have experienced a decline in their ability to offer both collective (identity) and selective social benefits. National parties have only limited options if they want to combat these trends, not least because it is local parties that traditionally have been the prime providers of selective social benefits. It is difficult to institute top–down changes in local party

TABLE 7.3 *Self-reported membership activity: party membership surveys**

	Canada 2003/4	Denmark 2000	Ireland FG 1999	Italy AN 2002	Germany 1998	Germany 2009	Netherlands 1999	Netherlands 2008	Norway 1991	Norway 2000	UK Conservative	UK Labour	UK Lib Dem
Local Meeting Attendance													
Don't attend	39	43	18	25	36	31				53		36	53
More than 1/month	10	30	14	45	6	6				52		30	
Time Spent on Party Activities/month													
None	39	56	55				57		55–79	4	46	50	54
5 hours or more	14	13	9				20#		6–28#	4	11	20	17

*Exact wording varies.
#"more than 5 hours."
Sources: see note 2 this chapter.

culture, and even harder to do so when these local parties are struggling merely to handle basic local and national electoral work. Perhaps as a result, the most visible party efforts to create new social benefits for party affiliates are ones that bypass local organizations in favor of non-geographic sub-communities.

Many of these new party communities are located on-line, with affiliates clustered together on Facebook or as Twitter or blog followers. Parties are most likely to use new technologies for top–down communications, but some also seek to use them to build group feeling by encouraging readers to participate in (party-moderated) on-line conversations about politics (cf. Ward and Gibson 2009, 29). Those who sign up for these groups can have frequent (sometimes daily) contact with party representatives and with fellow party supporters. This electronic companionship far exceeds the amount of contact that traditional party members have with their fellow members: even the most active party members probably attend party meetings only once or twice a month. The social benefits of on-line communities are different than, and not in competition with, the traditional social benefits provided by party meetings that end in the pub, or by local party annual dinners.

Parties' efforts to create on-line communities have met with mostly modest success, at least if they are judged in terms of increasing intra-party conversations. Table 7.4 shows one measure of the impact of such initiatives, the amount of interaction on party Facebook pages during one month in spring 2011 (a month when none of the countries held national elections). This measure shows whether members were taking advantage of this forum to share their opinions and create interactive communities. The Facebook pages shown in this table are a subset of the seventy surveyed in Chapter 6. For each country, it includes the two most popular party pages (as measured by the number of "likers"). The most striking feature of this table is the low amount of activity on these pages: few readers contributed in even the most minor of ways (adding a "like" to a posting). The ratio of passive to active members within the on-line communities seems even higher than activity rate among traditional party members. Some of these parties had thousands or even tens of thousands of Facebook friends, but only a handful of individuals used the platform's potential for two-way communication. These findings mirror other studies which have found that party members have been slow to embrace parties' interactive media (Gibson and Ward 2009; Jackson and Lilleker 2009; Kalnes 2009).

To get a sense of how a platform such as Facebook could be used to foster a virtual party community, it is instructive to look at supporter behavior in a party that started on-line, the German Pirate Party. In mid-2012 this protest party had 34,000 dues-paying members, and over 40,000 Facebook likes, a ratio of Facebook friends to formal members that was

Making Membership Rewarding

TABLE 7.4 *Activity on popular party Facebook pages, spring 2011*

		Total Facebook "Likers"	Average likes/post	Average posts/week
Australia	Labor	4,311	19	8.3
	Liberal	17,377	25	14.8
Austria	Socialists	9,724	39	8.5
	Freedom Party	85,508	579	9.5
Belgium	VlamsBelang (Nationalists)	8,148	5	34.8
	Groen (Flemish Greens)	8,583	29	9.5
Canada	Liberal	12,184	46	3.3
	Conservative	11,603	62	3.5
Denmark	Red Green	9,571	118	7.5
	Socialist People's Party	9,707	56	4.0
France	Socialists	18,396	71	27.8
	National Front	31,941	34	92.5
Germany	Social Democrats	18,784	75	21.8
	B90/Greens	19,668	81	17.5
	Pirates*	40,439	538	40.0
Greece	New Democracy	16,800	42	5.0
	SYRIZA (Coalition of the Radical Left)	1,767	0	24.3
Ireland	Labour Party	5,580	19	10.8
	Fine Gael	5,330	32	19.5
Italy	Left Party	44,808	32	48.8
	People of Freedom	33,028	69	22.3
Netherlands	D66	8,944	38	2.3
	GreenLeft	14,677	19	20.0
New Zealand	National Party	54,432	124	14.3
	Green Party	5,489	21	6.3
Norway	Conservative Party	7,769	11	12.0
	Progress Party	26,577	121	11.5
Portugal	Socialists	1,571	16	14.8
Spain	Popular Party	30,847	550	46.3
	Socialists	26,875	258	35.5
Sweden	Social Democrats	19,559	83	4.8
	Moderates	16,503	10	10.5
Switzerland	Social Democratic Party	2,990	21	0.6
	Christian Democratic People's Party	461	1	1.4
United Kingdom	Conservative	134,519	207	0.4
	Labour	97,583	110	2.2

Averages for four weeks of activity, Mar. 2011.
Includes party Facebook pages only, not leader pages.
* Jan. 2012.

considerably higher than that in most other parties. In addition, as Table 7.4 shows, its Facebook supporters were much more active than those in other parties. The number of daily "likers" on the Pirates' Facebook page averaged in the hundreds, as opposed to the single or double digits common in more established parties. This comparison gives a sense of what was *not* happening in most of the other parties in terms of interactive communication.

In short, as of 2011 few parties had been able to use this particular medium to create interactive on-line communities for digital affiliates. These data do not tell us about usage of other digital discussion platforms, or about participation in member-only on-line forums. However, there is no reason to think that these are much more heavily used. Electronic communities could potentially transform the experience of digital affiliation by inserting political conversations into supporters' daily lives and leisure time, but so far party supporters have shown only weak interest in using two-way communication opportunities. Those who enrolled in these ways were far more likely to receive messages than to send them.

A few national parties have tried to create new exclusive social benefits for sustainers by creating national donors clubs for those who contribute regularly, or in above-average amounts. Parties advertise these benefits alongside their appeals for donations, noting, for instance, that donor club members will receive benefits such as special lapel pins and invitations to events with political leaders. Such benefits are reserved for donors, and donors do not have to be members to receive them. As of early 2012, this model was most developed in Britain. The British Labour Party advertised a donor club with a membership minimum of £1,200 annually, offering benefits such as invitations to exclusive receptions. The British Conservative Party's web page advertised seven different levels of donor clubs, each with increasing benefits and increasingly exalted titles. Threshold contribution levels for these clubs ranged from £250 to £50,000 per annum. Parties could also use such clubs to reward sustained support rather than large one-time gifts. For instance, in 2012 Canada, a country with low limits on annual political contributions, the Liberal Party ran the Laurier Club for donors who pledged to contribute at least $100 per month. Club members received invitations to special events, a newsletter, and a club pin. Overall, however, such donor clubs were rare. As of early 2012, only seven out of the 109 party web pages alerted donors that gifts above a certain level, or gifts made on a standing-order basis, might qualify them for special benefits or honors.

It is likely that most parties find it politically unwise—and perhaps not economically rewarding—to publicize special honors for wealthier supporters. The political dangers of such a strategy were underscored in 2012, when the British Conservative Party's donor clubs drew unfavorable press scrutiny. They were derided as "pay for access" schemes. The party eventually bowed to public pressure and revealed the names of the top-level donors who had dined with the Prime Minister under this scheme (Watt 2012). Nevertheless, the party maintained these clubs, at least in the short term. A year later the Conservative Party's web pages continued to promote these clubs, including the £50,000 minimum "Leader's Group." Donors at this level were offered invitations to join Prime Minister David Cameron "and other senior figures from the Conservative Party at dinners, post-PMQ lunches, drinks receptions, election result events and important campaign launches."[9] This example illustrates how parties could encourage financial or other participation by offering exclusive benefits, ones that are available only to a small number of supporters or members.

Even aside from such exclusive benefits, and from digital communities, local political parties probably continue to provide social benefits for some who choose to get involved. Alternative leisure opportunities have not altogether eliminated the appeal of working with like-minded fellow citizens. The weakening of local party organizations has not erased the camaraderie these organizations provide for some members. Party activists form ties that may prompt them to continue paying dues even if they become less actively involved. The big change is that few contemporary parties are in a position to attract many members *primarily* for the social events or social honors that they offer; meanwhile, far fewer attempt to attract them by appealing to cleavage group identity.

CHANGING ECONOMIC AND MATERIAL BENEFITS

Political parties always have attracted supporters with promises of material improvements. Most of these promises involve collective policy goods, but some parties also promise more selective material benefits to their closest supporters. As with social benefits, contemporary political parties now have fewer options to inspire party membership with prospects of either collective or selective material benefits.

Collective Material Benefits (Cell 4): Economic Promises

Parties' electoral appeals routinely include promises of material improvement, be this by helping the economy as a whole, or by altering specific public services, taxes, or regulations. Such electoral messages may inspire some supporters with a sense of shared purpose that leads to political activity. In themselves, however, collective material benefits should be insufficient to motivate individual membership, because the person who joins or makes a contribution to the cause is no more or less likely to receive the benefits than anyone else.

From a strictly economic calculus, selective material benefits seem to offer potentially stronger tools for motivating party membership. Selective material rewards may be inclusive, offered to all party members, or they may be more exclusive, ones for which party membership is a necessary, but not sufficient, requirement.

Selective and Inclusive Material Benefits (Cell 5)

Parties have a long history of offering members economic benefits derived from group economies of scale. For instance, early mass parties enabled their members to take advantage of mutual-aid opportunities, including insurance schemes, burial societies, consumer co-operatives, and educational courses. These were valuable benefits in states which provided few welfare services. Many of these specific rewards became obsolete as living standards improved, and as states assumed responsibility for education and health services. Parties with tens of thousands of members still remain well-placed to bargain for consumer discounts for their members. Consumer benefits promoted by parties in 2011 included member-only credit cards, travel deals, good rates on automobile insurance, purchasing clubs, and free e-mail accounts.[10] Most of these deals offered modest potential savings, in no way equivalent to the selective benefits generally associated with patronage, but even small economic benefits could make membership more attractive by offsetting the (low) costs of enrollment and renewal.

Parties that offer such consumer benefits seldom mentioned them in web page discussions about why visitors should enlist as party members. This may indicate that most parties view these services more as incentives for membership renewal than as recruiting deals. The UK is one of the few countries where several party web pages actively promoted the consumer benefits of party membership. The Labour Party began offering its members a party credit card as early as the 1980s, sporting a picture of the House of Commons. This offer was particularly valuable in that decade, when credit card access was limited in Britain. In 2011 the Labour Party still offered members a credit card, along with other benefits such as discounted telephone service. The British Conservative Party introduced a consumer discount club in the 1990s (the "Affinity Scheme"). At first this was aimed only at party members, but by 2011 the party was offering it to all enrolled supporters: the party's enrollment web page highlighted these benefits as one reason that supporters should sign up as registered friends of the Conservative Party, even if they did not become full-fledged traditional members.

Few membership surveys have asked members whether they personally value such consumer discounts. However, a German member survey posed a related question, asking whether members thought that parties should offer consumer benefits in order to boost recruiting. In reply, most existing party members rejected the idea, with 72 percent of respondents expressing disapproval. The highest level of support for the idea was found in the Bavarian CSU, but even here only 17 percent of respondents approved of it (Laux 2011b, 172). The opinions expressed by current German party members do not rule out that consumer incentives might actually appeal to those who have not previously joined; they do not even tell us whether existing members would take advantage of such benefit schemes. However, they do show that Germany's current party members dislike the idea of promoting decisions about party membership in terms of economic self-interest. If those attitudes are widespread, it may explain why parties have been slow to develop their potential for providing consumer discounts. To the extent that current and potential members want to view their membership as a political act, or as an affirmation of identity, emphasizing the consumer benefits of membership could detract from its overall value.

Selective and Exclusive Material Benefits (Cell 6)

Patronage and clientelism are the most common systems for providing party members (and sometimes other recognized supporters) with selective economic rewards. Of the two types of benefits, patronage is more likely to be distributed by political parties, whereas clientelism generally refers to relations between voters and individual politicians. The common characteristic of patronage systems is that they direct state resources on the basis of political affiliation or support (Kopecký et al. 2012; Kopecký and Scherlis 2008). In traditional patronage relations, supplicants pay benefactors with their political support. These practices are usually distinguished from outright corruption, in which parties or politicians receive *financial* payments in return for favorable policy outcomes or public resources.

Traditional patronage was often based on the political rationing of access to public services such as school or university places, beds in public hospitals, or government permits and licenses. In patronage systems, party membership may help individuals move ahead in the queues for public services. This type of patronage has always been more available to parties in government (at some level), although in a few countries (most notably Austria), parties have divvied up access to state resources in ways that minimize the impact of electoral results. Over time, however, options to use state resources as political rewards have dwindled as states have routinized the distribution of public services, thus reducing opportunities for political intervention. Similarly, the professionalization of public bureaucracies drastically decreased the numbers of state jobs that were under partisan political control. Among the countries in this study, patronage-based distribution of government jobs remained most prominent at the beginning of the twenty-first century in Austria, Portugal,

Spain, Italy, and Greece. Many of these jobs were located at regional or local levels. Yet even in these countries the use of public sector jobs for political patronage was on the wane by this time. This decline was soon accelerated by crisis-induced austerity plans that rapidly shrank the size of the public sector (Gomez and Verge 2012; Jalali et al. 2012; Müller and Steininger 1994).

What remain are systems in which patronage hiring is too limited to stimulate many people to join parties, but which still may attract those seeking partisan political careers (as opposed to wanting other public sector jobs). Even downsized and de-politicized public sectors retain a few appointments that may be reserved for active partisans, including senior aides to legislators and regional councilors, staff for legislative party groups, and top positions within some government ministries. In addition, parties' extra-parliamentary organizations and party-linked foundations may also expect their staff to hold party membership. These positions may not be numerous, but their impact on party enrollment may exceed their actual number if every possible appointment inspires two or three people to join in hopes of future employment.

Parties also offer members opportunities for career advancement that do not rely on state resources, such as chances for professional networking. As already noted, younger party members regularly name career ambitions as one of their motives for joining a political party. This motive is particularly strong among the most active members (Bruter and Harrison 2009, 68; Young and Cross 2007). It was found even in countries such as Canada and the UK, which offered relatively few patronage appointments in the public sector. Such studies suggest that parties have scope to boost their recruiting appeal by increasing their offerings of these types of selective economic benefits. For instance, they could sponsor special career networking events for students and younger members, or promote political skill-building courses as career training that has uses outside the political realm. In this case, the selective economic benefit promised by party membership would be the prospect of increased future earnings. Parties could provide such benefits without incurring great costs to themselves

CONCLUSION: PARTY AFFILIATION AS A POLITICAL ACT

The discussions in this chapter have exposed some of the roots of parties' recruiting woes. Perhaps most importantly, parties that have moved away from identification with well-defined social groups can no longer rely on collective social benefits to inspire membership. In catch-all parties, party membership is no longer an identity badge that reinforces membership in a distinct community. These parties can offer selective economic and social benefits, but the real and relative value of these has waned due to changes in patronage opportunities, and due to changing social circumstances. New technologies do not seem particularly promising as ways to offer alternative social benefits, because parties have had little success so far in attracting large numbers of supporters to their on-line communities. The exception has been small and new parties, which have used on-line tools to rapidly build support bases. Yet it is too early to say whether newer parties can translate these on-line affiliations into longer-term commitments. Even if social and material benefits are not particularly important recruiting incentives, they possibly are more important for both new and established parties in providing reasons for existing members to continue to pay dues.

In contrast, political motivations seem to be playing an increasing role in motivating partisans to formally affiliate with a party. Among these, it is selective political benefits that seem most likely to inspire party enrollment. In the democracies studied here, only a few contemporary parties attract supporters primarily based on collective fervor for particular leaders or ideas, including anti-immigrant and separatist-nationalist parties. Such parties have seen electoral upsurges, but few have translated political enthusiasm into long-term membership commitments. On the other hand, new types of selective and inclusive political benefits are emerging as important tools for stimulating party affiliation and intra-party participation. The next chapter examines how they have been used, and their apparent impacts on party enrollment.

NOTES

1. This is close to Epstein's argument that class consciousness was crucial for explaining socialist parties' organizational success: "Organizationally, then, one should expect parties to be small, weak, and intermittent in comparison with many other associations... Where this is not the case and parties are organizationally strong, despite the absence of patronage, it is reasonable to seek the explanation in unusual circumstances—such as the class consciousness of a large social sector supporting a socialist party" (1968: 103).
2. This section summarizes discussions of membership motivations found in the following reports on party membership surveys: *Canada 2000* Bloc Quebeçois, Canadian Alliance, Liberals, NDP, Progressive Conservatives (Cross and Young 2004; Young and Cross 2002); *Canada 2003/04*, young party members in

Bloc Quebeçois, Liberals, NDP (Young and Cross 2007; Young and Cross 2008); *Denmark 2012* all 9 parties that campaigned in 2011 election (Kosiara-Pedersen 2013); *2000* all 10 parties represented in legislature (Hansen 2002; Pedersen et al. 2004); *Ireland 1999* Fine Gael (Gallagher and Marsh 2002; Gallagher and Marsh 2004); *Germany 1998 and 2009*, all parties in federal legislature (5 and 6 respectively) (Spier et al. 2011); *Italy 2001* National Alliance (Ignazi and Bardi 2006); *Netherlands 1999* CDA, D66, PvdA and VVD (Holsteyn et al. 2000; Koole et al. 2011); *2008* 9 parties (den Ridder 2014); *Norway 1991 and 2000* all 7 national parties in national legislature (Heidar and Saglie 2003); *UK* Conservatives 1992 (Whiteley et al. 1994), Labour 1989/90 (Seyd and Whiteley 1992), Liberal Democrats 1998 (Whiteley et al. 2006); Young party members in *2007* in 15 parties in *France, Germany, Hungary, Norway, Spain, and the UK* (Bruter and Harrison 2009).

3. 16.9% vs. 11.5%
4. In Germany, Canada, Ireland, and the UK.
5. Young Canadian party members were a bit different, with the majority in Canada attributing their membership to having been asked to join (Young and Cross 2007: 12). The question was not asked of young party members in the multi-country study, so it is unclear whether this is a broader pattern.
6. It should be noted that most of these countries have weak traditions of patronage politics. The picture might be different in countries where parties have more control over the dispersal of state benefits, not just because more people may reasonably expect to directly benefit from party affiliation, but also because patronage traditions may make it more socially acceptable to acknowledge such motives.
7. Austria is one country where these types of organizations remain important. Milieu organizations are distinct from intra-party organizations for women, youth, farmers, etc., groups which have statutory recognition and possibly some representation in party conferences or party executive boards.
8. In the 1950s the British Young Conservatives had a reputation for successful match-making that was held to be partly responsible for its recruiting success in this decade (Black 2008).
9. <www.conservatives.com/donate/donor_clubs.aspx>, accessed Jan. 2013. For the largest donors who receive access to party leaders, such benefits are politically problematic precisely because they seem likely to confer selective material rewards as well as social status.
10. The latter type of benefit could be especially helpful to the party that offers it, because it gives members a strong incentive to renew (in order to retain the e-mail account), and because it ensures that the party has a current e-mail address for these members.

8

Making Membership Meaningful

Political Benefits

Whatever else has changed, political parties remain central political players in parliamentary democracies. Individual parties may face greater political uncertainty as voter loyalty diminishes and as new challengers emerge, but collectively political parties continue to dominate competition for political offices at all levels. They structure behavior in legislatures, and they define voters' choices at the polls (Dalton et al. 2011). Because of their central political roles, parties have the ability to offer supporters substantively important opportunities for political participation. In response to declining membership enrollments, some parties have been doing just this, expanding and publicizing opportunities for affiliated supporters to influence party decisions. Such changes in intra-party culture are some of the most important features of the ongoing evolution of contemporary party organizations. They not only alter incentives for participation within parties. They also potentially redefine relations between party leaders and party supporters, creating new incentives and opportunities for elites to cultivate the party's organizational grassroots. These changes may transform long-held views about the ways that parties' extra-parliamentary organizations fit into representative processes.

This chapter investigates parties' efforts to use new political benefits to bolster the perceived value of partisan participation. These are the benefits depicted in the lowest row of Table 7.1 (repeated in Table 8.1). As the evidence will show, some of the new opportunities have proven highly popular, and may enable parties to meaningfully connect with, and mobilize, wider swathes of their potential voters. Yet some of these new procedures also pose risks for parties, threatening to undermine party cohesion by expanding internal competition. Moreover, the recruiting impact of the new procedures varies according to the rules that govern them, especially the rules that define the party *demos*.

TABLE 8.1 *Benefits for party members and supporters*

	Collective: Members and Others	Selective & Inclusive: All Members	Selective & Exclusive: Some Members
Political	7. **Positive:** advance a cause **Negative:** oust current government or combat political threat	8. **Influence:** party decisions **Information** **Self-actualization**	9. **Influence:** party and government decisions **Office:** party, public, or quasi-public jobs

For full table, see Chapter 7.

COLLECTIVE POLITICAL BENEFITS (CELL 7): STIRRING POLITICAL PASSIONS

As with the other benefits shown in Table 8.1, some of the political goods that parties offer are collective, while others selectively accrue to some or all who are active within the party. For most political parties, their fundamental and distinctive product is the promise of collective political rewards. Party volunteers receive the same policy benefits as other citizens in similar circumstances, though possibly the members value these benefits more than others. Engagement on behalf of a collective benefit may be reinforced by more selective side-payments, such as feelings of self-esteem that come from working for a cause in which one believes (so-called expressive benefits; Seyd and Whiteley 1992: 107). Party leaders and party platforms may be most able to inspire participation based on collective political benefits if they offer populist or ideological visions, or if they portray competitors in dire terms. We would expect such effects to peak prior to a tight election, or at times of perceived political crisis, when voters receive messages from multiple sources exhorting them to show their political colors. Such fervor is likely to wane after elections, as party supporters face the potentially disillusioning realities of electoral defeat or coalition compromises.

It is hard to directly measure the impact of collective political benefits on the supply of members. However, we do know that many party members claim to be inspired by them. As Chapter 7 showed, when party members are surveyed about the best reasons for joining a party, or why they themselves joined, the most frequently mentioned reasons are political ones. Whether or not survey responses accurately model individual membership decisions, it is striking how many members describe membership in political terms. The similarity of responses from existing members across such a wide range of parties suggests the paramount importance of collective political considerations when parties are trying to recruit new members: opportunities to be part of a bigger movement are still capable of inspiring political

Making Membership Meaningful

involvement even in a less ideological age. Such benefits are probably particularly important in newly created parties, be those Green parties in the 1980s or internet-based parties in the 2000s. These parties stir passions by challenging the established political order, and often have organizational structures that reflect the wider political changes that they advocate. On the other hand, while enthusiasm over party aims may prompt an initial wave of enrollments for these new parties, they probably need to offer something besides collective political benefits if they want those members to stay involved. This is one reason why more selective political benefits may be valuable to both new and established parties, because they can give supporters a reason to maintain their affiliation even if—or maybe particularly if—they become disillusioned with the party leader or with particular party policies. In Hirschman's terms, members may be more likely to stick around if exit is not the only alternative to loyalty (1970).

SELECTIVE POLITICAL BENEFITS (CELL 8): INFORMATION AND INFLUENCE

Parties can offer members and other registered supporters several types of selective political benefits, including privileged political information and influence within the parties. Many parties have been expanding opportunities for supporters to get involved in partisan projects, and to have a direct say in party decisions. Yet in keeping with the multi-speed affiliation models, they are not necessarily confining these new benefits to traditional members alone. The relation between the new participation opportunities and membership recruiting is thus a complex one.

Political Information

Among the possible selective political benefits that party membership may provide are opportunities and resources to become more educated about local, national, or international affairs. Current party members did not express much interest in receiving such benefits, and few parties emphasized them as a recruiting incentive. Of the party web pages which listed reasons for supporters to become members, only about 20 percent mentioned enhanced access to political information and education (see Table 7.2). These web pages might just note that members become better informed about politics; others described special training courses for members. To the extent that they made such offers, parties were emphasizing a role that was once central for some of them, that of providing political education. As Chapter 6 described, many parties have been using new technologies to rapidly expand their offerings of political news and information, and to expand the audience for this news. Yet the bulk of these offerings are not restricted to party members, but are instead used to attract new kinds of affiliates. In short, while parties might opt to use digital access to political information as a selective benefit for traditional membership, relatively few are choosing to do so.

Direct Action

Another type of selective political benefit that parties could offer is the opportunity to make a difference through personal political actions. For instance, in addition to recruiting campaign volunteers, local parties could enlist members to help with civic welfare causes, such as cleaning up a beach or playground, planting trees, or fundraising for a local charity. National parties could organize more large-scale partisan political actions, such as involving members in petition drives or rallies to support or oppose pending legislation.

Encouraging members and other supporters to become more politically involved might seem to be a fundamental purpose of extra-parliamentary party organization. If so, that was difficult to discern from the national party web pages. Only 15 percent of them advertised specific direct action opportunities for members or other supporters. The most common options were to participate in party-organized demonstrations, or to sign and circulate petitions. A few web pages encouraged party volunteering by posting a form enabling would-be helpers to register their interest, or by inviting them to send an e-mail offering their services. Under either method, someone from a local party was supposed to contact them about how to get involved. These forms were available to all supporters, regardless of their membership status. Using web pages to solicit volunteer help was more common in some countries than others. In Australia, Canada, Denmark, the Netherlands, and the United Kingdom multiple parties included volunteer forms or links on their web pages to encourage individuals to get directly involved with party work; elsewhere, at most one party used their web pages in this way. These examples aside, party web pages seldom highlighted individual political involvement as a reason to join, or made much effort to enlist web page visitors in party activities.

Influence within the Party

In contrast, many political parties have made important and highly visible changes in the opportunities they offer members to influence party affairs. Relevant reforms include introducing new procedures for policy discussions, and expanding the use of intra-party ballots for party decisions. Given that current members claim to place high value on the political rewards of membership, these changes seem likely to motivate current and potential members.

It is not new for party members to be given a say in party decisions. As Chapter 3 described, in the nineteenth century both liberal and socialist parties drew inspiration from the subscriber-democracy organizational models used by many civil society associations. In such organizations, leaders were formally accountable to dues-paying members. In practice, of course, inequalities of wealth and privilege did not vanish in these organizations. Moreover, party legislators tended to dominate the popular organization in electorally successful parties. Nevertheless, many parliamentary democracies have had parties of the left and the right whose rituals and statutes paid homage to the ideal of party organization as a miniature representative democracy, with members at the foundation of pyramidal accountability structures. Local and national parties organized in this way held annual or biennial meetings at which leaders presented activity and financial reports; members or their delegates then voted on accepting the reports, and on endorsing the leaders. For these types of parties, the national party conference was the highest party organ, though conferences generally delegated their day-to-day authority to small executive councils. Setting aside the question of how these parties operated in practice, the main point is that statutes in many parties have long given individual party members some role at the base of representative structures.

Thus, intra-party democracy in a representative guise is nothing new; indeed, it is an ideal espoused and practiced by some parties for over a century. What is new is the way that some parties are trying to expand opportunities for individual members to exercise a more direct impact on party decisions. These efforts take two main forms: giving interested members more opportunities to shape party policy priorities, and giving members the right to vote on important party decisions.

Policy Consultation

In recent years some parties have experimented with new ways to boost members' participation in policy formation. One way to do this is by establishing or expanding policy consultation forums, giving interested members a chance to attend live meetings and on-line forums to discuss policy options and priorities. Parties can use nationally organized consultation exercises to supplement more traditional policy discussions within local parties and within party conferences. Well-publicized consultations can burnish the credentials of campaign manifestos and other policy documents, showing the party to be responsive to supporters' priorities. As such, they may appeal to parties which have reduced their reliance on ideology or group goals to justify party priorities. Party members may be given special access to these processes, even if parties also use consultation exercises to reach out to groups and individuals from outside the party sphere.

Examples from established parties in Britain and Australia show how parties can modify traditional practices to incorporate individual supporters into national-party policy processes. Since the mid-1990s, the three largest British parties and the two biggest Australian parties have held a variety of consultation exercises to collect input from interested party supporters outside of (or in addition to) constituency party debates. For instance, the British parties have run regional policy forums in parallel to constituency party discussions, with the results said to feed into national policy process (Gauja 2009; Ward et al. 2003). The Australian Labor Party has held on-line and in-person policy consultation forums, open to members and registered supporters (Gauja 2013, 101). All these exercises offered opportunities for members with strong policy interests to learn about and discuss policy options, even if they did not provide them with much direct influence over ultimate decisions.

Giving members (and sometimes other supporters) a more decisive say in policy-making was a hallmark of the Green and Alternative parties that emerged in the 1980s. These parties' core values emphasized grassroots participation. As a result, their structures often eschewed delegate democracy in favor of more inclusive decision-making. This could mean holding conventions in which all interested supporters could attend and vote, sometimes regardless of membership status (see Koelble 1989 and Poguntke 1987 on the German Greens, and Burchell 2001 on Green Parties in Sweden, Austria, and Britain). When geography made it impractical to hold all-member meetings, parties experimented with other means to give members a decisive role in policy decisions. For instance, in the 1980s the Australian New Democrats, a small "Alternative" party, published structured policy debates in the party magazine and then held all-member postal votes on the issues (Gauja 2005). In Canada in the 1980s, the Reform Party pioneered voting with then-new technologies (automated phone voting, later internet voting) in order to give members a direct say in party policies. In the Netherlands, both alternative and traditional parties have opened policy-making processes by inviting all interested members to participate in party conference discussions. The Dutch D66 and Green Left parties opened up their party conferences in this way by 2001. The Dutch Liberal Party (VVD) and Christian Democrats (CDA) soon emulated them (Voerman 2006, 221). Such a solution is most feasible for parties in geographically compact countries, and with small memberships. However, the Dutch CDA, with its tens of thousands of members, proved that it is possible for even large parties to open internal conferences to all members—as long as turnout remains low.

In the twenty-first century some parties began experimenting with on-line options for involving members (and in some cases, other supporters) in policy discussions. These have ranged from informal exercises, probably not monitored by party leaders, through to very structured debates. In practice, parties have preferred the former to the latter, soliciting opinions in ways that allow for broad comments but probably have little impact on the direction or details of party policies. For example, many parties use their digital platforms to encourage readers to comment on topical debates. They may post a controversial topic on the party Facebook page, or they may place a poll on the party homepage and invite readers to cast a vote for or against issues in the news. More formally, some parties have used websites to foster debate by presenting differing views about key policy issues, and then inviting comments (cf. the British Labour Party's policy consultation exercise in 2006, or the New Zealand Labor Party's "Grassroots Labour" network; Gauja 2013, 110). These on-line consultations have the potential to involve a large number of party members in policy debates. However, so far members and other supporters have shown little interest in any of these types of political exercises, perhaps because they see little evidence that their opinions would have much impact. For instance, in early 2012 only ten of the 109 parties in this study included questionnaires on their web pages to solicit visitors' opinions on specific policies. Even when parties did provide opportunities for input, response rates were probably quite low. As Chapter 7 showed, discussions on party Facebook pages generally elicit few comments. Similarly, although there was quite a bit of publicity surrounding the British Labour Party's 2006 on-line policy consultation, only 343 comments were posted on the consultation website in its first four months (Gauja 2009, 9).

In other words, while new technologies and new policy-making networks may offer party members opportunities to discuss—and possibly influence—party policy outside the confines of local party meetings, the low participation rates in both conventional and on-line forums suggest that these types of political membership benefits have limited appeal. Even if they did, they would not necessarily encourage traditional membership recruiting, because few of them have been designed as *selective* membership benefits. Most of the on-line forums permit non-member participation, though participants may need to affiliate in some way (as Facebook group members, microblog recipients, etc.). Despite loose participation rules, so far these policy consultation exercises have attracted only limited interest from members or other supporters; this implies that they have done little to expand the circles of affiliated partisans.

Voting on Party Decisions

In contrast, members and potential members have shown much more interest in a different type of selective political benefit: the opportunity to vote in intra-party elections. In recent years many parties have introduced or expanded their use of such ballots. In doing so, they have been supplementing their representative structures with internal direct democracy. The high participation rates in intra-party elections suggest that such initiatives hold real promise for stimulating grassroots partisan participation. Whether such participation translates into increased party membership, and how it affects power relations within parties, will depend, in part, on the access rules that govern the ballots.

Parties' recent experiments with intra-party ballots have been influenced by surging support for using direct democracy to settle controversial public decisions, as well as by growing popular suspicion of partisan elites. By the 1990s, many parliamentary democracies were making greater use of national referendums to settle policy questions that cut across traditional party lines. These included issues of morality (divorce, abortion), and changes in constitutions or other major political institutions (European Union treaties, electoral systems, constitutional monarchy, etc.) (Scarrow 2001; Setala 1999). The growing use of these procedures at both national and subnational levels reaffirmed the sovereignty of individual citizens, and their capacity to make complex and weighty decisions. In this context, some established parties began experimenting with giving individual members a more direct say over their internal policy and personnel decisions.

In practice, most party ballots have been about personnel rather than policy, perhaps because policy decisions are less suited to yes/no voting. Nevertheless, some parties have turned to this procedure to settle policy questions, particularly when party leaders wanted to be sure that they had the backing of the membership. For instance, in 2004 the internally divided French Socialist Party held its first membership ballot on a policy issue, to decide the party's position ahead of the 2005 national referendum on a European Constitutional Treaty. The Danish Socialist People's Party held a ballot on the same topic a few weeks later (Sussman 2007, 2). In Germany, in the 1990s and early 2000s, five of the six parties represented in the German Bundestag changed their statutes to allow for intra-party ballots on policy issues. As of 2012 only the FDP and B90/Greens had used these instruments.[1] In 2013, the SPD made its first use of a party-wide membership ballot to answer a policy question, in this case holding a membership ballot on the party's proposed coalition agreement with the CDU and CSU.

Table 8.2 gives details about these and other policy ballots held by national parties in the nineteen countries of this study from 1990 to 2012. The brevity of the list makes clear that such procedures are far from common, even when policy is broadly defined to include questions about party mergers and party statutes. In other words, opportunities to vote on party policies are too rare to constitute much of an incentive to join or stay in a political party. Yet the other message of this table is that party members appear to find these opportunities meaningful, perhaps because almost all of the ballots dealt with issues of high internal importance. Member turnout in these ballots averaged over 50 percent.[2]

Making Membership Meaningful 183

In the past two decades at least a few parties have also expanded political benefits for members by giving them more direct roles in selecting national legislative candidates. In some countries, party members have long had a say in such decisions, especially where crucial parts of the candidate selection process are conducted at the local level (for example, in Canada or Finland). Elsewhere, trends towards expanding members' direct roles in these processes have been evident at least since the 1960s (Bille 2001; Scarrow et al. 2000). Oft-cited examples of this include the British Conservative and Labour parties moving in the 1990s to give individual members more direct say over candidate choices, in some cases even allowing participation by postal ballot (Hopkin 2001; Mikulska and Scarrow 2010). In Germany's mixed-member electoral system, local parties have been increasingly opting to involve all members in selecting district candidates, rather than having them selected by delegates at a regional meeting (Reiser 2011). The extent of the changes is hard to assess because of limited cross-national longitudinal data about candidate selection processes. Where they occur, such procedural changes create new incentives for supporters to join or at least stay in the party, and for would-be candidates to enlist their supporters as voting-eligible members. The magnitude of the incentives would depend on the extent of actual competition in specific contests, and on the accessibility of membership—how easy is it for supporters to join the party primarily for the purpose of participating in candidate selection decisions?

One of the most remarkable and widespread organizational changes in the past two decades among the parties in these nineteen countries has been the growing use of party-wide ballots for selecting party leaders and top party candidates. Prior to 1990 it was almost unknown for parties to ballot members as part of the leadership selection process. (A few Belgian parties and the newly formed Canadian Reform Party were the main exceptions.) As Figure 8.1 shows, by the second decade of the twenty-first century,

TABLE 8.2 *Participation in party policy votes, 1990–2012*

Country	Year	Party	Vote Topic	Member Turnout %
Belgium	1993	Socialist (SP)	Party manifesto	46.4
Belgium	1996	PSC	Party renewal	48.3
Belgium	2002	PSC	Party name	25.0
France	2004	PS	European Constitutional Treaty	80.0
Germany	1995	FDP	Wire tapping	42.0
Germany	1997	FDP	Conscription	19.5
Germany	2003	B90/Greens	Party leadership structure	56.6
Germany	2007	PDS die Linke	Merger with WASG	82.6
Germany	2007	WASG	Merger with PDS die Linke	57.0
Germany	2011	FDP	Euro insurance fund	31.6

Source: see Appendix A8.2.

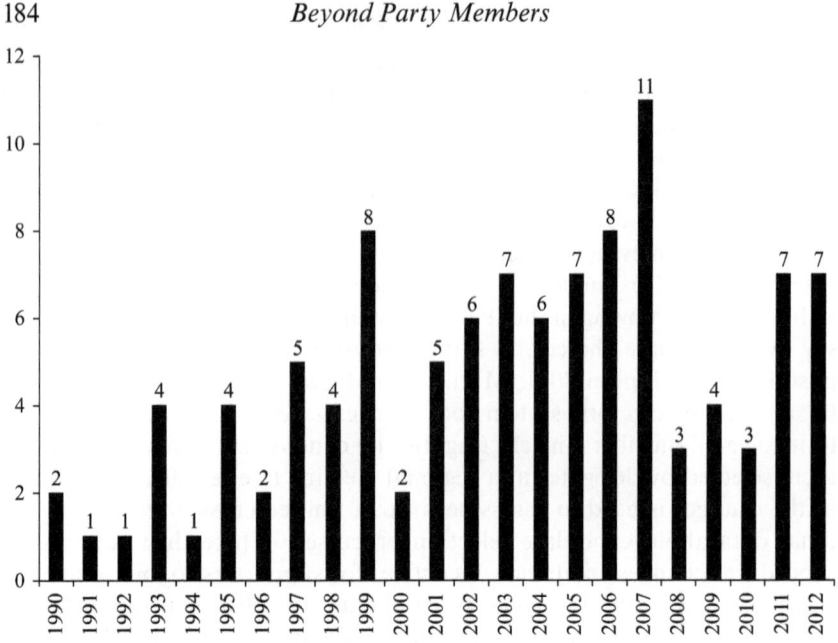

FIGURE 8.1 Use of intra-party leadership ballots, 1990–2012, 15 countries

leadership ballots had become much more common (Cross and Blais 2012; Kenig 2009b). The votes depicted in this figure are to select parties' top electoral candidates, positions which carry various job titles (including party chair, party leader, party list-leader). Use of leadership ballots more than doubled between the first and the second half of this period.[3] From the years 1990 through 2000, parties in these nineteen countries held at least thirty-four leadership ballots. In the next eleven years, from 2001 through 2012, they held at least seventy-three.

This growth was not evenly spread across the countries, as Table 8.3 shows. In four countries, there had been no party-wide ballots for leadership positions as of 2012 (Austria, Norway, Sweden, and Switzerland). Conversely, in seven of the countries, several parties had already used such ballots, in some cases multiple times. These national usage patterns suggest that within-country contagion may play a big role in popularizing this procedure. However, contagion may also transcend national borders. For instance, the French Socialists' presidential primary in 2011 drew international media attention, not only because it came on the heels of a high-profile scandal,[4] but also because almost 2.9 million voters participated in this intra-party ballot. Other parties likely took note, especially because the party's mobilization for the primary fed into a successful campaign to unseat an incumbent president.

TABLE 8.3 *Number of parties using leadership ballots, 1990–2012*

Australia	1
Austria	0
Belgium	12
Canada	8
Denmark	3
Finland	1
France	4
Germany	2
Greece	2
Ireland	2
Italy	2
Netherlands	4
New Zealand	1
Norway	0
Portugal	3
Spain	1
Sweden	0
Switzerland	0
United Kingdom	3

The final section of this chapter will look more closely at evidence of the popularity of these ballots, and at the potential for parties to use them as recruiting tools. First, however, the next section finishes the discussion of membership incentives by considering the supply of political benefits which are both selective and exclusive—those which are reserved for only a portion of the membership.

EXCLUSIVE POLITICAL BENEFITS (CELL 9): STATUS AND OFFICE-HOLDING

One of the distinguishing characteristics of political parties is that they compete to win public offices. A corollary of this characteristic is that they need to find candidates who are willing to compete on their behalf, and to serve if elected. Parties also need to find candidates to compete for and hold offices within the party. Most of the parties included in this study have traditionally reserved both kinds of candidacies for party members; as such, the need to supply candidates can itself become a recruiting stimulus for the party. The number of candidate slots may constitute a demand-side floor for local party membership, with local party leaders having strong and recurring incentives to recruit a supply of suitable (or at least willing) volunteers to fill party slates.

Opportunities to stand for office are also a supply-side recruiting stimulus whenever personal political ambition spurs individuals to join. Yet it is hard to know how much of a lure this is. Party web pages seldom list the prospect of candidacy as a reason for supporters to enlist: only six of the party web pages mentioned opportunities to stand for office among their enrollment arguments (see Table 7.2). Likewise, in party member surveys it is primarily younger members who admit to having joined in hopes of becoming a candidate or having a political career (Bruter and Harrison 2009; Young and Cross 2007).

Whatever the supply-side attractions of candidacies, parties cannot do much to alter the number of viable electoral offices available to members, particularly in regards to opportunities outside of the party organization. The number of public elective offices is mostly determined by the structure of regional and local government. On the other hand, parties can control whether they use candidacy opportunities to recruit new members, or whether they reserve them for long-standing members. If parties take the latter route, as has traditionally been the case in most membership-based parties, the link between recruiting and candidacy is quite indirect. Under these circumstances, access to office-holding benefits probably has a very minimal impact on party membership numbers, though aspiration for public office may inspire a few members to join and stay active over many years.

So far this chapter has examined parties' options for enhancing the attractiveness of membership by increasing the political benefits offered to members. It has shown that one trend towards doing this is to increase the use of intra-party ballots to settle important issues of policy and personnel. The final section of this chapter looks more closely at the relationship between such ballots and party membership recruiting. It argues that participation rules determine the extent to which these ballots are likely to stimulate supporters to enlist. They also may affect the results of the contests.

DEFINING THE PARTY *DEMOS*: HOW PARTICIPATION RULES AFFECT MEMBERSHIP

One of the key questions to ask about intra-party ballots concerns the eligible electorate: who is the party *demos*? In answering this question, it is useful to go beyond the binary distinction between closed (member-only) and open (all-voter) primaries. Because voting procedures interact with eligibility rules, it is more accurate to describe the electorate for intra-party

Making Membership Meaningful 187

decisions by placing it along the dimensions of *inclusion* and *access* (Hazan and Rahat 2010, 39–47). *Inclusion* describes formal eligibility to participate in the decision. No ballots are needed at the narrowest end of the inclusion spectrum, because decisions are made by a single leader or a very small group. At the other end are decisions in which a much larger number of supporters may participate. The continuum drawn by Hazan and Rahat shows the most inclusive party processes as those which are open to all eligible voters. In fact, some parties go even further than this, permitting participation by certain non-citizens who are ineligible to vote in national elections, or by citizens who are younger than the voting age.

Access describes the procedural hurdles that must be navigated by those who are eligible to vote in parties' elections. These can include advanced-registration requirements, monetary payments, and the time and effort required to cast a ballot (e.g. postal ballots vs. in-person voting). *Access* and *inclusion* are not identical traits, and they do not necessarily move together. Parties can be highly accessible even if they are not particularly inclusive. For instance, parties which hold member-only ballots can make it easy or difficult to fulfill membership requirements. They can grant instant voting rights to those who join on the day of the poll, or they can impose long probationary periods before new members obtain full voting rights. Conversely, parties can open ballots to non-member supporters, but they can make it difficult to take advantage of these opportunities, for example by limiting voting to those who attend an all-day candidates' meeting.

The expanded use of intra-party ballots should have the greatest impact on party membership recruiting when participation rules are exclusive (member-only contests), but when accessibility is broad (low fees, short or no probationary periods). Under these circumstances, supporters who get interested in the contest during the intra-party campaign can easily join in order to participate. Political competitors and their supporters also have big incentives to selectively recruit in hopes of influencing the outcome. Conversely, intra-party votes should provide a weaker recruiting stimulus when access is highly restricted, for example, when the probationary period closes before the contestants have been announced.

Table 8.4 gives a sense of the variety of recent party practices regarding inclusion and access for intra-party leadership ballots. This table includes each contest as a separate case, because parties can (and often do) change eligibility requirements from ballot to ballot. It includes all the ballots listed in Figure 8.1 for which information about procedural rules could be located. Because of incomplete information, this is only a sample of cases, but it is big enough to illustrate variations in party practices regarding access and inclusion in intra-party ballots. At one extreme of (non-)accessibility was the Portuguese Socialist Party, in which new members needed to wait eighteen

TABLE 8.4 *Access and inclusion in party leadership ballots, 1990–2012*

Access: Waiting Periods	
None: Day of Vote Registration	10.5%
1 Day–30 Days	23.7%
1 Month–6 Months	44.7%
6 Months+–12 Months	0.0%
More than 1 Year*	21.1%
N = 38	
Inclusion:	
Member only	88.9%
Members and other supporters	11.1%
N = 63	

Elections of party leaders, party list leaders, and presidential candidates. Cases for which rules were discernible.
* Seven of the eight cases were Portuguese PS (eighteen-month waiting period).

months before gaining internal voting rights. At the other extreme were parties which allowed participation by members who enrolled on or close to polling day, such as the Greek New Democracy in 2009 (election day membership), the Canadian Alliance in 2000 (one week in advance) and the Dutch D66 in 2006 (four weeks in advance). Few parties had probationary periods that exceeded a year, but many had waiting periods seemingly designed to prevent voting by members who might join after an internal contest was in full swing. Such probationary rules make it less likely that membership ballots will stimulate membership recruiting, but they do not entirely rule this out. For example, if the contest date is known well in advance, such as for primaries ahead of scheduled general elections, supporters of internal candidates could recruit like-minded members ahead of probationary deadlines.

Table 8.4 also shows that party ballots differ in their degree of inclusiveness, particularly in whether non-members are eligible to vote. By far the most common rule is to restrict voting to traditional members (although access rules may make membership easy to obtain). Nevertheless, about 10 percent of the leadership ballots were conducted under rules that allowed participation by those who were not full-fledged dues-paying members. Some parties opened their contests to non-members in order to boost their populist credentials or to broaden their electoral appeal. Others did so for more pragmatic reasons, particularly if they were too new to have established an organized membership. The latter was the case in Italy in 2005 and 2007, when two center-left parties held open parties to select their top candidates for national elections. For these new electoral coalitions, holding inclusive primaries was as much a matter of identifying and rallying potential supporters as it was about choosing candidates. (Indeed, even though these were technically contested votes, in both cases the likely outcome was widely known in advance.)

Making Membership Meaningful

Yet it is not only new parties that have expanded their selectorates beyond traditional membership bounds. Most strikingly, in 2011 the French Socialist Party (PS) opted to use an open primary to select its candidate for the 2012 presidential election. This was a shift from the party's 1995 and 2006 member-only presidential primaries. In 2011, would-be participants could register in advance or on election day by signing a declaration of support for the party and paying a €1 fee.[5] Those who registered could opt in to receive information from candidates and from the PS itself. This second step meant that non-member participants potentially joined the party's ongoing news audience.[6] This intra-party contest attracted a great deal of interest. Over 2.8 million people cast a ballot in the Socialist primary, a number which was equivalent to 44 percent of the votes cast for PS candidates in the first round of the 2007 legislative elections. In 2011 the French Greens also held an inclusive primary, open to registered "cooperators" as well as members. Cooperators were supporters who enrolled on-line by paying a reduced fee (€10), and endorsing a "statement of ecological principles." The candidate nominated by this small party had no chance of winning the presidential ballot, but participation was nevertheless relatively high: the equivalent of 77 percent of the party's members, or 3 percent of the votes received by the party's legislative candidates in 2007.

Do Party Ballots Make Membership More Attractive?

Does the expanded use of intra-party ballots help parties to recruit and/ or retain members? Two kinds of evidence shed light on these questions. The first is whether members are actually taking advantage of the new voting opportunities. If not, it would seem unlikely that ballots are shifting the calculus of membership decisions. In addition, where data are available we can examine more direct evidence of instances where membership numbers have changed in response to intra-party voting opportunities.

Participation in Intra-Party Ballots

How popular are opportunities to participate in ballots to help select party leaders? If these internal ballots generate more enthusiasm than traditional party activities, then they would seem to be drawing favorable attention from more than just the usual core of activists. If so, it would be plausible to argue that such ballots are possibly helping to boost membership recruiting and retention. This potential bonus would seem to be particularly promising if ballots continue to generate high participation over multiple uses—in other words, after the procedures lose their novelty value.

It is difficult to calculate and compare turnout levels in intra-party contests because of inconsistencies in the available data, and because of differences in the eligibility rules. Parties use different systems for reporting participation rates (if they report these at all). Sometimes they publish turnout figures but do not give the number of ballots cast. Sometimes they report the absolute number of voters but do not say how many were eligible to cast votes. The denominator can be inferred from party membership figures, but this is an imprecise measure, especially if membership figures are published months prior to, or after, the contest. Moreover, for parties with very accessible contests (e.g. same day membership registration), and for ones which have very inclusive rules (open to non-members), actual party membership is a conceptually misleading denominator. In these cases, turnout figures might reasonably be measured against the number who *could have* participated. The difficulties of generating comparable figures make all measures of turnout in intra-party elections inevitably imprecise.

Despite these problems, it is still useful to calculate rough measures of turnout to assess general levels of partisan mobilization generated by intra-party ballots. This study uses two such measures, dubbed Member Turnout and Voter Turnout. Member Turnout calculates ballot participation as a proportion of party membership.[7] Voter Turnout calculates participation relative to the votes the party received in a proximate national election. This denominator estimates a reasonable upper limit on intra-party participation.[8]

Table 8.5 uses these two measures to summarize participation patterns in intra-party leadership votes from 1990 to 2012, including all contests for which at least one of these measures could be obtained. The top row shows that median Member Turnout levels for intra-party contests were high in comparison with members' participation in other party activities, as reported in Chapter 7. Figure 8.2 reinforces this message: most ballots

TABLE 8.5 *Turnout in party leadership ballots, 1990–2012 median participation rates*

		N
Member Turnout*	49.5%	88
Member Turnout contested elections	57.7%	56
Member Turnout minus "open" elections	48.6%	84
Voter Turnout**	2.3%	99
Voter Turnout contested elections	2.7%	64
Voter Turnout minus "open" elections	2.3%	92

"Open" elections: open to non-members and to same-day registrants.
* Denominator is number of party members reported for that year, or calculated from party's own figures on turnout of eligible members.
** Denominator is number of voters in national legislative election held in same year as party vote, or most recent previous election.

Making Membership Meaningful 191

have generated Member Turnout rates of well over 50 percent. Moreover, as the second line of Table 8.5 shows, participation was higher in contested elections. This is the pattern we would expect if members see these opportunities as political benefits: members are most likely to participate when something important is at stake.

Comparing Member Turnout rates is problematic, because access and inclusion rules vary so widely. Where access to the event is most open, the denominator (eligible members) may increase drastically on election day, as new members enroll. Where participation rules are very inclusive (i.e. open to non-members), Member Turnout figures could be over 100 percent because the universe of eligible participants is much larger than the denominator (party members). One remedy for both problems is to use party voters as the denominator, on grounds that this figure approximates the maximum number of people who might plausibly participate in an intra-party ballot. Yet this denominator is also imperfect, not least because of possible links between election results and the use of intra-party ballots: in some cases, the decision to use a ballot may reflect a party's poor showing in a prior election; in other cases, the use of a ballot could increase the party's votes in a subsequent election. Neither measure is perfect for estimating a party's potential support independent of ballot use, but given that so many other factors also influence party support, the measure that is closest to the time of the internal ballot is probably the best. Despite the problems with the denominator, Voter Turnout is an informative measure when comparing participation across party elections with wide variations in access and inclusiveness.

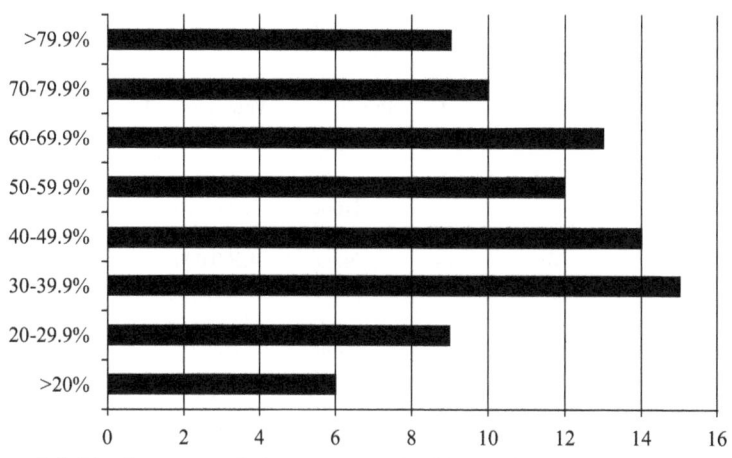

FIGURE 8.2 Member turnout in intra-party leadership elections, 1990–2012, 15 countries. See text for explanation of calculation

Sources: Table A8.1 and A8.2

As the lower rows of Table 8.5 show, median Voter Turnout in intra-party leadership ballots has been just over 2 percent of party supporters, which is about what we would expect if parties enroll about 5 percent of the electorate as members, and if about half of these members participate in the vote. There are, however, some interesting outliers in these figures, as shown in Table 8.6. This table lists the seven intra-party ballots which attracted the highest Voter Turnout. Hundreds of thousands, or even millions, of supporters participated in these contests. All but one of the high participation ballots used highly inclusive rules, allowing participation by registered non-members. The Greek New Democracy vote in 2009 was the exception, restricting voting to members. However, it permitted would-be participants to join on election day. Most of the high participation contests enhanced accessibility by charging low registration fees, ranging from €1 to a high of €6 for the PASOK in 2012. The very high participation figures shown in Table 8.6 suggest that intra-party ballots are capable of rousing a large percentage of party supporters to register ties to a party, and to actively participate in its internal affairs.

It might be argued that high participation in these relatively new procedures is not predictive of future patterns, because the initial use is likely to have a novelty value. One way to test that hypothesis is by asking whether participation rates have declined in parties which held multiple intra-party contests. Table 8.7 shows average turnout levels for parties which have conducted at least three party-wide leadership ballots, comparing turnout in the first contests with the mean for subsequent contests. These figures do not support the suggestion that ballot

TABLE 8.6 *High participation leadership ballots*

Year	Party	Contest?	Include non-mbrs?	Pre-registration?	Votes cast	Mbr turnout %*	Voter turnout %*
Italy							
2007	Democratic Party	Yes	Yes	None	3,400,000		17.9
2005	The Union	Yes	Yes	None	4,300,000		22.6
2012	Center-Left	Yes	Yes	21 days	3,110,210		22.7
Greece							
2009	New Democracy	Yes	No	None	782,000	223.0	26.1
2007	PASOK	Yes	Yes	None	769,000	79.0	28.2
2012	PASOK	No	Yes	None	240,000		28.8
France							
2011	Socialists	Yes	Yes	None	2,860,157	143.0	44.4

*See Table 8.5 and text for explanations of Member Turnout and Voter Turnout.

Making Membership Meaningful 193

TABLE 8.7 *Sustained Member Turnout in intra-party elections (%)*

Country	Party	First Election	Mean Others	Number of Elections
Belgium	CVP	36.0	27.4	3
Belgium	PRL	16.6	27.8	5
Belgium	PSC	45.5	54.4	3
Belgium	VLD	43.8	34.0	4
Canada	NDP	28.0	52.4	3
France	PS	53.3	110.0	3
Netherlands	PvdA	54.0	51.7	3
Portugal	CDS-PP	22.5	26.7	3
Portugal	PS	65.0	41.5	8
Portugal	PSD	37.2	61.9	4
United Kingdom	Liberal Democrats	71.9	66.1	4

participation declines after the novelty wears off. Indeed, in many cases participation was higher in later contests, possibly because there was growing campaigning by rival candidates as they gained experience with intra-party ballots.

In short, participation in intra-party ballots has been high compared to participation in other types of intra-party activities, and interest in these contests is not a one-time affair. These figures suggest that party members and other supporters have responded positively to new participation opportunities, and that they are willing to pay some costs to take part in politically meaningful events. Participation increases when access rules are most relaxed, but supporters also participate in large numbers when costs are higher. Given this, is there any direct evidence that intra-party ballots have been helping parties to boost memberships?

Intra-Party Ballots and Membership Recruiting

The best way to judge the recruiting impact of intra-party contests would be to examine monthly membership data for parties before they hold such contests. If ballot opportunities increase interest, membership should surge immediately prior to the voting eligibility deadline. Unfortunately, parties seldom release monthly enrollment figures.[9] More anecdotal information from a small number of cases suggests that voting opportunities do prompt supporters to enroll, at least in some circumstances. For instance, the UK Labour Party added 32,000 members during its 2011 leadership contest, a surge of over 20 percent. This was notable growth for a party that had just suffered a big electoral defeat. In France, leadership ballots were credited with spurring membership growth in two big parties in the early part of the twenty-first century. In 2006, the French Socialist Party gained almost 100,000 members ahead of a contest to select the party's presidential candidate, with growth boosted by the combination of a well-publicized and contested leadership ballot, a reduction in membership fees, and an active recruiting campaign. In the same period, membership surged in the French Socialists' rival, the UMP. In this party, too, recruiting seemed to be boosted by the prospect of a leadership ballot, even though in this case the ballot was more of a ratification than a contest (Dolez and Laurent 2007; Ivaldi 2007).

In these cases, national parties deliberately and successfully used internal ballots to stimulate membership growth. Another example of growth prompted by an intra-party contest comes from the Israeli Labor Party in 2011. This party is not otherwise included in this study, but its experience is pertinent, because it shows how membership ballots may stimulate recruiting even under seemingly unfavorable circumstances, and in ways that may not have been intended. Access to this member-only contest was limited due to a long probationary period. Nevertheless, 57,000 of the approximately 80,000 members who were eligible to participate had registered within the year prior to the ballot. Most were enlisted by campaigners for the five competing candidates, who enrolled supporters ahead of the probationary deadline. While these new members may have been a boon for particular candidates, the new enrollees did not necessarily help the party. Indeed, they became the focus of controversy, including allegations of registration fraud (Rolef 2011). Some Canadian candidate intra-party elections have also produced accusations of unseemly mobilization by candidates who arrange transportation to constituency selection meetings, and who may even pay registration fees for new members (Cross 2004, 66).

MEMBERSHIP ACCESS AND POLITICAL BENEFITS

These examples suggest that, as members are empowered to make more politically consequential decisions, parties will need to pay more attention to normative questions about the relations between members and other party supporters: who *should* have the right to decide party priorities and to select party personnel? Decisions about access and inclusion rules must answer whether current party members have more at stake in a party than those who join merely to participate in a party ballot. They also must decide whether there are enduring party priorities or community values to which the members themselves must be loyal. If answers to both questions are positive, parties may limit participation to those who have demonstrated their long-term commitment to party values. If not, however, parties may be willing to be more flexible in granting participation opportunities.

The high participation rates in internal ballots suggest that these political opportunities are indeed valued by current members and by non-member supporters. This means that parties have significant opportunities to use participation privileges as recruiting incentives. However, they may have to make some tough choices about how best to use them, especially whether to employ them to identify and mobilize large groups of supporters ahead of a general election, or as rewards to motivate smaller groups of loyal long-term members. From the perspective of multi-speed parties, which are cultivating varied types of affiliates, restricting participation to long-term dues-paying members may not be the preferred choice. For these parties, the goal may be to involve non-members in intra-party contests, but to do so in ways that make it most likely that the party can remobilize them in the general elections. This means getting them registered so that the party can keep on communicating with them. On the other hand, parties which are more focused on preserving traditional membership may restrict participation to those who are more than opportunistic affiliates. At the least, they may want to design contests so that the votes of long-term members count for more. For instance, they could use two-stage primaries, in which members pick the top two candidates, and all supporters are invited to participate in the run-off election between them.[10]

Such tradeoffs bring us back to the normative models outlined in the first chapter. Questions about inclusiveness and access to party decision-making are not just questions about electoral strategies. They are also, and perhaps above all, questions about the sources of party legitimacy, and the role (if any) that party members play in conferring this. Whether and how instant members threaten party identity depends in part on whether the party views itself as representing a cleavage group, club-defined interests, or the entire potential electorate. In the former cases, the charge against instant members is that they may not understand or share predefined group interests, and that they are therefore likely to support candidates who do not represent the party's "true" interest. In the latter case, the only reasonable objection to instant members and non-member primaries is that they enable infiltration by voters who might maliciously attempt to harm the parties' electoral chances. Put differently, whether it is appropriate for parties to offer highly inclusive participation benefits in order to encourage enlistment may depend on how they conceive the role of the traditional members—as stakeholders, fans, or group members.

NOTES

1. The FDP held three such ballots between 1995 and 2011, the first of which was held before the mechanism was inserted into the party statutes. The first two were called by the national party leadership; the third was triggered by a membership petition.
2. See section below for a discussion of how turnout has been calculated for internal ballots.
3. The ballots tallied in this figure and in other tables and figures in this chapter include all national-level party-wide ballots for which the author could find records, looking only at parties represented in national legislatures. Sources include party web pages, newspaper articles, and scholarly articles, as detailed in the appendix to this chapter. As of the writing of this book there were no comprehensive repositories containing standardized historical data on intra-party elections in all these countries. Because of this, participation data are incomplete, and the data set may be missing a few ballots. However, there is no reason to suspect any systematic bias in the missing data.
4. A scandal that prompted front-runner Dominique Strauss-Kahn to withdraw from the intra-party contest shortly before candidate nominations closed.
5. Minors who would be eligible to vote by the Presidential election, foreign members of the PS, and French citizens living abroad needed to register approximately three months in advance. This could be done on-line.
6. Due to French laws covering the storage of political information, the party could retain contact information after the ballot only for the supporters who separately signed up to receive party communications.
7. Either from turnout rates reported by the party, or if these were unavailable, by dividing the number of ballots cast by party membership numbers from the year in which the contest was held.
8. The denominator for Voter Turnout is the number of votes the party received in a national election held the same year as the party's internal contest, or in the closest prior year. For presidential elections this is party vote share in the presidential election (first round, if there is a run-off); for parliamentary systems this is vote share in elections to the lower house of the national legislature.
9. One study which uses annual data to study European Social Democratic parties concluded that opportunities for membership voting did not affect recruiting success (Scholte 2011). However, the short-term effects of membership ballots may be difficult to discern in annual membership numbers. One of the rare studies based on monthly affiliation figures comes from Brazil, a country outside the parameters of this book. This study found that such party registration peaked in the year prior to an election, and that growth was strongest in municipalities with contested party primaries (Speck 2013, 2014). This kind of pattern is what we would expect if mobilization for intra-party contests encourages partisan enlistment.
10. The Italian Democratic Party used a variant of this system in leadership elections in 2009 and 2013. The first round of voting was open to members only, whereas the second round was open to all supporters.

TABLE A8.1 *Leadership and policy ballots, 1990–2012: turnout*

Country	Year	Party	Office	Member Turnout %*	Voter Turnout %*
Australia	1990	Australian Democrats	Party leader	Missing	Missing
Australia	1991	Australian Democrats	Party leader	Missing	Missing
Australia	1993	Australian Democrats	Party leader	Missing	Missing
Australia	1997	Australian Democrats	Party leader	Missing	Missing
Australia	2001	Australian Democrats	Party leader	83.0	0.3
Australia	2002	Australian Democrats	Party leader	50.0	Missing
Australia	2004	Australian Democrats	Party leader	Missing	Missing
Belgium	1990	PRL	Party leader	16.6	1.3
Belgium	1992	PRL	Party leader	19.5	1.4
Belgium	1993	CVP	Party leader	36.0	4.3
Belgium	1993	SP	Referendum	46.4	5.0
Belgium	1993	VLD	Party leader	43.8	4.9
Belgium	1994	PSC	Party leader	45.5	3.5
Belgium	1995	PRL	Party leader	14.5	0.8
Belgium	1995	VLD	Party leader	34.7	3.5
Belgium	1996	CVP	Party leader	34.1	3.8
Belgium	1996	PSC	Party leader	63.9	4.7
Belgium	1996	PSC	Referendum	48.3	3.5
Belgium	1997	PRL	Party leader	40.0	2.3
Belgium	1997	SP	Party leader	63.1	6.3
Belgium	1997	VLD	Party leader	40.6	4.0
Belgium	1998	PSC	Party leader	44.9	2.9
Belgium	1999	CVP	Party leader	20.7	2.5
Belgium	1999	PRL	Party leader	37.0	2.3
Belgium	1999	PS	Party leader	38.7	6.4
Belgium	1999	SP	Party leader	48.9	6.1
Belgium	1999	VLD	Party leader	26.7	2.3
Belgium	2000	VU	Party leader	59.0	2.6
Belgium	2001	SP.A	Party leader	56.4	6.1
Belgium	2001	VLD	Party leader	32.8	2.8
Belgium	2002	CD&V	Party leader	24.8	2.5
Belgium	2002	PSC	Referendum	25.0	1.3
Belgium	2003	CD&V	Party leader	23.1	2.3
Belgium	2003	CDH	Party leader	67.6	3.7
Belgium	2003	MR	Party leader	31.0	1.4
Belgium	2003	PS	Party leader	35.0	3.4
Belgium	2003	SP.A	Party leader	48.5	3.0
Belgium	2004	CD&V	Party leader	50.6	4.8
Belgium	2004	MR	Party leader	50.7	2.0
Belgium	2004	SPIRIT	Party leader	60.0	0.0

(Continued)

TABLE A8.1 *(Continued)*

Country	Year	Party	Office	Member Turnout %*	Voter Turnout %*
Belgium	2004	VLD	Party leader	37.3	2.7
Belgium	2005	SP.A	Party leader	48.6	0.0
Belgium	2007	PS	Party president	30.3	3.3
Belgium	2007	SP.A	Party president	44.6	3.8
Belgium	2007	Spirit	Party leader	32.3	0.3
Belgium	2008	CD&V	Party chair	Missing	1.7
Belgium	2008	MR	Party leader	26.5	1.2
Belgium	2008	Open VLD	Party leader	23.6	2.0
Belgium	2009	CDH	Party leader	Missing	2.3
Belgium	2009	Open VLD	Party leader	Missing	2.7
Belgium	2010	CD&V	Party chair	Missing	3.9
Belgium	2011	MR	Party leader	53.0	3.0
Canada	1995	NDP	Party leader	28.0	2.4
Canada	1997	Bloc Quebeçois	Party leader	45.0	3.5
Canada	1998	Progressive Conservatives	Party leader	52.0	2.0
Canada	2000	Alliance	Party leader	60.0	3.7
Canada	2002	Canadian Alliance	Party leader	71.0	2.7
Canada	2003	Liberals	Party leader	25.0	2.5
Canada	2003	NDP	Party leader	54.0	4.1
Canada	2004	Conservatives	Party leader	Missing	2.4
Canada	2006	Greens	Party leader	Missing	0.5
Canada	2012	NDP	Party leader	50.7	1.4
Denmark	2005	SocDems	Party leader	88.0	5.2
Denmark	2005	Socialist Peoples Party	Party leader	78.6	3.0
Finland	2011	Green League	Party leader	65.0	2.0
France	1995	PS	Presidential nominee	53.3	0.6
France	1998	RPR	Party president	81.5	1.1
France	1999	RPR	Party president	63.1	0.9
France	2003	PS	Party leader	77.0	1.6
France	2004	PS	Consultative plebiscite	80.0	1.6
France	2006	PS	Presidential nominee	81.5	3.9
France	2007	UMP	Presidential nominee	69.1	2.0
France	2011	L'europe Ecologiste Verts	Presidential nominee	77.3	4.5
France	2011	PS	Presidential nominee	14300.8	44.4
France	2012	UMP	Party leader	58.9	1.8
Germany	1993	SPD	Party leader	56.7	3.0
Germany	1995	FDP	Referendum: wire tapping	43.1	2.2

Germany	1997	FDP	Referendum: conscription	19.5	Missing
Germany	2003	B90/Greens	Referendum: separation of party & elected office	56.6	0.6
Germany	2007	PDS die Linke	Merger with WASG	82.6	1.2
Germany	2007	WASG	Merger with PDS die Linke	57.0	Missing
Germany	2011	FDP	Referendum: Euro insurance fund	31.6	0.3
Germany	2012	Greens	Top candidates	61.7	Missing
Greece	2007	PASOK	Party leader	79.0	28.2
Greece	2009	New Democracy	Party leader	223.4	26.1
Greece	2012	PASOK	Party leader	Missing	31.8
Ireland	2002	Labour	Party leader	88.1	2.0
Ireland	2007	Greens	Party leader	60.0	0.8
Ireland	2011	Greens	Party leader	71.6	1.3
Italy	2005	The Union	Party leader	n.a.	22.7
Italy	2007	Democratic Party	Secretary	n.a.	17.9
Italy	2009	Democratic Party	Secretary	56.4	3.8
Italy	2012	Center-Left Coalition	Secretary	n.a.	Missing
Netherlands	2002	CDA	Party chair	"Over 50%"	2.2
Netherlands	2002	PvdA	List leader	54.0	2.2
Netherlands	2003	VVD	Party chair	13.5	0.4
Netherlands	2005	PvdA	Party chair	34.8	0.8
Netherlands	2006	D66	List leader	47.0	2.0
Netherlands	2006	VVD	List leader	74.0	2.0
Netherlands	2012	CDA	Party leader and list leader	54.9	Missing
Netherlands	2012	PvdA	Party chair	68.6	2.0
New Zealand	1995	Greens	Party leader	Missing	Missing
Portugal	1999	PS	General secretary	65.0	3.1
Portugal	2001	PS	General secretary	43.0	2.2
Portugal	2002	PS	General secretary	15.0	0.7
Portugal	2004	PS	General secretary	48.0	1.8
Portugal	2005	CDS-PP	General secretary	14.3	1.2
Portugal	2006	PS	General secretary	27.0	1.0
Portugal	2006	PSD	General secretary	37.2	1.2
Portugal	2007	CDS-PP	General secretary	21.9	1.8
Portugal	2007	PSD	General secretary	60.7	1.3
Portugal	2008	CDS-PP	General secretary	31.4	0.4

(Continued)

TABLE A8.1 *(Continued)*

Country	Year	Party	Office	Member Turnout %*	Voter Turnout %*
Portugal	2008	PSD	General secretary	58.9	2.7
Portugal	2009	PS	General secretary	36.0	1.2
Portugal	2010	PSD	General secretary	66.2	3.1
Portugal	2011 (July)	PS	General secretary	34.3	2.3
Portugal	2011 (March)	PS	General secretary	87.5	1.8
Spain	1998	PSOE	Top candidate	54.0	2.2
United Kingdom	1999	Liberal Democrats	Party leader	62.0	1.0
United Kingdom	2001	Conservative	Party leader	79.1	3.1
United Kingdom	2005	Conservative	Party leader	78.0	2.3
United Kingdom	2006	Liberal Democrats	Party leader	72.2	0.9
United Kingdom	2007	Liberal Democrats	Party leader	64.0	0.7
United Kingdom	2010	Labour	Party leader	72.0	1.4

TABLE A8.2 *Leadership and policy ballots, 1990–2012: sources*

Country	Year	Party	Source
Australia	1990	Australian Democrats	
Australia	1991	Australian Democrats	
Australia	1993	Australian Democrats	
Australia	1997	Australian Democrats	
Australia	2001	Australian Democrats	<http://australianpolitics.com/news/2001/01-04-07a.shtml>
Australia	2002	Australian Democrats	"Andrew Bartlett Elected Leader Of Australian Democrats" http://australianpolitics.com/news/2002/10/02-10-05.shtml
Australia	2004	Australian Democrats	
Belgium	1990	PRL	Wauters 2009
Belgium	1992	PRL	Wauters 2009
Belgium	1993	CVP	Wauters 2009
Belgium	1993	Socialist (SP)	Wauters 2009
Belgium	1993	VLD	Wauters 2009

Country	Year	Party	Source
Belgium	1994	PSC	Wauters 2009
Belgium	1995	PRL	Wauters 2009
Belgium	1995	VLD	Wauters 2009
Belgium	1996	CVP	Wauters 2009
Belgium	1996	PSC	Wauters 2009
Belgium	1996	PSC (Christ Dems)	Wauters 2009
Belgium	1997	PRL	Wauters 2009
Belgium	1997	SP	Wauters 2009
Belgium	1997	VLD	Wauters 2009
Belgium	1998	PSC	Wauters 2009
Belgium	1999	CVP	Wauters 2009
Belgium	1999	PRL	Wauters 2009
Belgium	1999	PS	Wauters 2009
Belgium	1999	SP	Wauters 2009
Belgium	1999	VLD	Wauters 2009
Belgium	2000	VU	Wauters 2009
Belgium	2001	SP.A	Wauters 2009
Belgium	2001	VLD	Wauters 2009
Belgium	2002	CD&V	Wauters 2009
Belgium	2002	PSC	Wauters 2009
Belgium	2003	CD&V	Wauters 2009
Belgium	2003	CDH	Wauters 2009
Belgium	2003	MR	Wauters 2009
Belgium	2003	PS	Wauters 2009
Belgium	2003	SP.A	Wauters 2009
Belgium	2004	CD&V	Wauters 2009
Belgium	2004	MR	Wauters 2009
Belgium	2004	SPIRIT	Wauters 2009
Belgium	2004	VLD	Wauters 2009
Belgium	2005	SP.A	Wauters 2009
Belgium	2007	PS	Wauters 2009
Belgium	2007	SP.A	Wauters 2009
Belgium	2007	Spirit	Wauters 2009
Belgium	2008	CD&V	<www.bpol.be/actuaArtikel.php?naam=200805171>
Belgium	2008	MR	<http://www.standaard.be/artikel/detail.aspx?artikelid=DMF19102008_083>
Belgium	2008	Open VLD	<http://www.hln.be/hln/nl/957/Belgie/article/detail/198849/2008/03/08/Bart-Somers-blijft-voorzitter-Open-Vld.dhtml>
Belgium	2009	CDH	<http://www.standaard.be/artikel/detail.aspx?artikelid=L52JJMCD>
Belgium	2009	Open VLD	<http://www.demorgen.be/dm/nl/5036/Wetstraat/article/detail/1038286/2009/12/05/Keulen-of-De-Croo-nieuwe-voorzitter-Open-Vld.dhtml>
Belgium	2010	CD&V	<http://www.standaard.be/artikel/detail.aspx?artikelid=DMF20101222_089>

(Continued)

TABLE A8.2 *(Continued)*

Country	Year	Party	Source
Belgium	2011	MR	<www.rtl.be/info/belgique/politique/771940/officialisation-de-l-election-de-charles-michel-a-la-tet-du-mr>
Canada	1995	NDP	Carty et al. 2000
Canada	1997	Bloc Quebecois	Kenig 2009b
Canada	1998	Progressive Conservatives	Carty et al. 2000
Canada	2000	Alliance	Ellis 2005
Canada	2002	Canadian Alliance	Cross 2004
Canada	2003	Liberals	Cross 2004
Canada	2003	NDP	Cross 2004
Canada	2004	Conservatives	<http://en.wikipedia.org/wiki/Conservative_Party_of_Canada_leadership_election,_2004>
Canada	2006	Greens	<http://en.wikipedia.org/wiki/Green_Party_of_Canada_leadership_election,_2006>
Canada	2012	NDP	Paul Mcleod, "Mulcair Wins NDP Leadership," *Chronicle Herald,* Mar. 24 2012, http://thechronicleherald.ca/canada/77153-mulcair-wins-ndp-leadership>. No date, "New Democratic Party leadership election, 2012," Wikipedia, <http://en.wikipedia.org/wiki/New_Democratic_Party_leadership_election,_2012>
Denmark	2005	SocDems	Participant number estimated based on Pedersen 2006 for turnout and van Biezen et al. 2012 for membership
Denmark	2005	Socialist Peoples Party	<http://www.dr.dk/nyheder/htm/baggrund/tema2005/Villy%20blev%20valgt/31.htm>; personal communication, Karina Pedersen
Finland	2011	Green League	Personal communication, Vesa Koskimaa
France	1995	PS	<http://fr.wikipedia.org/wiki/Primaire_pr%C3%A9sidentielle_socialiste_de_1995>
France	1998	RPR	Vanessa Schneider, "Les Militants RPR plebiscent leur president," Dec. 12 1998, Liberation.fr <www.liberation.fr/evenement/0101265198-les-militants-rpr-plebiscitent-leur-president-candidat-unique-philippe-seguin-obtient-95-des-voix>, accessed Aug. 2008
France	1999	RPR	<www.liberation.fr/politiques/01013000980-presidence-du-rpr-ainsi-soit-elle-alliot-marie-l-emporte-avec-62-7-des-voix-devant-delevoye>

France	2003	PS	<http://www.france-politique.fr/chronologie-ps.htm>
France	2004	PS	Wagner 2008
France	2006	PS	<http://www.france-politique.fr/chronologie-ps.htm>
France	2007	UMP	<fr.wikipedia.org/wiki/primaires_pr%C3%A9sidentielles_de_1%27UMP_en_2007>
France	2011	L'europe Ecologiste Verts	<http://fr.wikipedia.org/wiki/Primaire_pr%C3%A9sidentielle_%C3%A9cologiste_de_2011>; <http://www.lefigaro.fr/politique/2011/06/06/01002-20110606ARTFIG00618-la-primaire-ecologiste-mode-d-emploi.php>
France	2011	PS	<http://www.france-politique.fr/chronologie-ps.htm>
France	2012	UMP	"La Commission proclame la victoire a Cope," <http://www.lefigaro.fr/politique/2012/11/16/01002-20121116LIVWWW00511-ump-cope-fillon.php>
Germany	1993	SPD	Thörmer and Einemann 2007
Germany	1995	FDP	<http://www.berliner-zeitung.de/archiv/fdp-mitglieder-fuer-lauschangriff—rechtspolitiker-schmidt-jortzig-als-nachfolger-benannt-justizministerin-tritt-zurueck,10810590,9053938.html>
Germany	1997	FDP	<http://www.neues-deutschland.de/artikel/686928.fdp-niederlage-fuer-gegner.html>
Germany	2003	B90/Greens	<http://www.faz.net/aktuell/politik/mitgliederbefragung-gruene-basis-hebt-trennung-von-amt-und-mandat-auf-1101796.html>
Germany	2007	PDS die Linke	<http://archiv2007.sozialisten.de/sozialisten/parteibildung/urabstimmung/pdf/ergebnis_urabstimmung_070519.pdf>
Germany	2007	WASG	<http://www.linksueberholen.de/linkewasgarchiv20052007/html/urabstimmung_ii.html>
Germany	2011	FDP	<http://www.zeit.de/politik/deutschland/2011-12/roesler-fdp-kommentar>
Germany	2012	Greens	<http://www.gruene.de/partei/urwahl/katrin-goering-eckardt-und-juergen-trittin-gewinnen-die-urwahl.html>
Greece	2007	PASOK	<http://en.wikipedia.org/wiki/Panhellenic_Socialist_Movement_leadership_election,_2007>

(Continued)

TABLE A8.2 *(Continued)*

Country	Year	Party	Source
Greece	2009	New Democracy	<http://en.wikipedia.org/wiki/New_Democracy_leadership_election,_2009>
Greece	2012	PASOK	"Venizelos to Tender Resignation," Marketall, Mar. 19 2012, <http://www.marketall.eu/economy-and-politics/3001-venizelos-to-tender-his-resignation-to-lead-pasok-party-to-upcoming-elections>; "Wanna Vote for New PASOK Leader? All You Need is Your ID and 2 Euro," Keep Talking Greece, Mar. 5 2012, <http://www.keeptalkinggreece.com/2012/03/05/wanna-vote-for-new-pasok-leader-all-you-need-is-your-id-and-e2>
Ireland	2002	Labour	Kevin Rafter, "Leadership Changes in Fine Gael and the Labour Party, 2002," *Irish Political Studies,* 18 (2002): 108–19
Ireland	2007	Greens	<http://www.rte.ie/news/2007/0717/greens.html>
Ireland	2011	Greens	<http://www.thejournal.ie/former-minister-eamon-ryan-elected-new-green-party-leader-144515-May2011>
Italy	2005	The Union	<http://en.wikipedia.org/wiki/The_Union_(political_coalition)#Primary_elections>
Italy	2007	Democratic Party	Pasquino 2009
Italy	2009	Democratic Party	<http://it.wikipedia.org/wiki/Elezioni_primarie_del_Partito_Democratico_(Italia)_del_2009>
Italy	2012	Center-Left Coalition	<www.primarieitaliabenecomune.it>
Netherlands	2002	CDA	Voerman 2006
Netherlands	2002	PvdA	Voerman 2006
Netherlands	2003	VVD	Voerman 2006
Netherlands	2005	PvdA	Voerman 2006
Netherlands	2006	D66	<http://nl.wikipedia.org/wiki/D66-lijsttrekkersreferendum_2006>
Netherlands	2006	VVD	<en.wikinews.org/wiki.Rutte_elected_leader_of_the_VVD>, accessed Aug. 2011
Netherlands	2012	CDA	<http://www.nrc.nl/nieuws/2012/05/18/sybrand-van-haersma-buma-wordt-de-lijsttrekker-van-het-cda>

Netherlands	2012	PvdA	<http://nl.wikipedia.org/wiki/Verkiezing_Partijleider_PvdA_2012>, "Verkiezing partijleider PvdA 2012"
New Zealand	1995	Greens	
Portugal	1999	PS	Lisi 2010
Portugal	2001	PS	Lisi 2010
Portugal	2002	PS	Lisi 2010
Portugal	2004	PS	Lisi 2010
Portugal	2005	CDS-PP	Lisi 2010
Portugal	2006	PS	Lisi 2010
Portugal	2006	PSD	Lisi 2010
Portugal	2007	CDS-PP	Lisi 2010
Portugal	2007	PSD	Lisi 2010
Portugal	2008	CDS-PP	Lisi 2010
Portugal	2008	PSD	Lisi 2010
Portugal	2009	PS	Lisi 2010
Portugal	2010	PSD	Lisi 2010
Portugal	2011 July	PS	<http://www.rtp.pt/noticias/index.php?article=463908&tm=9&layout=121&visual=49>
Portugal	2011 Mar.	PS	<http://www.agenciafinanceira.iol.pt/politica/socrates-directas-ps-eleicoes-congresso-tvi24/1242454-4072.html>
Spain	1998	PSOE	<http://www.lanacion.com.ar/94681-sorpresivo-triunfo-de-borrell-en-las-primarias-del-psoe>
UK	1999	Liberal Democrats	<www.cix.co.uk/-rosenstiel/elections/all-member/htm>
UK	2001	Conservative	<www.parliament.uk/documents/commons/lib/research/briefings/snpc-01366.pdf>
UK	2005	Conservative	<www.parliament.uk/documents/commons/lib/research/briefings/snpc-01366.pdf>
UK	2006	Liberal Democrats	<wikipedia.org/wiki/Liberal_Democrats_leadership_election_2006>
UK	2007	Liberal Democrats	<http://en.wikipedia.org/wiki/Liberal_Democrats_leadership_election,_2007>
UK	2010	Labour	<http://www.bbc.co.uk/news/uk-politics-11412031>

*See Table 8.5 and text for explanations of Member Turnout and Voter Turnout.

9

The Consequences of Organizational Change

This book has examined the changing relations between political parties and their members, seeking to understand why an overall drop in party enrollment has coincided with a widespread increase in the rights enjoyed by individual members. The developments described in this book have shed light on this puzzle. They depict a pattern of organizational evolution that has come almost full circle, with a more individualistic model of party activity replacing the group-based and subscriber-democracy templates first popularized by parties in the late nineteenth and early twentieth centuries. The new partisan models define organizational aims in terms of accountability to electoral markets. They prioritize the mobilization of individuals, not of self-identified social groups. In this new environment, parties are experimenting with ways to boost loyalty and partisan interest among key supporters, including, but not limited to, traditional party members. These initiatives may create new conflicts within party organizations, not least because the new forms of affiliation are often layered on top of traditional membership structures.

The most prominent of the new affiliation options are the light members and news audience members introduced in Chapter 2. Both types of affiliates are potentially more numerous than traditional party members, but they are likely to have much looser partisan ties. In cultivating an audience to follow party newsletters, blogs, and Facebook postings, parties are returning to their much earlier role of providing news designed to shape opinions and strengthen a political community. In trying to activate followers to share party news with their friends, they are seeking to mobilize a new generation of digital ambassadors, adding electronic outreach to more traditional forms of community presence.

Whether these digital opportunities represent deliberate strategies or are merely adopted in imitation of social trends, such efforts may precipitate a wider shift in how parties approach grassroots support. Parties adopting this new perspective would be more interested in electoral outcomes than in maintaining traditional structures. In practical terms, this means that they would be more interested in what their active supporters do than in whether or not they hold party membership. According to this more functional orientation, traditional members are not the only source of help for party efforts. Instead, parties should also seek to engage non-member affiliates to donate to the party, to volunteer, and to get involved in party debates. Those who affiliate provide parties with valuable new data about their supporters, information which parties can potentially use for multiple purposes, particularly in technologically sophisticated campaigns. When parties create new affiliation options, they reach out to supporters who may not be seeking long-term organizational commitments, but who are nevertheless interested in connecting with a party, and possibly in shaping its future. Parties' recent efforts in this direction complement other changes which may increase the supply of traditional members by reducing the procedural costs of joining. Most importantly, membership in many parties is now a commodity that can be purchased on-line from the national party, not one that can only be obtained by connecting with a local party branch.

A second and related area of organizational change is the expanding use of intra-party ballots for making important party decisions. As the figures in Chapter 8 showed, the number of parties using internal ballots for leadership and party decisions has grown rapidly since the 1990s. These changes in party practices seem to have twin aims: making parties more popular by burnishing their democratic (or sometimes populist) credentials, and giving supporters more incentives to get active within their preferred party.

Usage numbers alone are not the only indicator of this revolution; the mere fact that a party debates whether to adopt such a procedure may signal underlying changes in prevailing understandings about how, and whom, parties represent. One way to understand the import of these changes is by returning to the second chapter's discussion of how party members fit into parties' narratives of representation, and its distinctions between party members as fans, adherents, community members, or stakeholders. These labels emphasized that only certain types of parties have regarded party members as key sources of legitimacy for party policies or personnel. Others have enrolled members, but have not assigned them central roles as guarantors of the quality of the party's political product. For instance, in some parties leaders or ideologies have defined and justified the party message. In them, members have been assigned the role of fans or even adherents: supporters may enroll in the party and work on its behalf because they like its message, but its leaders are not accountable to them and the members are not arbiters of party policy. Cleavage parties traditionally ascribed a larger role to members in defining aims or selecting leaders, but their input was usually indirect and channeled into representative structures. Their influence was limited by non-negotiable group aims. In any of these parties, giving members a greater *direct* say in party decisions is not a minor procedural switch: it represents a revised understanding of the members' role in establishing party legitimacy. For cleavage parties and for subscriber democracy parties, including *non*-members in party decisions represents an even greater change, because it overturns long-held assumptions about who should have the last word in defining party aims and values.

These organizational changes have emerged as established parties try to hold onto shrinking support bases, and as new parties have been pushing to enter already crowded political markets. In an era of austerity and policy convergence, parties have limited scope to win votes by promising to fund expensive new programs, so they must seek other ways to attract vote-winning support. This may be one reason why parties of all types have shown increasing interest in making their internal structures part of their electoral appeal, for instance by highlighting how their structures keep party leaders in touch with popular concerns. In adopting these approaches, parties move towards the ethos of political market parties, touting practices which keep them attentive to the wide swathes of voters who are their potential customers.

To understand the implications of these changes, it is important to bear in mind the main argument of the first part of this book, that there was never a universal golden age of mass membership parties. The idea of membership-based organizing found growing support among democratic parties in the twentieth century, but efforts to implement this idea often lagged far behind party organizational aspirations. Some parties did enroll relatively large numbers of supporters. However, even in them only a small percentage of members were active partisan participants. This buffers the impact of declining membership numbers, particularly for parties that can succeed in using multi-speed organizational approaches to mobilize non-traditional affiliates. Such supporters could undertake many of the jobs once ascribed to party members (donating, volunteering for campaigns, transmitting party messages into local communities). Yet while resource substitution strategies could help some parties conduct successful campaigns, in the longer term their use could also revive questions about how democratic parties ought to function, and about how parties' internal processes should mesh with the constitutional structures of representative democracies.

MULTI-SPEED MEMBERSHIP AND PARTY CHANGE

The changes described in the preceding chapters are not monolithic, nor do they have an undifferentiated impact. Their importance for specific parties depends to some extent on what preceded them. As Panebianco (1988) and others have argued, party origins matter, not least because organizational changes tend to be incremental. New organizational modes are more likely

Consequences of Organizational Change 209

to be layered on top of old ones rather than to immediately displace them. Because of this, their effects should be gradual, not dramatic. Nevertheless, it is possible to make some general predictions about where the impact of these changes is most likely to be felt: in reshaping the composition of active partisans, in redistributing influence within parties, and in altering incentives for party cohesion.

Patterns of Partisan Participation and Mobilization

Membership-based political parties are organizations that foster participatory linkage, encouraging participation by those who might otherwise be left out of the political process (Lawson 1980). Partly through their efforts to recruit and mobilize their supporters, some parties have helped to offset socio-economic disparities in civic participation (on donating, see Ponce and Scarrow 2011; on voting, see Verba et al. 1978: 115–17). One question to ask about the new, more individualistic, types of party affiliation is whether they are likely to be similarly effective in encouraging political participation and communication, including by those whose economic and social resources make them less disposed to participate in civic life (Rogers 2005: 605–6). Another question concerns the sheer volume of participation: can new modes of partisan affiliation effectively encourage previously passive supporters to more actively participate in the political realm, for instance by engaging in on-line political discussions?

When answering the latter question, it is important to start from realistic baselines. As Chapter 4 showed, in most countries parties have never enrolled more than about 5–10 percent of eligible voters. And as Chapter 5 showed, most traditional party members have had only loose ties with their local parties: fewer than half of the enrolled members report attending monthly party meetings or actively campaigning. Given these small numbers, new organizational approaches do not have to generate a great deal of extra activity to replicate previous levels of partisan engagement. They could reach these levels in many ways, including by mobilizing digital affiliates to join local campaign teams, or to regularly forward parties' electronic messages to their friends. It is quite plausible that parties which offer multiple affiliation opportunities could enroll at least 3 percent of their supporters as traditional members, while affiliating another 3 percent in other ways, ranging from cyber-militants to news audience members. Many of these might be digitally affiliated partisans who are largely passive within the organization, but who receive frequent digital messages from the party. Their organizational ties to the party might be weak, but this was also true of many traditional members in the hey-day of membership organizing.

What is different now is that parties can have frequent contact with even internally passive supporters, and can encourage them to share party messages. This expands party networks of potential opinion leaders. At election times, parties may be able to mobilize their usually inactive digital affiliates to provide financial support or to volunteer for local campaigns. Such mobilization could help parties to offset the decline in volunteer support and personal campaigning once provided by traditional members. In communities which never had large membership parties, or where members were largely passive except during campaigns, parties could approximate past levels of community engagement by activating a relatively modest number of digital affiliates.

What is less clear is whether a multi-speed affiliation approach could be as effective as traditional party structures in offsetting resource-based disparities in political participation. This is hard to test, in part because participation patterns are likely to be affected by other changes that are occurring at the same time, particularly the weakening of cleavage-based politics. On the one hand, it seems likely that affiliation strategies based on digital contacts could exacerbate resource-based participation disparities. Internet access has spread rapidly in high-income countries, mitigating some of the initial fears about the emerging digital divide (Cruz-Jesus et al. 2012; Norris 2003). Nevertheless, resource-linked access and usage differences remain, and less-educated citizens are less likely to take advantage of on-line participation opportunities (Bovens and Wille 2010; Schlozman et al. 2010). These differences suggest that parties' digital mobilization efforts might reinforce existing inequalities in partisan participation.

On the other hand, party options for digital affiliation and digital participation might reduce other types of inequalities in traditional party membership, including the under-representation of women, young people, and ethnic minorities (Acik 2013; Marien et al. 2010; Oser et al. 2013; Scarrow and Gezgor 2010). Members of these groups may find it more congenial to participate in on-line partisan activity than to visit local party meetings, especially if the latter have the reputation of being bastions of male activists from dominant ethnic groups. Many of the parties that have been promoting new digital affiliation options have explicitly done so in hopes of connecting with their younger supporters.

How likely is it that these organizational changes will also affect the ideological composition of the participant pool? This question is particularly pertinent given the trend towards granting traditional members, and sometimes other affiliates, more say over party decisions. Despite the plausibility of John May's "Special Law of Curvilinear Disparity" (1973), which predicts that active party members will be more ideologically extreme than party office-holders or non-member supporters, past studies of parties in parliamentary democracies have found little evidence of this type of ideological distribution (Kitschelt 1989; Norris 1995; Scarrow and Gezgor 2010). These studies call into question May's premise that only ideological extremists would find membership benefits attractive enough to offset the costs of joining and being active. Yet even if May were right, sophisticated ideological extremists might still be pragmatic enough to take account of anticipated electoral effects when selecting candidates. Though there is not yet much evidence about the ideological impact of new decisions procedures, a few studies of British politics suggest that traditional members may make centrist decisions when they are included in party decisions about candidate selection and leadership selection (Mikulska and Scarrow 2010; Quinn 2010). One possible reason is that intra-party ballots have generated high interest, meaning that it is not just the most passionate of party members who have been participating. As yet, there is not enough research to understand the likely consequence of rule changes in this area. However, as Chapter 8 made clear, future research in this area should avoid simple distinctions between "closed" and "open" procedures; instead, it should take account of the full range of access and inclusion rules, because these rules potentially shape the size and ideological composition of the party selectorate.

Intra-Party Dynamics: Accountability and Influence

At their heart, decisions about how to circumscribe the party *demos* are decisions about the distribution of influence, and about who holds ultimate authority in party affairs. Subscriber-democracy parties portray members as the basis of party legitimacy. Indeed, some of the strongest advocates of this view of party legitimacy have described democratically organized membership parties as the essential foundation of, and precondition for, political democracy (cf. Abendroth 1964). Of course, this is a disputed view. Others have argued that what matters for representative democracy is that there is competition between parties, thus giving voters clear choices. According to the latter view, the degree of democracy within the parties is secondary or even irrelevant.[1] Yet even among those who argue that democratic parties should practice internal democracy, there is no consensus about whether such democracy needs to be limited to formal members. If a party aspires to represent the entire electorate, rather than a well-defined segment of it, why should responsibility for party decisions be delegated to self-selected members, rather than to all party voters? In multi-speed parties, uncertainty about the normative source of authority—members or all supporters—has the potential to increase tensions between different types of affiliates.

This tension may be most evident in discussions about who should participate in intra-party ballots. If a major purpose of such ballots is to encourage supporters to enlist and stay enrolled, participation should be limited to long-term members. Such rules would emphasize the privileged role of committed party members as the chief stakeholders in the party. If, however, the priority is to use such ballots to bolster a party's political credibility and increase pre-election mobilization, there are good reasons to maximize ballot participation, whether by allowing registered non-members to participate, or by allowing new members to enroll and vote on the day of the party contest.

These decisions may be related to the important question of who wins and who loses when parties begin to make greater use of internal ballots. Some would describe the likely outcome as precisely what parties generally claim it to be: a shift of political influence from the center to the grassroots of the party, be that to all members or to all supporters. The German political scientist Klaus Detterbeck espoused this point of view when he argued that the surrender of powers to party members is the price that parties must pay if they want to retain members:

> In short, parties are facing a dilemma. One option is to accept the declining membership numbers and the corresponding drawbacks. They can attempt to compensate for this blood loss in other ways, for instance with more state resources. In return, the party leaders can wind up with more room to maneuver. The alternative is that they try to accommodate the expanded participation demands of politically-interested citizens, for instance by moving strongly in the direction of direct democracy or by giving delegate committees more effective control. They would thereby reduce the autonomy of party elites within bargaining networks. (2009: 84)[2]

From this perspective, insofar as the multi-speed party is accompanied by an increase in intra-party democracy (however the *demos* is defined), it is likely to represent a big shift in influence within the party, one that reduces the control of party elites.

There are two common counter-arguments to this view. The first is that so-called democratization of party decisions actually empowers party leaders at the cost of mid-level elites and activists within parties. The other is that such reforms tend to disempower *both* party leaders and activists, transferring control to an amorphous and potentially fickle party electorate. The first view has been expressed most clearly by advocates of the Cartel Party hypothesis, who decry "the apparent democratization of the party through the introduction of such devices as postal ballots or mass membership meetings at which large numbers of marginally committed members or supporters...can be expected to drown out the activists" (Katz and Mair 2009: 759). The second view is usually adopted by those who fear that highly accessible voting procedures ("instant members," etc.) will empower those who do not share a long-term commitment to party success or to established party values. This is viewed as harmful to the democratic process, because by undermining party cohesion and identity, it is likely to produce parties that are less able to implement their goals even if they do win elections (Hazan and Rahat 2010; Cross and Blais 2012).

In addition to the effects of intra-party ballots, it is likely that existing party factions and organized subgroups will lose influence if parties move away from narratives that portray representation as the balancing of group interests. In parties with corporate membership, and in those with internal representation of group interests (women's sections, youth organizations, trade unions), parties had depicted themselves as responsive to, and representative of, distinct social interests. In moving towards models in which the *ultima ratio* is provided by individual affiliates—including instant members and light members—or by the entire electorate, parties are moving away from a more pluralist vision of electoral competition as a contest between organized groups and their representatives. Instead, they have embraced the idea of parties as representatives of individual interests. Even when parties recognize subgroup interests, they may be more likely to do so in ways which emphasize individual traits rather than group action. For instance, they may seek to boost female candidacies by adopting "zippered" candidate lists, not by giving women's sections greater roles in selecting or vetting female candidates. The influence of other internal factions is also likely to wane, except for those that prove to be adept in campaigning for intra-party ballots. These changes could exacerbate conflicts among party leaders, who must now publicly compete for the votes of individual members rather than just conducting backroom negotiations with leaders of regional parties or party subgroups.

Party Cohesiveness

These same forces may also alter relations between party leaders, legislators, and legislative candidates. On the one hand, the new affiliation options potentially strengthen central party organizations by building up national party networks. This continues a trend towards creating stronger direct links between traditional members and central parties, a development that has been evident ever since parties began compiling central databases of party members. Most national parties, and some individual national party leaders, now can communicate directly with national networks of party members, friends, and followers. Centralized communications may produce stronger ties between individual party supporters and national political figures, but they potentially make it less likely that supporters will develop personal ties with local legislators and with local party organizers.

To the extent that central parties control the organizational resources that help candidates to get elected or re-elected, these shifts increase incentives for individual politicians to toe the party line (cf. Tavits 2013: chs 4 and 5).

On the other hand, the new organizing style can produce tensions that work in the opposite direction, potentially undermining party unity. The most important of these are changes which open up the procedures for selecting party candidates and party leaders. Using public competitions to decide party affairs brings intra-party conflicts out of backrooms and party conferences, into a much harsher media glare. To work effectively as demonstrations of democratic openness, such contests must offer real choices, and should include an airing of differences. Opening up party debates may make a party look more democratic, but hard-fought leadership contests run the risk of providing ammunition for a party's electoral competitors. They also can increase the autonomy of individual politicians by encouraging contestants in party ballots to construct personal support organizations, and to do their own fundraising (see Scarrow 2013).

Finally, to the extent that new organizational models are focused on building national digital networks, they may encourage parties to neglect their local-level organizations. Multi-speed organizing strategies do not *necessarily* erode local organizational networks. Indeed, it is possible to organize them in ways that simultaneously strengthen local parties (for instance, by using national party websites to help identify would-be volunteers for local campaigns). However, to the extent that new affiliation modes remain focused on national party brands and the personalities of national leaders, they could contribute to a vertical decoupling of partisan mobilizing.

MULTI-SPEED MEMBERSHIP PARTIES AND REPRESENTATIVE DEMOCRACIES

Multi-speed structures have emerged as an outgrowth of parties' efforts to connect with citizens who are turning their backs on traditional modes of partisanship. Ironically, some of the obstacles to the full-fledged emergence of multi-speed membership parties are laws that define and protect party roles in representative democracies. These laws have become more complex in the past half-century, in part because the spread of public subsidies for political parties created new reasons to codify what a party is. In addition, some key justifications for giving parties public subsidies—arguments about parties performing vital public functions—have also been used to justify the increasing regulation of parties' internal affairs. In this view, tax-payer-supported parties should be democratically accountable, including by having democratic and transparent internal structures. As a result, some countries have written party laws and election laws that define parties in terms of the ideal of subscriber-democracy parties (van Biezen and Borz 2012). For instance, party registration rules may require parties to have a minimum number of individual members. Rules for distributing party subsidies may be tied to the number of dues-paying members, or may require parties which receive subsidies to give certain rights to party members. Some of these rules could potentially limit the development of multi-speed parties because they legally reinforce the dominant status of traditional members. At the least, where they exist they give parties strong grounds for continuing to invest in traditional membership, whatever other structures also develop.

Regardless of how parties define their *demos*, parties' newfound interest in securing intra-party mandates for important decisions is likely to affect the practice of politics in parliamentary democracies. First, using ballots to settle internal disputes over leadership and policy is likely to shorten the time-frame for policy invention and implementation. Especially when cleavage-based parties adopt intra-party ballots, they are moving away from the idea that party decisions are motivated by long-term commitments to party platforms or ideologies. Intra-party democracy provides immediate legitimacy for party leadership choices, or for decisions about specific policies, but it also implies that alternative decisions would be equally valid, as long as they were endorsed by an intra-party ballot. This puts leaders in a potentially weak political position once they are elected. This can be a particular problem during economic or other crises, when there are no painless solutions. Even if party rules do not provide for deselection of a sitting leader, leaders selected by an intra-party ballot will find it more difficult to bolster their authority by portraying themselves as the guardian of the party's underlying aims—because it is the supporters who are empowered to define these aims. If intra-party responsiveness winds up stifling policy innovation, parties' internal democratization potentially has the longer-term effect of increasing popular dissatisfaction with existing parties (Kitschelt 2000: 142).

A second consequence of the move towards intra-party democracy is that such contests may reduce party loyalty, because they may dilute the support of those who backed losing internal candidates. In addition, electoral volatility may increase as internal competition becomes more personalized, especially if parties become more identified with particular leaders than with long-term party aims. Moreover, politicians with personal followings and personal resources may be more likely to defect after an internal loss, either by forming new parties or by switching between existing ones. Thus, while intra-party ballots may temporarily boost partisan participation, and even party membership, parties face a longer-term challenge of reinforcing the partisan convictions of these newfound activists, so that they are not just supporters of a particular candidate.

Political market parties define their primary loyalty to the voters at large, rather than to their members or to a specific ideology or group. This raises a question of who should be allowed to participate within their decision-making processes. The examples in Chapter 8 clearly showed that parties have acted like lightly regulated private associations when it comes to setting participation rules for their internal elections; in this area they have not seemed to face the same constraints as public utilities (van Biezen 2004). Party participation rules have varied widely even within a single country, and have varied over time within a single party. Furthermore, some parties have felt free to include as decision-makers those who are ineligible to vote in the general election (primarily: resident foreigners and minors, or corporate entities). Such expansive decisions may become less common if parties come to understand their contests as vehicles for competition among individual voters, rather than as arenas for contending ideologies or group interests.

These possibilities are a reminder that the impact of changes in parties' internal structures may be felt far beyond the boundaries of the individual parties. They have the potential to reshape established practices of representative democracy. Yet departures from tradition are not necessarily a bad thing. One way of describing these changes would be to interpret them as signs of parties' increasing responsiveness to public concerns. Parties are reacting to citizens' impatience with politics-as-usual by giving them new ways to connect with politics. Whether these reforms can inspire increased partisan activism has yet to be seen, but it would be foolish to lightly dismiss these adaptations as signs of decline rather than signs of organizational vitality. Indeed, it may be archaic to insist that the only right way to organize politics is through representation by subscriber-democracy parties, in which leaders are accountable to a small group of members rather than to the wider party electorate.

That said, the evidence presented in this book has shown that traditional party membership is far from obsolete. In many contemporary parties, memberships remain useful reservoirs of volunteers, opinion leaders, candidates, and donors. Because of this, competitive parties have meaningful incentives to recruit them. Parties' recognition of the utility of enrolled members helps to explain one of the puzzles examined in this book, the seemingly paradoxical increase in individual party members' political rights at the same time that overall memberships are shrinking. Yet evidence presented in the preceding chapters has also shown that parties are increasingly offering their supporters other channels of partisan engagement and communication that can complement, or substitute for, traditional party membership. Parties' efforts to expand affiliation options are likely to further erode the distinctions between various types of partisan participants.

Whether, and in which realms, parties' multi-faceted recruiting efforts will succeed, are separate questions. At the least, evidence presented here suggests that members and potential members still respond to the enrollment rewards that parties can offer, particularly to the political opportunities. Parties' roles in government make their voluntary organizations uniquely attractive organizations for those who desire to make a difference in politics. Even citizens with an anti-politics leaning often form organizations that put up candidates and therefore function as anti-government *parties*, not merely as anti-government *movements*. Parties can offer their supporters unique opportunities for ongoing political engagement. The recurring electoral cycle also gives parties frequent chances to strengthen various types of bonds with supporters, who may be motivated to sign up for newsletters or give a donation or become a member as a result of the positive and negative rhetoric of high-profile campaigns.

Such developments suggest several lessons for those who are trying to track the evolution of parties' organizational resources and internal power structures. First, we should use dynamic models of party activism, studying supporters over time as they move between multiple and overlapping circles of activity, and studying party efforts to expand specific spheres. Second, researchers may profit from viewing party support activity as a functional output, a product that can be increased or reduced by various organizational arrangements, rather than using traditional membership numbers as the primary indicator of partisan activism. This means looking not only at the activities of dues-paying members, but also at how parties engage non-member supporters in partisan activities. Using more differentiated frameworks for understanding partisan activism should make it easier to identify important changes in membership-based political parties. It also should aid comparisons between active party supporters across regimes and parties which have used different models of partisan mobilization, including those not based on formalized membership.

Employing frameworks that encompass party members alongside other active supporters means abandoning exaggerated notions of the past dominance of membership-based party organizing. It also means giving more attention to the multiple ways that democratic parties can use, and are using, organization and affiliation to motivate citizens' political engagement across multiple civic arenas. These perspectives switch the focus away from laments for the passing of an era of party-structured politics, towards more nuanced assessments of the ways that parties' organizational efforts affect political participation and electoral outcomes. Recognizing the multiple meanings of party membership, and the many alternative forms of party affiliation, will facilitate truly comparative studies of party organization and partisan participation, ones which cross temporal and institutional boundaries. In short, party scholars as well as party organizers may have much to gain by "going" beyond party members.

NOTES

1. Perhaps most famously E. E. Schattschneider, who argued that "Democracy is not to be found *in* the parties but *between* the parties" (1942: 60).
2. Author's translation.

References

Abendroth, Wolfgang. 1964. "Innerparteiliche- und innerverbandliche Demokratie als Voraussetzung der politischen Demokratie." *Politische Vierteljahresschrift*, 5: 308–38.
Aberg, Martin. 2011. *Swedish and German Liberalism: From Factions to Parties, 1860–1920*. Lund: Nordic Academic Press.
Acik, Necla. 2013. "Reducing the Participation Gap in Civic Engagement: Political Consumerism in Europe." *European Sociological Review*, 29(6): 1309–22.
Aldrich, John. 1995. *Why Parties?* Chicago: Chicago University Press.
Aldrich, John. 2011. *Why Parties? A Second Look*. Chicago: Chicago University Press.
Allardt, Erik, and Pertti Pesonen. 1960. "Citizen Participation in Political Life: Finland." *International Social Science Journal*, 12(1): 27–39.
Allern, Elin Haugsgjerd. 2010. *Political Parties and Interest Groups in Norway*. Colchester: ECPR Press.
Allern, Elin Haugsgjerd. 2012. "Appointments to Public Administration in Norway: No Room for Political Parties." In Petr Kopecký, Peter Mair, and Maria Spirova (eds), *Party Patronage and Party Government in European Democracies*. Oxford: Oxford University Press, 272–93.
Amr, Dima, and Rainer Lisowski. 2001. "Political Finance in the Old Dominions (Australia and Canada)." In Karl-Heinz Nassmacher (ed.), *Foundations for Democracy*. Baden-Baden: Nomos Verlag, 53–72.
Andeweg, Rudy, and Galen A. Irwin. 1993. *Dutch Government and Politics*. Basingstoke: Macmillan.
Banti, Alberto Mario. 2000. "Public Opinion and Associations in Nineteenth-Century Italy." In Nancy Bermeo and Philip Nord (eds), *Civil Society Before Democracy*. Princeton: Princeton University Press, 43–59.
Barnes, Samuel, Max Kaase, and Klaus Allerbeck. 1979. *Political Action: Mass Participation in Five Western Democracies*. Beverly Hills, CA: Sage.
Bartolini, Stefano. 1983. "The Membership of Mass Parties: The Social Democratic Experience, 1889–1978." In Hans Daalder and Peter Mair (eds), *Western European Party Systems: Continuity and Change*. London: Sage Publications, 177–220.
Bartolini, Stefano. 2000. *The Political Mobilization of the European Left, 1860–1980*. Cambridge: Cambridge University Press.
Bermeo, Nancy, and Philip Nord, eds. 2000. *Civil Society Before Democracy*. Princeton: Princeton University Press.
Bille, Lars. 2001. "Democratizing a Democratic Procedure: Myth or Reality?" *Party Politics*, 7(3): 363–80.
Billordo, Libia. 2003. "Party Membership in France: Measures and Data-Collection." *French Politics*, 1(1): 137–51.

Black, Lawrence. 2008. "The Lost World of Young Conservatism." *Historical Journal*, 51(4): 991–1024.

Bonander, Frederik. 2009. *Party Membership and State Subsidies: A Comparative Study*. Örebro (Sweden): Örebro Studies in Political Science.

Bovens, Mark, and Anchrit Wille. 2010. "The Education Gap in Participation and its Political Consequences." *Acta Politica*, 45(4): 393–422.

Bruter, Michael, and Sarah Harrison. 2009. *The Future of our Democracies: Young Party Members in Europe*. New York: Palgrave Macmillan.

Bulmer-Thomas, Ivor. 1967, 2nd edn. *The Growth of the British Party System*, i. *1640–1923*. London: John Baker.

Burchell, Jon. 2001. "Evolving or Conforming? Assessing Organisational Reform within European Green Parties." *European Journal of Political Research*, 24(3): 113–34.

Carstairs, Andrew. 1980. *A Short History of Electoral Systems in Western Europe*. London: George Allen.

Carty, R. Kenneth. 1981. *Party and Parish Pump: Electoral Politics in Ireland*. Waterloo, Ontario: Wilfred Laurier University Press.

Carty, R. Kenneth, and Munroe Eagles. 1999. "Do Local Campaigns Matter? Campaign Spending, the Local Canvass and Party Support in Canada." *Electoral Studies*, 18(1): 69–87.

Carty, R. Kenneth, William Cross, and Lisa Young. 2000. *Rebuilding Canadian Party Politics*. Vancouver: University of British Columbia Press.

Casas-Zamora, Kevin. 2005. *Paying for Democracy: Political Finance and State Funding for Parties*. Colchester: ECPR Press.

Christensen, Dag Arne. 1997. "Adaptation of Agrarian Parties in Norway and Sweden." *Party Politics*, 3(3): 391–406.

Chubb, Basil. 1970. *The Government and Politics of Ireland*. Stanford CA: Stanford University Press.

Clark, Peter B., and James Q. Wilson. 1961. "Incentive Systems: A Theory of Organizations." *Administrative Science Quarterly*, 6: 129–66.

Costa Pinto, António, and Pedro Taveres de Almeida. 2000. "On Liberalism and the Emergence of Civil Society in Portugal." In Nancy Bermeo and Philip Nord (eds), *Civil Society Before Democracy*. Princeton: Princeton University Press, 3–22.

Cox, Gary. 1987. *The Efficient Secret: The Cabinet and the Development of Political Parties in Victorian England*. Cambridge: Cambridge University Press.

Cross, William. 2004. *Political Parties*. Vancouver: UBC Press.

Cross, William, and André Blais. 2012. *Politics at the Centre: The Selection and Removal of Party Leaders in Anglo Parliamentary Democracies*. Oxford: Oxford University Press.

Cross, William, and Lisa Young. 2004. "The Contours of Political Party Membership in Canada." *Party Politics*, 10(4): 427–44.

Cruz-Jesus, Frederico, Tiago Oliveira, and Fernando Bacao. 2012. "Digital Divide across the European Union." *Information and Management*, 49(6): 278–91.

Daalder, Hans. 2001. "The Rise of Parties in Western Democracies." In Larry Diamond and Richard Gunther (eds), *Political Parties and Democracy*. Baltimore: Johns Hopkins University Press, 40–51.

Dachs, Herbert. 1995. "Das Parteiensystem." In Emmerich Talos et al. (eds), *Handbuch des politischen Systems Österreichs: Erste Republik 1918–1933*. Vienna: Manszsche- und Universitätsbuchhandlung, 43–149.

Dalton, Russell J. 1996. *Citizen Politics*. Chatham, NJ: Chatham House.

Dalton, Russell, and Steven Weldon. 2005. "Public Images of Political Parties: A Necessary Evil?" *West European Politics*, 28(5): 931–51.

Dalton, Russell, David Farrell, and Ian McAllister. 2011. *Political Parties and Democratic Linkage*. Oxford: Oxford University Press.

Delwit, Pascal. 2009. *La Vie politique en Belgique de 1830 à nos jours*. Brussels: UB lire.

Diamond, Larry, and Richard Gunther. 2001. "Types and Functions of Parties." In Larry Diamond and Richard Gunther (eds), *Political Parties and Democracy*. Baltimore: Johns Hopkins University Press, 3–39.

Di Mascio, Fabrizio. 2012. "Party Patronage in Italy: A Matter for Solitary Leaders." In Petr Kopecký, Peter Mair, and Maria Spirova (eds), *Party Patronage and Party Government in European Democracies*. Oxford: Oxford University Press, 229–49.

Dolez, Bernard, and Annie Laurent. 2007. "Une primaire à la française." *Revue française de science politique*, 57(2): 133–61.

Duebber, Ulrich, and Gerard Braunthal. 1963. "West Germany." *Journal of Politics*, 25(3): 774–89.

Drysch, Thomas. 1993. "The New French System of Political Finance." In Arthur Gunlicks (ed.), *Campaign and Party Finance in North America and Western Europe*. Boulder, CO: Westview Press, 155–77.

Duggan, Christopher. 2000. "Politics in the Era of Depretis and Crispi, 1870–96." In Nancy Bermeo and Philip Nord (eds), *Civil Society Before Democracy*. Princeton: Princeton University Press, 154–80.

Duverger, Maurice. 1954. *Political Parties*, tr. Barbara and Robert North. New York: John Wiley & Sons.

Edwards, Bryce. 2003. "Political Parties in New Zealand: A Study of Ideological and Organisational Transformation." Ph.D Thesis, University of Canterbury, New Zealand.

Eley, Geoff. 2002. *Forging Democracy: The History of the Left in Europe, 1850–2000*. Oxford: Oxford University Press.

Ellis, Faron. 2005. *The Limits of Participation*. Alberta: University of Calgary Press.

Engelmann, Frederick, and Mildred Schwartz. 1975. *Canadian Political Parties: Origin, Character, Impact*. Englewood Cliffs, NJ: Prentice Hall.

Epstein, Leon D. 1956. "British Mass Parties in Comparison with American Parties." *Political Science Quarterly*, 71(1): 97–125.

Epstein, Leon D. 1968. *Political Parties in Western Democracies*. New York: Praeger.

Ertman, Thomas. 2000. "Liberalization, Democratization, and the Origins of 'Pillarized' Civil Society in Nineteenth-Century Belgium and the Netherlands." In Nancy Bermeo and Philip Nord (eds), *Civil Society Before Democracy*. Princeton: Princeton University Press, 155–78.

Evans, Ellen L. 1999. *The Cross and the Ballot: Catholic Political Parties in Germany, Switzerland, Austria, Belgium and the Netherlands, 1785–1985*. Boston: Humanities Press.

Fisher, Justin, Edward Fieldhouse, and David Cutts. 2014. "Members are Not the Only Fruit: Volunteer Activity in Political Parties." *British Journal of Politics and International Relations*, 16(1): 75–95.

Gallagher, Michael, and Michael Marsh. 2002. *Days of Blue Loyalty: The Politics of Membership of the Fine Gael Party*. Dublin: PSAI Press.

Gallagher, Michael, and Michael Marsh. 2004. "Party Membership in Ireland: The Members of Fine Gael." *Party Politics*, 10(4): 407–25.

Gash, Norman. 1977. *Politics in the Age of Peel: A Study in the Technique of Parliamentary Representation*. Hassocks, Sussex: Harvester Press.

Gauja, Anika. 2005. "The Pitfalls of Participatory Democracy: A Study of the Australian Democrats' GST." *Australian Journal of Political Science*, 40(1): 71–85.

Gauja, Anika. 2009. "Moving Beyond the Membership? The Transformation of Party Organisations, Policy Outsourcing and the Creation of Supporters' Networks." Paper presented at American Political Science Association Meetings, Toronto.

Gauja, Anika. 2013. *The Politics of Party Policy: From Members to Legislators*. Basingstoke: Palgrave Macmillan.

Gibson, Rachel, and Stephen Ward. 2009. "Parties in the Digital Age: A Review Essay." *Representation*, 45(1): 87–100.

Gillespie, Richard. 1989. *The Spanish Socialist Party: A History of Factionalism*. Oxford: Clarendon Press.

Goldstein, Robert. 1983. *Political Repression in the Nineteenth Century*. London: Croom Helm.

Goldstein, Robert. 1989. *Political Censorship of the Arts and the Press in Nineteenth-Century Europe*. Basingstoke: Macmillan.

Gomez, Raul, and Tania Verge. 2012. "Party Patronage in Spain: Appointments for Party Government." In Petr Kopecký, Peter Mair, and Maria Spirova (eds), *Party Patronage and Party Government in European Democracies*. Oxford: Oxford University Press, 316–34.

Grüner, Erich. 1977, 2nd edn. *Die Parteien in der Schweiz*. Bern: Francke Verlag.

Gunther, Richard, and Larry Diamond. 2003. "Species of Political Parties: A New Typology." *Party Politics*, 9(2): 167–99.

Haegel, Florence. 1998. "Conflict and Change in the Rassemblement pour la République." In Piero Ignazi and Colette Ysmal (eds), *The Organization of Political Parties in Southern Europe*. Westport, CT: Praeger, 26–42.

Hanham, H. J. 1978. *Elections and Party Management: Politics in the Time of Disraeli and Gladstone*. Hassocks, Sussex: Harvester Press.

Hansen, Bernhard. 2002. *Party Activism in Denmark: A Micro Level Approach to a Cross-Sectional Analysis of the Correlates of Party Activism*. Aarhus, Denmark: University of Aarhus Department of Political Science.

Harmel, Robert, and Kenneth Janda. 1994. "An Integrated Theory of Party Goals and Party Change." *Journal of Theoretical Politics*, 6(3): 259–87.

Hartleb, Florian. 2013. "Anti-Elitist Cyber Parties?" *Journal of Public Affairs*, 13(4): 355–69.

Hazan, Reuven, and Gideon Rahat. 2010. *Democracy within Parties: Candidate Selection Methods and their Consequences*. Oxford: Oxford University Press.

Heidar, Knut, and Jo Saglie. 2003. "A Decline of Linkage? Intra-Party Participation in Norway 1991–2000." *European Journal of Political Research*, 42(6): 761–86.

Heidenheimer, Arnold. 1963. "Comparative Party Finance: Notes on Practices and Toward a Theory." *Journal of Politics*, 25(4): 790–811.

Hellman, Ollie. 2011. *Political Parties and Electoral Strategy*. Basingstoke: Palgrave Macmillan.

Hering, Gunnar. 1992. *Die politische Parteien in Griechenland 1821–1936*, 2 vol. Munich: R. Oldenbourg Verlag.

Hiebl, Ewald. 2006. "The Instrumentalization of *Buergerlichkeit*." In Graeme Morton, Boudien de Vries, and R. J. Morris (eds), *Civil Society, Associations and Urban Places*. Aldershot: Ashgate, 56–76.

Hirschman, Albert O. 1970. *Exit, Voice and Loyalty*. Cambridge, MA: Harvard University Press.

Hoffman, Stefan-Ludwig. 2003. "Democracy and Associations in the Long Nineteenth Century: Towards a Transnational Perspective." *Journal of Modern History*, 75(2): 269–99.

Hofnung, Menachem. 1996. "Public Financing, Party Membership and Internal Party Competition." *European Journal of Political Research*, 29(1): 73–86.

Hofnung, Menachem. 2008. "Unaccounted Competition: The Finance of Intra-Party Elections." *Party Politics*, 14(6): 726–44.

Holsteyn, Joop van, Ruud Koole, and Jan Elkink. 2000. *Rekrutering en representatie in een representatief bestel*. Leiden: Departement Politieke Wetenschap.

Hopkin, Jonathan. 2001. "Bringing the Members Back In? Democratizing Candidate Selection in Britain and Spain." *Party Politics*, 7(3): 343–61.

Hopkin, Jonathan. 2004. "The Problem with Party Finance: Theoretical Perspectives on the Funding of Party Politics." *Party Politics*, 10(6): 627–51.

Huard, Raymond. 1996. *La Naissance du parti politique en France*. Paris: Presses de la Fondation Nationale des Sciences Politiques.

Huard, Raymond. 2000. "Political Association in Nineteenth-Century France: Legislation and Practice." In Nancy Bermeo and Philip Nord (eds), *Civil Society Before Democracy*. Princeton: Princeton University Press, 135–53.

Hughes, Colin. 1963. "Australia." *Journal of Politics*, 25(4): 646–63.

Ignazi, Piero, and Luciano Bardi. 2006. "Gli iscritte ad Alleanza nazionale: Attivi ma frustrate." *Polis*, 20(1): 31–58.

Inglehart, Ronald. 1990. *Culture Shift in Advanced Industrial Society*. Princeton: Princeton University Press.

Irving, R. E. M. 1979. *The Christian Democratic Parties of Western Europe*. London: George Allen & Unwin.

Ivaldi, Gilles. 2007. "Presidential Strategies, Models of Leadership and the Development of Parties in a Candidate-Centred Polity: The 2007 UMP and PS Presidential Nomination Campaigns." *French Politics*, 5(3): 253–77.

Jackson, Nigel, and Darren Lilleker. 2009. "Building an Architecture of Participation? Political Parties and Web 2.0 in Britain." *Journal of Information Technology and Politics*, 6(3–4): 232–50.

Jalali, Carlos, Patricia Silva, and Diogo Moreira. 2012. "Party Patronage in Portugal: Treading in Shallow Water." In Petr Kopecký, Peter Mair, and Maria

Spirova (eds), *Party Patronage and Party Government in European Democracies*. Oxford: Oxford University Press, 294–315

Jennings, M. Kent, et al. 1990. *Continuities in Political Action*. Berlin: Walter de Gruyter.

Johnston, Ron, and Charles Pattie. 2003. "Do Canvassing and Campaigning Work? Evidence from the 2001 General Election in England." *British Elections and Parties Review*, 13(1): 248–73.

Judt, Tony. 2007. *Postwar: A History of Europe since 1945*. New York: Random House.

Jupp, James. 1964. *Australian Party Politics*. London: Melbourne University Press.

Kalnes, Oyvind. 2009. "Norwegian Parties and Web 2.0." *Journal of Information Technology and Politics*, 6(3–4): 251–66.

Kalyvas, Stathis. 1996. *The Rise of Christian Democracy in Europe*. Ithaca, NY: Cornell University Press.

Karp, Jeffrey, Susan Banducci, and Shaun Bowler. 2008. "Getting out the Vote: Party Mobilization in Comparative Perspective." *British Journal of Political Science*, 38(1): 91–112.

Katz, Richard S. 1990. "Party as Linkage: A Vestigial Function?" *European Journal of Political Research*, 18(1): 143–61.

Katz, Richard S., and Peter Mair, eds. 1994. *How Parties Organize*. London: Sage Publications.

Katz, Richard S., and Peter Mair, eds. 1995a. *Party Organizations: A Data Handbook*. London: Sage.

Katz, Richard S., and Peter Mair. 1995b. "Changing Models of Party Organization and Party Democracy: The Emergence of the Cartel Party." *Party Politics*, 1(1): 5–28.

Katz, Richard S., and Peter Mair. 2009. "The Cartel Party Thesis: A Restatement." *Perspectives on Politics*, 7(4): 753–66.

Katz, Richard S., et al. 1992. "The Membership of Political Parties in European Democracies, 1960–1990." *European Journal of Political Research*, 22(3): 329–45.

Kenig, Ofer. 2009a. "Democratization of Party Leadership Selection: Do Wider Selectorates Produce More Competitive Contests?" *Electoral Studies*, 28(2): 240–7.

Kenig, Ofer. 2009b. "The Democratization of Party Leaders' Selection Methods: Canada in Comparative Perspective," Canadian Political Science Association Conference, May 27–29, Ottawa, Canada

Kenig, Ofer, et al. 2013. "Shifting Political Sands: When Politicians, Voters and [Even] Party Members are on the Move." Presented at conference on Party Members, University of Copenhagen, 6–7 June.

Kertzer, David. 2000. "Religion and Society, 1789–1892." In John Davis (ed.), *Italy in the Nineteenth Century 1796–1900*. Oxford: Oxford University Press, 179–205.

Kirchheimer, Otto. 1966. "The Transformation of the Western European Party Systems." In Joseph LaPalombara and Myron Weiner (eds), *Political Parties and Political Development*. Princeton: Princeton University Press, 177–200.

Kitschelt, Herbert. 1988. "Organization and the Strategy of Belgian and West German Ecology Parties: A New Dynamic of Party Politics in Western Europe?" *Comparative Politics*, 20(2): 127–54.

Kitschelt, Herbert. 1989. "The Internal Politics of Parties: The Law of Curvilinear Disparity Revisited." *Political Studies*, 37(3): 400–21.

Kitschelt, Herbert. 2000. "Citizens, Politicians and Party Cartelization: Political Representation and State Failure in Post-Industrial Democracies." *European Journal of Political Research*, 37(2): 149–79.

Klein, Markus, Ulrich von Alemann, and Tim Spier. 2011. "Warum brauchen Parteien Mitglieder?" In Tim Spier et al. (eds), *Parteimitglieder in Deutschland: Die Potsdamer Parteimitgliederstudie*. Wiesbaden: VS Verlag, 18–29.

Koelble, Thomas. 1989. "Party Structures and Democracy." *Comparative Political Studies*, 22(2): 199–216.

Koliopoulos, John S., and Thanos M. Veremis. 2002. *Greece: The Modern Sequel*. New York: New York University Press.

Koole, Ruud. 1994. "The Vulnerability of the Modern Cadre Party in the Netherlands." In Richard Katz and Peter Mair (eds), *How Parties Organize: Change and Adaptation in Western Democracies*. London: Sage, 278–303.

Koop, Royce. 2011. *Grassroots Liberals: Organizing for Local and National Politics in Canada*. Vancouver: UBC Press.

Kopecký, Petr, and Peter Mair. 2012. "Party Patronage as an Electoral Resource." In Petr Kopecký, Peter Mair, and Maria Spirova (eds), *Party Patronage and Party Government in European Democracies*. Oxford: Oxford University Press, 3–16.

Kopecký, Petr, and Gerardo Scherlis. 2008. "Party Patronage in Contemporary Europe." *European Review*, 16(3): 355–71.

Kopecký, Petr, Peter Mair, and Maria Spirova, eds. 2012. *Party Patronage and Party Government in European Democracies*. Oxford: Oxford University Press.

Korisis, Hariton. 1966. *Die politischen Parteien Griechenlands: Ein neuer Staat auf dem Weg zur Demokratie 1821–1910*. Hersbruck: Verlag Karl Pfeiffer.

Kosiara-Pedersen, Karina. 2013. "For Limited Use Only: Participation among Danish Party Members." Paper presented at "Towards More Multifaceted Understandings of Party Membership," 6–7 June, University of Copenhagen.

Krouwel, Andrae. 1999. *The Catch-All Party in Western Europe 1945–1990*. Amsterdam: Vrije Universiteit.

Ladner, Andreas. 2001. "Swiss Political Parties: Between Persistence and Change." *West European Politics*, 24(2): 123–44.

Larmour, Peter J. 1964. *The French Radical Party in the 1930s*. Stanford, CA: Stanford University Press.

Laux, Annika. 2011a. "Was motiviert Parteimitglieder zum Beitritt." In Tim Spier et al. (eds), *Parteimitglieder in Deutschland: Die Potsdamer Parteimitgliederstudie*. Wiesbaden: VS Verlag, 61–78.

Laux, Annika. 2011b. "Was wünschen sich die Mitglieder von ihren Parteien?" In Tim Spier et al. (eds), *Parteimitglieder in Deutschland: Die Potsdamer Parteimitgliederstudie*. Wiesbaden: VS Verlag, 158–78.

Laven, David, and Lucy Riall, eds. 2000. *Napoleon's Legacy: Problems of Government in Restoration Europe*. Oxford: Berg.

Lawson, Kay, ed. 1980. *Political Parties and Linkage*. New Haven: Yale University Press.

Leonardi, Robert, and Douglas Wertman. 1989. *Italian Christian Democracy*. New York: St Martin's Press.

Lewitzki, Markus. 2011. "Das Internet in Parteiform: Wie segelt die Piratenpartei?" University Duisburg-Essen School of Governance: <http://regierungsforschung.de/data/070111_regierungsforschung.de_lewitzki_piraten.pdf>.

Little, Conor, and David M. Farrell. 2013. "Political Failure and Party Change? The Case of Fianna Faíl." Paper presented at American Political Science Association Annual Meetings, Chicago, 29 Aug.–1 Sept.

Lisi, Marco. 2010. "The Democratisation of Party Leadership Selection: The Portuguese Experience." *Portuguese Journal of Social Science*, 9(2): 127–48.

López Pintor, Rafael, Maria Gratschew, and Tim Bittiger. 2004. *Voter Turnout in Western Europe since 1945*. Stockholm: International Idea.

McKenzie, R. T. 1955. *British Political Parties*. Melbourne: William Heinemann.

Mackie, Thomas, and Richard Rose. 1974. *The International Almanac of Electoral History*. New York: Free Press.

Mackie, Thomas, and Richard Rose. 1991, 3rd edn. *The International Almanac of Electoral History*. London: Macmillan.

Mair, Peter. 1987. *The Changing Irish Party System*. New York: St Martin's Press.

Mair, Peter, and Ingrid van Biezen. 2001. "Party Membership in Twenty European Democracies, 1980–2000." *Party Politics*, 7(1): 5–21.

Margetts, Helen. 2006. "The Cyber Party." In Richard S. Katz and William Crotty (eds), *Handbook of Party Politics*. London: Sage Publications, 528–35.

Marien, Sofie, Marc Hooghe, and Ellen Quintelier. 2010. "Inequalities in Non-Institutionalised Forms of Political Participation: A Multi-Level Analysis of 25 Countries." *Political Studies*, 58(1): 187–213.

Marschall, Stefan. 2001. "Parteien und Internet—auf dem Weg zu internet-basierten Mitgliederparteien." *Aus Politik und Zeitgeschichte*, 10: 38–46.

May, John. 1973. "The Opinion Structure of Political Parties: The Special Law of Curvilinear Disparity." *Political Studies*, 21(2): 135–51.

Michels, Robert. 1959 (1915). *Political Parties*, tr. Eden and Cedar Paul. New York: Dover Publications.

Mikulska, Anna, and Susan Scarrow. 2010. "Assessing the Political Impact of Candidate Selection Rules: Britain in the 1990s." *Journal of Elections, Public Opinions and Parties*, 20(3): 311–33.

Milne, R. S. 1966. *Political Parties in New Zealand*. London: Oxford University Press.

Morris, Robert J. 1990. *Class, Sect and Party: The Making of the British Middle Class, Leeds 1820–1850*. Manchester: Manchester University Press.

Morris, Robert J. 2000. "Civil Society, Subscriber Democracies, and Parliamentary Government in Great Britain." In Nancy Bermeo and Philip Nord (eds), *Civil Society Before Democracy*. Princeton: Princeton University Press, 111–33.

Morton, Graeme, Boudien de Vries, and R. J. Morris, eds. 2006. *Civil Society, Associations and Urban Places*. Aldershot: Ashgate.

Moss, Warner. 1933. *Political Parties in the Irish Free State*. New York: Columbia University Faculty of Political Science.

Müller, Wolfgang C. 1993. "After the 'Golden Age': Research into Austrian Political Parties since the 1980s." *European Journal of Political Research*, 23(4): 439–63.

Müller, Wolfgang C. 1994. "The Development of Austrian Party Organizations in the Post-War Period." In Richard S. Katz and Peter Mair (eds), *How Parties Organize*. London: Sage, 51–79.

Müller, Wolfgang C., and Barbara Steininger. 1994. "Party Organisation and Party Competitiveness: The Case of the Austrian People's Party, 1945–1992." *European Journal of Political Research*, 26(1): 1–29.

Murschetz, Paul. 1998. "State Support for the Daily Press in Europe: A Critical Appraisal." *European Journal of Communication*, 13(3): 291–313.

Nassmacher, Karl-Heinz ed. 2001. *Foundations for Democracy: Approaches to Comparative Political Finance*. Baden-Baden: Nomos, Verlagsgesellschaft.

Nassmacher, Karl-Heinz, ed. 2009. *The Funding of Party Competition: Political Finance in Twenty-Five Democracies*. Baden-Baden: Nomos.

Neumann, Sigmund. [1932] 1965. *Die Parteien der Weimarer Republik*. Stuttgart: W. Kohlhammer Verlag.

Niedermayer, Oskar, ed. 2012. *Die Piratenpartei*. Berlin: Springer DE.

Nipperdey, Thomas. 1961. *Die Organisation der deutschen Parteien vor 1918*. Düsseldorf: Droste Verlag.

Noelle-Neumann, Elisabeth. 1980. *Die Schweigespirale: öffentliche Meinung-unsere soziale Haut*. Munich: Piper.

Norris, Pippa. 1995. "May's Law of Curvilinear Disparity Revisited." *Party Politics*, 1(1): 29–47.

Norris, Pippa. 1999. *Critical Citizens: Global Support for Democratic Government*. Oxford: Oxford University Press.

Norris, Pippa. 2003. *Digital Divide: Civic Engagement, Information Poverty, and the Internet Worldwide*. Cambridge: Cambridge University Press.

Nousiainen, Jaako. 1971. *The Finnish Political System*, tr. John H. Hodgson. Cambridge, MA: Harvard University Press.

OSCE/ODIHR. 2011. *Guidelines on Political Party Regulation*. Warsaw: OSCE Office for Democratic Institutions and Human Rights.

Oser, Jennifer, Marc Hooghe, and Sofie Marien. 2013. "Is Online Participation Distinct from Offline Participation?" *Political Research Quarterly*, 66(1): 91–101.

Ostrogorski, Moisei. [1902] 1982. *Democracy and the Organization of Political Parties*, i. England, ed. and abridged Seymour Martin Lipset. New Brunswick, NJ: Transaction Books.

Overacker, Louise. 1952. *The Australian Party System*. New Haven: Yale University Press.

Overacker, Louise. 1968. *Australian Parties in a Changing Society: 1945–67*. Melbourne: F. W. Cheshire.

Panebianco, Angelo. 1988. *Political Parties: Organization and Power*, tr. Marc Silver. Cambridge: Cambridge University Press.

Pappas, Takis. 1999. *Making Party Democracy in Greece*. London: Macmillan.

Pasquino, Gianfranco. 2009. "The Democratic Party and the Restructuring of the Italian Party System." *Journal of Modern Italian Studies*, 14(1): 21–30.

Passarelli, Gianluca, and Dario Tuorto. 2013. "Being Activists in Two Atypical Parties. The Italian Northern League and Movement 5 Stars." Paper presented at American Political Science Association Annual Meetings, Chicago, 29 Aug.–1 Sept.

Passigli, Stefano. 1963. "Italy." *Journal of Politics*, 25(4): 718–36.
Pedersen, Karina. 2006. "The 2005 Danish General Election: A Phase of Consolidation." *West European Politics*, 28: 1101–8.
Pedersen, Karina, et al. 2004. "Sleeping or Active Partners? Danish Party Members at the Turn of the Millennium." *Party Politics*, 10(4): 367–84.
Pelizzo, Riccardo. 2004. *The Changing Political Economy of Party Membership*. Singapore: Singapore Management University.
Picard, Robert G., and Mikko Grönlund. 2003. "Development and Effects of Finnish Press Subsidies." *Journalism Studies*, 4(1): 105–19.
Pierre, Jon, Lars Svåsand, and Anders Widfeldt. 2000. "State Subsidies to Political Parties: Confronting Rhetoric with Reality." *West European Politics*, 23(3): 1–24.
Pinto-Duschinsky, Michael. 1981. *British Political Finance 1830–1980*. Washington, DC: American Enterprise Institute.
Poguntke, Thomas. 1987. "The Organization of a Participatory Party: The German Greens." *European Journal of Political Research*, 15(6): 609–33.
Poguntke, Thomas, and Susan Scarrow. 1996. "The Politics of Anti-Party Sentiment." *European Journal of Political Research*, 29(3): 257–62.
Ponce, Aldo, and Susan Scarrow. 2011. "Who Gives? Partisan Donations in Europe." *West European Politics*, 34(5): 997–1020.
Putnam, Robert. 2001. *Bowling Alone: The Collapse and Revival of American Community*. New York: Simon & Schuster.
Quinn, Thomas. 2010. "Membership Ballots in Party Leadership Elections in Britain." *Representation*, 46(1): 101–17.
Reiser, Marion. 2011. "'Wer entscheidet unter welchen Bedingungen über die Nominierung von Kandidaten?' Die innerparteilichen Selektionsprozesse zur Aufstellung in den Wahlkreisen." In Oskar Niedermeyer (ed.), *Die Parteien nach der Bundestagswahl 2009*. Wiesbaden: Verlag für Sozialwissenschaften, 237–59.
Reiter, Howard L. 1989. "Party Decline in the West: A Skeptic's View." *Journal of Theoretical Politics*, 1(3): 325–48.
Ridder, Josje den, Ruud Koole, and Joop van Holsteyn. 2011. "Join the Party! Party Members of Dutch Political Parties." Paper prepared for conference, Centre for Voting and Parties, University of Copenhagen, 3–4 Feb.
Robson, J. L. 1967. *New Zealand: The Development of its Laws and Constitution*. London: Stevens & Sons.
Rogers, Ben. 2005. "From Membership to Management? The Future of Political Parties as Democratic Organisations." *Parliamentary Affairs*, 58(3): 600–10.
Rokkan, Stein, and Jean Meyriat. 1969. *International Guide to Electoral Statistics*. The Hague: Mouton.
Rolef, Susan Hattis. 2011. "Labor Drive Invites Corruption," *Jerusalem Post online*, 7 June: <www.jpost.com/opinion/op-edcontributors/article/aspx?id=228211> (accessed July 2012).
Rosenblum, Nancy L. 2008. *On the Side of the Angels*. Princeton: Princeton University Press.
Rustow, Dankwart. 1955. *The Politics of Compromise: A Study of Parties and Cabinet Government in Sweden*. New York: Greenwood Press.

Sainsbury, Diane. 1983. "Functional Hypotheses of Party Decline: The Case of the Scandinavian Social Democratic Parties." *Scandinavian Political Studies*, 6(4): 241–60.

Salmon, Philip. 2002. *Electoral Reform at Work: Local Politics and National Parties, 1832–1841*. Woodbridge, Suffolk: Boydell & Brewer.

Scarrow, Susan. 1996. *Parties and their Members*. Oxford: Oxford University Press.

Scarrow, Susan. 2000. "Parties without Members? Party Organization in a Changing Electoral Environment." In Russell Dalton and Martin Wattenberg (eds), *Parties without Partisans: Political Change in Advanced Industrial Democracies*. Oxford: Oxford University Press, 79–101.

Scarrow, Susan. 2001. "Direct Democracy and Institutional Design: A Comparative Investigation." *Comparative Political Studies*, 34(6): 651–65.

Scarrow, Susan. 2002. *Perspectives on Political Parties: Classic Readings*. New York: Palgrave Macmillan.

Scarrow, Susan. 2006. "Party Subsidies and the Freezing of Party Competition: Do Cartel Mechanisms Work?" *West European Politics*, 29(4): 619–39.

Scarrow, Susan. 2011. "Carrots and Sticks, Chickens and Eggs: Understanding Variations in Party Finance Regulatory Systems." Paper presented at IPSA/ECPR Conference, São Paolo, Brazil.

Scarrow, Susan, and Burcu Gezgor. 2010. "Declining Membership, Changing Members? European Political Party Members in a New Era." *Party Politics*, 16(6): 832–43.

Scarrow, Susan, Paul Webb, and David Farrell. 2000. "From Social Integration to Electoral Contestation." In Russell Dalton and Martin Wattenberg (eds), *Parties without Partisans*. Oxford: Oxford University Press, 129–53.

Schattschneider, E. E. 1942. *Party Government*. New York: Holt, Rinehart, Winston.

Schlesinger, Joseph. 1991. *Political Parties and the Winning of Office*. Ann Arbor: University of Michigan Press.

Schlozman, Kay Lehman, Sidney Verba, and Henry E. Brady. 2010. "Weapon of the Strong? Participatory Inequality and the Internet." *Perspectives on Politics*, 8(2): 487–509.

Scholte, Sara. 2011. *Stoppt mehr Partizipation den Mitgliederverlust? Mitgliederentwicklung und innerparteiliche Mitbestimmung bei sozialdemokratischen Parteien in Europa*. Berlin: Friedrich Ebert Stiftung.

Selle, Per, and Lars Svåsand. 1991. "Membership in Party Organizations and the Problem of Decline of Parties." *Comparative Political Studies*, 23(4): 459–77.

Setala, Maija. 1999. "Referendums in Western Europe—A Wave of Direct Democracy?" *Scandinavian Political Studies*, 22(4): 327–40.

Seyd, Paul, and Patrick Whiteley. 1992. *Labour's Grass Roots*. Oxford: Clarendon Press.

Sorauf, Frank. 1960. "The Silent Revolution in Patronage." *Public Administration Review*, 20: 28–34.

Soucy, Robert J. 1991. "French Fascism and the *Croix de Feu*: A Dissenting Interpretation." *Journal of Contemporary History*, 26(1): 159–88.

Speck, Bruno Wilhelm. 2013. "Nem ideológica, nem oportunista: A filiaçao partidária no contexto pré-eleitoral no Brasil." *KA Cadernos*, 2: 37–60.
Speck, Bruno Wilhelm. 2014. "Neither Ideological nor Pragmatic: Party Membership as a Device for Intra-party competition in Brazil." Paper presented at ECPR Joint Sessions, 11–15 Apr.
Sperber, Jonathan. 1997. *The Kaiser's Voters: Electors and Elections in Imperial Germany*. Cambridge: Cambridge University Press.
Sperber, Jonathan. 2005. *The European Revolutions, 1848–1851*. 2nd ed. Cambridge: Cambridge University Press.
Spier, Tim et al. eds. 2011. *Parteimitglieder in Deutschland: Die Potsdamer Partei mitgliederstudie*. Wiesbaden: VS Verlag.
Spourdalakis, Michael. 1988. *The Rise of the Greek Socialist Party*. London: Routledge.
Statistische Bundesamt. 2011. *Statistisches Jahrbuch 2011 für die Bundesrepublik Deutschland*. Berlin.
Strikwerda, Carl. 1997. *A House Divided: Catholics, Socialists, and Flemish Nationalists in Nineteenth-Century Belgium*. Lanham, MD: Rowman & Littlefield.
Strom, Kaare, and Lars Svåsand. 1997. "Political Parties in Norway: Facing the Challenges of a New Society." In Kaare Strom and Lars Svåsand (eds), *Challenges to Political Parties: The Case of Norway*. Ann Arbor: University of Michigan Press, 1–32.
Sundberg, Jan. 1987. "Exploring the Basis of Declining Party Membership in Denmark: A Scandinavian Comparison." *Scandinavian Political Studies*, 10(1): 17–38.
Sundberg, Jan. 1995. "Finland: Nationalized Parties, Professionalized Organizations." In Richard S. Katz and Peter Mair (eds), *How Parties Organize*. London: Sage, 158–84.
Sussman, Gary. 2007. "Are Party Ballots Approximating National Referendums?" *Representation*, 43(1): 1–18.
Tavits, Margit. 2012. "Organizing for Success: Party Organizational Strength and Electoral Performance in Postcommunist Europe." *Journal of Politics*, 74(1): 83–97.
Tavits, Margit. 2013. *Post-communist Democracies and Party Organization*. Cambridge: Cambridge University Press.
Tenfelde, Klaus. 2000. "Civil Society and the Middle Classes in Nineteenth Century Germany." In Nancy Bermeo and Philip Nord (eds), *Civil Society Before Democracy*. Princeton: Princeton University Press, 83–108.
Therborn, Göran. 1988. "A Unique Chapter in the History of Democracy: The Social Democrats in Sweden." In Klaus Misgeld, Karl Molin, and Klas Amark (eds), *Creating Social Democracy A Century of the Social Democratic Labor Party in Sweden*. University Park, PA: Pennsylvania State University Press, 1–34
Thörmer, H., and Einemann, E. 2007. *Aufstieg und Krise der Generation Schröder*. Marburg: Schüren
Totz, Daniel. 2012. "Mitglieder gesucht: Die Reform der SPD-Parteiorganisation." In Alexandra Bäcker and Philip Erbentraut (eds), *Mitteilungen des Instituts für deutsches und internationals Parteienrecht und Parteienforschung*, 18, 72–85.
Treib, Oliver. 2012. "Party Patronage in Austria: From Reward to Control." In Petr Kopecký, Peter Mair, and Maria Spirova (eds), *Party Patronage and Party Government in European Democracies*. Oxford: Oxford University Press, 31–53.

Tweede Kamer der Staaten-General. 2011. *Financiering politiekepartijen.* 's-Gravenhage: 32 634, no. 2.
van Biezen, Ingrid. 2000. "Party Financing in New Democracies Spain and Portugal." *Party Politics*, 7(1): 5–21.
van Biezen, Ingrid. 2004. "Political Parties as Public Utilities." *Party Politics*, 10(6): 701–22.
van Biezen, Ingrid, and Petr Kopecký. 2001. "On the Predominance of State Money: Reassessing Party Financing in the New Democracies of Southern and Eastern Europe." *Perspectives on European Politics and Society*, 2(3): 401–29.
van Biezen, Ingrid, and Daniela Romée Piccio. 2013. "Shaping Intra-Party Democracy: On the Legal Regulation of Internal Party Organizations." In William Cross and Richard S. Katz (eds), *The Challenges of Intra-Party Democracy*. Oxford: Oxford University Press, 27–48.
van Biezen, Ingrid, Peter Mair, and Thomas Poguntke. 2012. "Going, Going... Gone? The Decline of Party Membership in Contemporary Europe." *European Journal of Political Research*, 51(1): 24–56.
Van Deth, Jan. 2000. "Interesting but Irrelevant: Social Capital and the Saliency of Politics in Western Europe." *European Journal of Political Research*, 37(2): 115–47.
Van Haute, Emilie. 2011a. "Party Membership: An Understudied Mode of Political Participation." In Emilie Van Haute (ed.), *Party Membership in Europe: Explorations into the Anthills of Party Politics*. Brussels: Editions de l'Université de Bruxelles, 7–22.
Van Haute, Emilie. 2011b. "Le CD&V (Christen-Democratisch & Vlaams)." In *Les Parties politiques en Belgique*. Brussels: Editions de l'Université de Bruxelles, 35–62.
Verba, Sidney, Norma Nie, and Jae-On Kim. 1978. *Participation and Political Equality*. Chicago: University of Chicago Press.
Vincent, J. R. 1976. *The Formation of the British Liberal Party 1857–1868*. London: Harvester Press.
Voerman, G. 2006. "Plebiscitaire partijen?" In *Jaarboek 2004: Documentatiecentrum Nederlandse Politieke Partijen*. Groningen: University of Groningen, 217–44.
Von Beyme, Klaus. 1985. *Political Parties in Western Democracies*, tr. Eileen Martin. Aldershot: Gower Publishing.
Von Beyme, Klaus. 2002. *Parteien im Wandel: Von den Volksparteien zu den professionaliserten Wählerparteien*. Wiesbaden: Westdeutscher Verlag.
Ward, Stephen, and Rachel Gibson. 2009. "European Political Organizations and the Internet: Mobilization, Participation and Change." In Andrew Chadwick and Philip N. Howard (eds), *Routledge Handbook of Internet Politics*. London: Routledge, 25–39.
Ward, Stephen, Rachel Gibson, and Wainer Lusoli. 2003. "Online Participation and Mobilisation in Britain: Hype, Hope and Reality." *Parliamentary Affairs*, 56(4): 652–68.
Ware, Alan. 2002. *The American Direct Primary: Party Institutionalization and Transformation in the North*. Cambridge: Cambridge University Press.
Warner, Carolyn. 2000. *Confessions of an Interest Group: The Catholic Church and Political Parties in Europe*. Princeton: Princeton University Press.

Watt, Nicholas. 2012. "David Cameron Publishes Details of Donor Dinners in Cash-for-Access Row." *Guardian*, 26 Mar.: <www.guardian.co.uk/politics/2012/mar/26/david-cameron-donor-dinners-cash-access> (accessed Jan. 2013).

Wauters, Bram. 2009. "Intra-Party Democracy in Belgium: On Paper, in Practice and through the Eyes of Members." Paper prepared for ECPR Joint Sessions, 14–19 Apr.

Webb, Paul. 2000. *The Modern British Party System*. London: Sage.

Weber, Max. [1919] 1946. "Politics as Vocation." In *From Max Weber: Essays in Sociology*, tr. and ed. H. H. Gerth and C. Wright Mills. New York: Oxford University Press, 77–128.

Wagner, Markus. 2008. "Debating Europe in the French Socialist Party: The 2004 Internal Referendum on the EU Constitution." *French Politics*, 6(3): 257–79.

Whiteley, Paul. 2011. "Is the Party Over? The Decline of Party Activism and Membership across the Democratic World." *Party Politics*, 17(1): 21–44.

Whiteley, Paul, and Patrick Seyd. 2002. *High-Intensity Participation: The Dynamics of Party Activism in Britain*. Ann Arbor: University of Michigan Press.

Whiteley, Paul, Patrick Seyd, and Antony Billinghurst. 2006. *Third Force Politics: Liberal Democrats at the Grassroots*. Oxford: Oxford University Press.

Whiteley, Paul, Patrick Seyd, and Jeremy Richardson. 1994. *True Blues: The Politics of Conservative Party Membership*. Oxford: Oxford University Press.

Widfeldt, Anders. 1997. *Linking Parties with People? Party Membership in Sweden 1960–1994*. Göteborg: Department of Political Science, Göteborg University.

Wiesendahl, Elmar, Uwe Jun, and Oskar Niedermayer. 2009. "Die Zukunft der Mitgliederparteien auf den Prüfstand." In Uwe Jun, Oskar Niedermayer, and Elmar Wiesendahl (eds), *Die Zukunft der Mitgliederpartei*. Opladen: Verlag Barbara Budrich, 9–30.

Williams, John R. 1956. *The Conservative Party of Canada*. Durham, NC: Duke University Press.

Wilson, James Q. 1973. *Political Organizations*. New York: Basic Books.

Young, Lisa, and William Cross. 2002. "Incentives to Membership in Canadian Political Parties." *Political Research Quarterly*, 55(3): 547–69.

Young, Lisa, and William Cross. 2007. *A Group Apart: Young Party Members in Canada*. Ottawa: Canadian Policy Research Networks.

Young, Lisa, and William Cross. 2008. "Factors Influencing the Decision of the Young Politically Engaged to Join a Political Party: An Investigation of the Canadian Case." *Party Politics*, 14(3): 345–69.

Index

access
   to ballots, 187–188, 194–195, 212–213
   membership, 129, 130–134, 137–138, 207
adherents, defined, 22
affiliates and affiliations
   bulls-eye model, 26–29
   digital affiliates, 166–168, 210, 214
   as gateways to traditional membership, 151–152
   modern modes, 29–32
   multi-speed index, 146–148, 154
   patterns of party connections, 29
   rights and obligations, 30–32, 137–138
   vs. traditional memberships, 135–136
   traits, 136–138
   value to parties, 206–207
   See also members; multi-speed membership approach
Alternative parties, 24, 180
Anti-Corn Law League, 46
anti-democratic movements, 57, 59–61
associational life, 37–40, 42, 162
atomic model analogy, 27, 32
austerity, 61, 111, 115–118, 127 nn. 9–10, 172, 208
Austria, 44, 92, 93, 96 n. 4, 174 n. 7

Belgium, 46, 53, 62, 162
benefits. *See also* incentives
Berlusconi, Silvio, 65
"Birmingham Model," 51
branding, 24–25
bulls-eye model of affiliation, 26–29

Cameron, David, 169
campaigns
   badges, 105–106
   campaign finance legislation, 52
   electoral strategy shifts, 162
   member vs. non-member participation, 103–108, 125, 126 nn. 3–4
   professionalization, 15, 17–18, 69, 103
   reliance on media, 73–74
   See also elections
Canada, 68 n.9, 174 n. 5
careerism, 158–159, 172, 186
Carlsbad Decrees of 1819, 44
Cartel Party hypothesis, 212
catch-all parties, 16, 24–25, 162, 173
Catholic parties, 42–43, 53, 58, 61–62
censorship, 44–45, 49
   See also legislation
centralization of affiliation modes, 136
civic associations, 37–40
cleavage representation parties, 21–23, 150, 162–163, 207–208
clientelism, 171
   See also donors clubs
closed primaries, defined, 186
cohesiveness, 213–214
communications
   digital affiliate mobilization, 210
   government censorship, 44–45, 49
   impacts on cohesiveness, 213–214
   information offerings as incentive, 177–178
   media campaigns, 73–74
   member ambassadors, 28, 122–125, 127 nn. 14–15, 145
   news audience, 31–32, 143–145, 189, 196 n. 6, 206
   social media, 30, 31, 141–143, 152 n. 9, 166–167, 181
Communist parties, 59–60, 152 n. 3
community ambassadors, 28, 122–125, 127 nn. 14–15, 145
concentric circle model, 26–29

Conservative Party (UK), 78–79, 168–169, 170
constitutional monarchies, 47
consumer discounts, 170–171
contributions, member
  fundraising, 117–120
  non-dues financial support, 117–120
  to party success, 101–102
  as replaceable resource, 123–126
  volunteerism, 103–109, 126 n. 2
  voter turnout, 120–122, 127 n. 13
  See also dues
cooperators, 138, 189
corporate membership. *See also* indirect membership
cost/benefit approach, 14–19, 29–32
cost categories, 129
cultural pressures, 18–19, 37–40, 42, 74, 161–162
cyber-members, 30, 65, 137–140, 166–168, 173
See also digital affiliates; technology

decline in party membership. *See also* enrollment change
definitional explanations for membership shifts, 77, 82–83, 91–92
demand-side explanations for membership levels, 15–19, 72–75, 86–91, 92–93, 185
demos, 175, 186–189, 211–213
digital affiliates, 137, 166–168, 210, 214
  See also cyber-members; technology
"digital ambassadors," 28, 145
direct action, 178
donations. *See also* financial support
donors clubs, 168–169, 174 n. 9
dues
  accounting methods, 114, 126 nn. 7–8, 127 n. 11
  concessionary rates, 130
  minimum rates, 115–118, 127 nn. 9–10
  in multi-speed membership approach, 129
  on-line payment, 132, 152 n. 2

value during austerity era, 111
Dutch Party for Freedom of Geert Wilders, 66, 131–132
Duverger, Maurice, 16, 26–29, 66, 109–110

economic consequences of membership
  benefits, 157, 169–173, 174 n. 10
  hardships, 61, 111, 115–118, 127 nn. 9–10, 172, 208
elections
  candidacy as membership incentive, 185–186
  candidate selection process, 183–185, 196 nn. 3–4
  competitiveness, 50, 56, 57, 68 n. 1
  demos determination, 175, 186–189, 210–211
  historical expansion of electorate, 47–49
  impact of changes on organizational needs, 41
  losses, 25
  voter turnout, 120–122, 125, 127 n. 13, 189–193, 197–205
  See also campaigns; enfranchisement; intra-party leadership and policy ballots
electoral economy approach, 20–25, 66–67
See also cost/benefit approach
electors/voters (bulls-eye model), 26–27
elite party type, 21, 22
enfranchisement
  competitive elections as result of, 50
  expansion, 47–49
  impact of changes on organizational needs, 41
  impact of expansion on electoral environments, 57
  voting age, 68 n.7, 96 n. 2, 152 n. 9, 196 n. 5
  of women, 68 n.6, 96 n. 12
enrollment change
  causes, 86–94
  factors, 72–76

historical realities, 36–37
hypothetical patterns, 75–76
implications, 3–5
importance of accurate baseline data, 94–95
overstatement of, 76–80
problems with data, 69–85
record cleaning, 81, 96 n. 13
recruiting, 159–160, 173, 174 n. 5, 176–177, 187–194
re-evaluation, 86–91
relative vs. absolute, 70–71
role of poor marketing, 160–161, 168, 170
substitutes for member contributions, 101, 123–126
supply-side explanations, 18–19, 74–75, 86, 90–91, 93–94
trends in, 94–95
enrollment data
cross-national comparisons, 91–95
definition of membership, 77, 82–83, 91–92
eligibility changes, 78–79, 83, 96 n. 3
importance of accurate baseline, 94–95
inflation in, 77, 80–81, 96 n. 2, 96 n. 11
measurement errors, 76–80
membership density, 70–71, 75, 87–89, 93, 97
problematic use of, 69–70
self-reported, 83–86, 96 nn. 4–9
totals by decade, 97
truncated series, 76
unreliable estimates, 77, 81–82
enrollment marketing, 160–161
Epstein, Leon, 16, 17, 173 n. 1
ethnic minorities, 210
See also cleavage representation parties
exclusive benefits of membership, 157–158, 168–169, 171–172
extra-parliamentary party organizations
formal separation from parliamentary wings, 52, 79
functional explanations, 40

historical development, 37, 47, 50, 53
impact on party growth, 54, 64
role in representative process, 175, 178
subsidies, 86, 89, 113

Facebook, 30, 31, 141–143, 152 n. 9, 166–167, 181
See also technology
fans
Facebook, 141–143
party type associations, 20–22, 25, 216
rightist parties, 65–66
fascism, 60–61
finances
campaign finance legislation, 52
costs, 129, 130, 137
cross-national comparisons, 149
economic inflation, 115–118, 127 nn. 9–10
sustainer affiliates, 31
financial support
donations other than dues, 127 n. 12, 168–169
inflated reporting, 126 n.8
member support, 109–120, 123, 125, 126 nn. 7–8, 127 nn. 9–12
minimum dues rates, 115–118, 127 nn. 9–10
non-dues member contributions, 117–120
from non-members, 119–120
on-line donations, 140–141
public subsidies, 73
See also dues
France, 44–45, 184, 189, 196 n. 6
franchise. See also enfranchisement
French Socialist Party (PS), 189, 196 n. 6
"friends," 30, 138
functional perspectives, 15–18, 40–41
fundraising, 117–120

generational changes, 73–75, 86
genetic theory, 16

German Pirates Party, 65, 138–139, 166–167
Germany, 52–54, 60, 170–171
Great Britain. *See also* United Kingdom (UK)
Green parties, 65, 180, 189
Grillo, Beppe, 139
group identity
  cleavage representation parties, 21–23, 150, 169, 207–208
  incentive, 157, 162–163, 176–177
  milieu organizations, 174 n. 7
  religion, 43
guest memberships, 138

Habsburg Empire, 38, 44, 68 n. 5
historical development
  associational life, 37–40, 42
  electorate expansion, 47–49, 52
  importance of baseline, 1–2, 34–35, 67, 208–209
  legislative obstacles, 44–47, 50–52
  membership party emergence, 51–55
  new participatory parties, 64–65
  popular mobilization, 55–61
  religious parties, 42–43, 53, 58, 61–62

ideals of party membership, 1–2, 35–37, 40, 43, 67, 94, 179
ideological approach, 20–25, 66–67
ideological party type, 21–22
ideology
  as incentive for membership, 159
  interaction with party goals, 21, 25–26
  organizations as reinforcements, 42–43
  recruitment benefit, 176–177
  See also group identity; narratives of legitimacy
incentives
  exclusive benefits, 157–158, 168–169, 171–172
  ideology, 176–177

inclusive benefits, 157–158, 164–168, 169–171
introduction, 156
marketing of, 160–161, 168, 170, 177, 178
material, 157, 169–173, 174 n. 10
selective benefits, 157–158, 163–172, 173
social, 157–159, 161–169, 172–173, 173 n. 1, 174 nn. 6–9
See also motives; rights; obligations
inclusion (participation), 187–188, 194–195, 196 n. 10, 211–213
inclusive benefits of membership, 157–158, 164–168, 169–171
indirect membership
  definition, 7
  early party focus, 42, 53–55
  shift away from, 56, 61–63, 66–67, 213
  socialist parties, 57–58
individualism
  impact on internal party dynamics, 182, 213
  prioritization over group identity, 57–58, 62–64, 206
  rise of, 18–19, 74
inflation
  of data, 77, 80–81, 96 n. 2, 96 n. 11
  economic, 115–118, 127 nn. 9–10
institutional pressures, 40–41
internet. *See also* technology
intra-party leadership and policy ballots
  demos determination, 175, 186–189, 210–211
  eligibility, 186–189
  implications of direct democracy, 207–208
  leadership ballots, 181–194, 196 nn. 1–4
  policy ballots, 179–181
  recruiting tool, 187–194
  risks, 175–176, 212–216
  voter turnout, 189–193, 197–205
Ireland, 45–46, 58, 64, 68 n. 11
issue-based appeals, 66–67
Italian Five Star Movement, 65, 139
Italy, 93–94, 162, 196 n. 10

Index

Kirchheimer, Otto, 16, 17, 24, 25

labor parties, 54, 54–56, 63, 78, 150, 181
labor unions, 7, 42, 44, 57–58, 63.
  See also indirect membership
Law on Association (France, 1808), 44–45
leaders and leadership
  accountability, 21–22, 179
  candidacy as membership incentive, 185–186
  clientelism, 171
  donor access to, 168–169, 174 n. 9
  empowerment by internal direct democracy, 212
  personalistic party focus, 20–21
  See also intra-party leadership and policy ballots
legislation
  anti-revolutionary, 44
  censorship, 49
  guarantees of free association, 49–51
  organizational statutes, 64
  political finance, 52
  restrictions on organizations, 38, 41, 44–45, 214–215
  trade union, 49–51
  See also specific legislation by name
legitimacy. *See also* narratives of legitimacy
Leninist cell-based structures, 59
light membership, 30, 138, 206
local party networks
  erosion, 162, 164, 213, 214
  historical development, 45–46, 51–53, 58, 68 n. 11
loyalty, 120–122, 125, 127 n. 13, 189–193

marketing, 160–161, 168, 170, 177–178
mass membership parties
  early adoption, 51–56
  emergence, 37–43
  enfranchisement, 47–51
  enrollment marketing, 160–161
  expansion of, 43–56
  ideal, vs. historical reality, 36–37, 56–59
  mobilization, 55–61
  obstacles, 44–47, 53–54
  organizational structure development, 51–56
  peak of, 61–67
  See also multi-speed membership approach
material incentives, 157, 169–173, 174 n. 10
May, John, 210–211
media
  campaign reliance on, 73–74
  government censorship, 44–45, 49
  member ambassadors, 28, 122–125, 127 nn. 14–15
  membership obsolescence, 17–18
  news audience, 31–32, 143–145, 177–178, 189, 196 n. 6, 206
  social media, 30, 31, 141–143, 152 n. 9, 166–167, 181
  See also technology
meetings, 106–108, 126 n. 3, 163–168
member/electorate (M/E) ratios, 70, 78, 87, 88, 89, 96 n. 1
members and membership
  in bulls-eye model, 26–27
  density of membership, 70–71, 75, 87–89, 93, 97
  historical development, 36–68
  inconsistent definitions, 77, 82–83, 91–92
  party motives for adoption, 14–32
  roles of membership, 20–25
  varieties of, 5–7
  See also contributions; enrollment change; enrollment data; motives; multi-speed membership approach
milieu organizations, 22, 53, 57–58, 162, 174 n. 7
  See also group identity
militants, 26–27
modes of party membership, 5–7
  See also affiliates and affiliations

motives
  membership, 158–160, 173, 173 n. 2, 174 n. 5
  party, for enrollment done, 14–19, 20–25, 29–32
  See also incentives; narratives of legitimacy
multi-speed membership approach
  assessments, 145–151, 152 n. 10
  consequences, 206–218
  dues reduction, 129
  emergence, 26–34
  as gateway to traditional membership, 151–152
  index, 146–148, 154
  introduction, 128–129
  model, 33, 136, 217
  new mobilization efforts, 209–210
  overview, 3, 32–36, 128
  party families, 147–148, 150–151, 153 n. 11
  procedural cost reduction, 129–134
  reputational cost reduction, 134–135
  See also affiliates and affiliations-myths, 2, 29, 36–37, 67, 94

narratives of legitimacy
  intra-party ballot impact, 207–208, 211
  organizational choice linkage, 42
  political market impact, 90
  recruiting impact, 175–176
  sources, 20–25
  value of membership, 67, 102, 150–151
National Front (France), 162–163
new parties
  competition for resources, 177, 215–216
  primaries as means of identifying supporters, 188
  retention of members, 177
  technology, 137, 139, 173
news distribution and audience, 31–32, 143–145, 177–178, 189, 196 n. 6, 206
newspaper taxes, 45, 49
non-member participation

  ambassadors, 123–125
  Facebook, 142–143
  financial support, 119–120
  implications of expansion, 207–208
  inclusion in party *demos,* 186–195, 196 nn. 6–10
  volunteerism, 103–108, 126 nn. 3–4
non-violent political mobilization, 46
Northern League (Italy), 162
Norwegian Farmers' Party, 52

O'Connell, Daniel, 45
on-line accessibility index, 148–150, 155
on-line populism, 65, 138–140
open primaries, defined, 186
opposition parties, fundraising, 118–119
organizational contagion, 16, 66
organizations
  as cultural products, 37–40
  electoral environment, 57–58, 162
  enfranchisement, 41, 47–51
  external benefit activities, 101–102
  historical exceptions to membership-based, 52–53
  as ideological reinforcement tools, 42–43
  impacts on cohesiveness, 213–214
  indications of vitality, 216–217
  individual membership adoption, 51–56
  internal benefit activities, 101–102
  non-hierarchical structures, 139–140
  obstacles to popular organization, 44–47, 53–54
  as solutions to problems, 40–41
  structural change in, 14, 206–218

Panebianco, Angelo, 16, 17, 19, 208
party-family differences, 147–148, 150–151
party friends, 30, 138
party membership. See also members and membership
party motives for enrollment, 14–25, 29–32. See also narratives of legitimacy

party sympathizers, 30, 138
party types, 20–25
patronage, 93–94, 171–172, 173 n. 1, 174 n. 6
personalistic parties, 20–21
policy making. *See also* intra-party leadership and policy ballots
political incentives
 collective, 157, 159–160, 176–177
 direct action opportunities, 178
 exclusive, 157
 inclusive, 157
 influence on party, 178–185
 information offerings, 177–178
 narratives of legitimacy, 175–176
 office-holding, 185–186
 risks, 157, 175–176
political market parties, 21, 24–25, 216
political moods, 90
political process parties, 21, 24
polls. *See also* survey methods
populism, on-line, 65, 138–140
Portugal, 81, 96 n. 13
press freedom, 44–45, 49
See also legislation
primaries, 186, 188–193
See also intra-party leadership and policy ballots
probationary membership, 132, 152 n. 3
procedural costs, 129, 130–134, 207
professionalization
 of parties, 15, 17–18, 69, 103
 of public bureaucracy, 171
professional networking, 158–159, 172, 186
project-oriented participation, 74
proportional representation, 41, 57
proporz, 93
psychological benefits, 157–158, 173 n. 1
public partisanship, 134–135
public subsidies, 73
punctuated equilibrium, 73–75, 86

rallies, 106–108, 126 n. 3
recruiting, 159–160, 173, 174 n. 5, 176–177, 187–194

Reform Bills (UK), 45–46
registries, membership, 63–64, 77
religious organizations, 42–43, 53, 58–59, 61–62
reputational costs, defined, 129
revolutions, 38, 44–45, 47, 57
rights and obligations, 30–32, 137–138
See also incentives

Schattschneider, E. E., 218 n.1
Second World War, 61, 66
secularization, 53
selective benefits, 157–158, 163–172, 173
Seyd, Patrick, 157
social clubs, 37–40, 162–163
social incentives, 157–159, 161–169, 172–173, 173 n. 1, 174 nn. 6–9
socialism
 elevation of mass party model, 39
 group identity, 163, 173 n. 1
 individual vs. indirect memberships, 57–58, 68 n. 10
 initial founding of, 49
 party structure development, 54–55
 trade unions, 63
social media, 30, 31, 141–143, 152 n. 9, 166–167, 181
See also media; technology
"Special Law of Curvilinear Disparity," 210–211
Stakeholders, 21, 24
stereotypes, 13, 163
subscriber-democracy parties
 change from civic to political purposes, 21, 23–24, 51–52
 emergence of, 39, 179
 importance of members, 211, 215–216
 modern adherents, 64–67
 non-member inclusion, 207–208
 replacement by individualist models, 206
subsidies, 73, 86–90, 96 n. 10
suffrage. *See* enfranchisement
supply-side explanations for membership levels
 benefits to parties, 14–15
 candidacy as incentive, 186

membership decline, 18–19, 74–75, 86, 90–91, 93–94
supporters
  bulls-eye model, 26–27
  campaign participation, 103–108, 125, 126 nn. 3–4
  financial contributions, 119–120
  voter turnout, 120–122, 127 n. 13
  See also affiliates and affiliations
sustainers, 31, 140
sympathizers, 30, 138

taxes, newspaper, 45, 49
technology
  cross-national adoption comparisons, 146–147
  cyber-members, 30, 65, 137–140, 166–168, 173
  digital affiliates, 137, 166–168, 210, 214
  "digital ambassadors," 28, 145
  dues and donations, 31, 132, 140–141, 152 n. 2
  effect on mobilization strategies, 151–152
  internet-based parties, 65
  media costs, 137
  mobilization tools, 206
  for news distribution, 31–32, 143–145, 178, 206
  on-line accessibility, 131–134, 148–150, 155
  party cohesiveness, 213–214
  policy consultations, 180–181
  web pages, 128–129
  See also media
top–down communication, 145, 166
trade unions, 7, 42, 44, 57–58, 63
See also indirect membership

trial memberships, 30, 138
Twitter, 31, 143

unions, 7, 42, 44, 57–58, 63
See also indirect membership
United Kingdom (UK), 44–46, 51–52, 54–55, 78–79, 103, 168–170

Venn diagrams, 33, 136, 217
virtual members, 30
volunteerism, 103–109, 125, 126 n. 2, 178
Voter Turnout, 120–122, 125, 127n13, 189–193, 197–205
voting age, 68 n. 7, 96 n. 3, 152 n. 9, 196 n. 5

Weber, Max, 15
web pages
  accessibility index, 148–150, 155
  as manifestos, 128–129
Whiteley, Paul, 157
Wilders, Geert, 66, 131
Wilson, James Q., 156–157
women, under-representation of, 210
women's suffrage, 68 n. 6, 96 n. 12
World War II, 61, 66

younger members
  careerism, 158–159, 172, 186
  generational changes, 73–75, 86
  matchmaking among, 174 n. 8
  participation preferences, 74, 210
  party referrals, 174 n. 5
  social benefits, 163–164
  voting age, 68 n. 7, 96 n. 3, 152 n. 9, 196 n. 5

Zeitgeist, 40